FATHER HUNGER

Father Hunger

Robert S. McGee

VINE
BOOKS

Servant Publications
Ann Arbor, Michigan

Vine Books is an imprint of Servant Publications especially
designed to serve Evangelical Christians.

Published by Servant Publications
P.O. Box 8617
Ann Arbor, Michigan 48107

Passages from Scripture used in this work, unless otherwise
indicated, are taken from the *Holy Bible, New International
Version.* Copyright © 1973, 1978, 1984, by International
Bible Society, Zondervan Bible Publishers. Used by permission.

The stories in *Father Hunger* are true and used with permission.
They have been gleaned from willing volunteers in a number of
places: Rapha Treatment Centers, support groups, fellow family
members, co-workers, and so forth. Their contribution is
invaluable. Of course, the names of all those who shared their
stories—and those of any relatives mentioned by name—have
been changed to protect their anonymity.

Cover design by Michael Andaloro

    02 03 04 05 16 15 14 13

Printed in the United States of America
ISBN 0-89283-818-3

Library of Congress Cataloging-in-Publication Data

McGee, Robert S.
    Father hunger / Robert S. McGee.
        p. cm.
    Includes bibliographical references.
    ISBN 0-89283-818-3
    1. Mental health—Religious aspects—Christianity. 2.
Fatherhood (Christian theology) 3. Father and child. 4. Spiritual
Life—Christianity. I. Title
    BT732.4.M25 1993
    261.8 358742—dc20   93-17059

Contents

15 60

117453

ACKNOWLEDGMENTS

A BOOK LIKE THIS ONE certainly requires more than a single author. So many people willingly sacrificed their time and emotional energy to make this manuscript much stronger than I could have done on my own. I am thankful for them all. I would especially like to thank:

- All the people who volunteered to share stories about their fathers. Many such stories were painful to tell. I sincerely appreciate your willingness to be honest and vulnerable in the hope of helping others identify and eliminate potential problems.
- Bill and Pat Elam, and all the volunteers who agreed to *repeated* interrogation at ELEEO Ministries meetings in St. Charles, Illinois. You prove three times a week that ELEEO does indeed mean "mercy in action." I would like to acknowledge you all by name, but respect your anonymity. You know (as does God) who you are.
- The people in our Rapha Treatment Centers who took on the added emotional burden of using their free time to answer even more questions about the pains of childhood.
- The staff members of our hospitals, who went out of their way to both accommodate our interviewers and protect their patients.
- Michael Meyer, our Community Relations Director, who helped get this project off the ground in the first place.
- Pat Springle, Stuart Rothberg, and the rest of the Rapha staff here in Houston. I depend on them more than I let them know.
- Ann Spangler, Beth Feia, and the good people at Servant Publications. I appreciate their vision for this very important project and their expertise at making the book the best it can be.
- Stan Campbell, who spent many hours interviewing people, researching information, and helping me to shape the contents of *Father Hunger.* He made a tremendous contribution to this book!

Finally, I would be remiss not to acknowledge the work of Jesus Christ in my life and those of so many of our counselees. In the kind of work I do, I am continually reminded of his promise: "My grace is sufficient for you, for my power is made perfect in weakness" (2 Cor 12:9). May we all become stronger as we better understand the hope Christ provides in spite of our weaknesses.

Introduction

IMAGINE FOR A MOMENT that you're at the airport, shortly before Christmas, waiting for a friend's plane to arrive. You can't help overhearing the conversation of two young women standing right behind you. One gushes to the other, "My dad is just about the most wonderful man you could ever know! He was always there when I needed him. He encouraged me, came to nearly all my school functions, and took us on adventurous family vacations every year. Christmas and other family holidays were some of the best times of my life. I can't wait until he gets here and we can spend more time with each other!"

You can tell by this woman's voice that she feels genuinely excited about her father's visit. Her comments automatically set into motion memories of your own relationship with your father. How might hearing such comments make you feel?

(a) warm and fuzzy: "I wish I could give *my* dad a big hug."
(b) depressed: "What I wouldn't give to start over again."
(c) angry: "Holiday shmaltz is so sickening!"
(d) confused: "Can this guy be for real?"
(e) jealous: "Why couldn't I have gotten one like that?"
(f) skeptical: "Obviously this woman is lying!"
(g) other:_____

If you chose the "warm and fuzzy" response, this book is not for you (although you may find it helpful to learn how lots of other people might react). If you chose any of the other answers, *Father Hunger* should interest you.

Some readers may ask, "Why another book about fathers? Doesn't the world have enough books about parenting already?"

I don't think so. I believe most of the books on the market are for those who want to be the best fathers they can be, or for those adult children who would have felt the warm fuzzies in the above situation. Personally, I could not respond that way. I've had my share of pain and suffering from the condition that has come to be labeled "father hunger." And I know that the people who come to Rapha for counseling repeatedly list this problem as a source of significant pain in their lives. While I have seen an article here or there, I haven't yet seen a book that deals with the topic in a thorough manner.

To tell you the truth, I wasn't particularly eager to tackle this subject. I can think of several books I would have preferred to write before this one. (People with father hunger aren't usually chatty about their pain.) But when Rapha was approached by Servant Publications to create a book on this topic, we all agreed that the time had come to deal with this sensitive and deeply important issue.

If you're looking for a "feel good" book about father and child relationships, this isn't it. If you and your father have had a little spat and are still holding a grudge against each other, find another resource to help you. This book is for: (1) people who as children didn't receive the quality and quantity of love they wanted and deserved from their fathers; and (2) others who currently relate to such people. And since fathers are only human, I have found that these two categories include almost everyone.

If children fail to receive enough love from their fathers, they carry the painful effects for a long time to come—usually for the rest of their lives. Our natural tendency is to block out the painful past. But the wound is too severe. While the hurt may be suppressed for a time, it will eventually emerge, frequently in unexpected and undesired ways. As we form relationships with a spouse or offspring or anyone else, the unresolved pain from the past will cause emotional havoc in the present.

My first goal in this book is to help you recognize and release any pent-up pain that is based on an inadequate relationship with your father. Not only must you think about things you've been trying so long to forget but also face other long-buried memories and emotions which will be dredged up in the process. In most cases, this will not be a pleasant or an easy task. If it's going to be painful, why do it? Because it can be even more painful (and emotionally devastating) to keep trudging on with your life, leaving such a deep wound to fester beneath the surface.

The second goal of this book, consequently, is to help the reader get past the pain and on the way to emotional health and freedom. If you identify the problem of father hunger in your own life, choosing to deal with it can be quite traumatic. Yet when you're finally able to quit dodging the feelings that haunt you, to confront the issue head-on, and to move forward with your life, the sensation can be incredibly freeing.

I urge you to "stay the course" as you read through this book. Because the problem of father hunger is so massive, answers won't come easily. They will come, but to find them you must first navigate some emotionally turbulent waters. To help you negotiate these rapids as smoothly as possible, I have chosen to divide this material into lots of shorter chapters. Each one deals with a specific aspect of father hunger so that you can chew on bite-sized chunks a little at a time. I have also included several questions for reflection at the end of each chapter, little snacks for thought.

The first section of this book (chapters one through four) provides an overview of the issue of father hunger. You will see why this has become such a major consideration for our society, as well as what it means on a personal level. The second section (chapters five through thirteen) delves into specific ways the problem can manifest itself. You will see the depth of pain and suffering which father hunger can cause when left unchallenged. And finally, the third section (chapters fourteen through twenty-five) provides insight into how victims or loved ones can address the problem of father hunger.

This book is liberally peppered with first-person accounts from those who have identified the problem in their own lives and are trying to do something about it. These stories are all true, gleaned from willing volunteers in a number of places: our Rapha Treatment Centers, support groups, fellow family members, co-workers, and so forth. (Of course, the names of all those who shared their stories—and those of any relatives mentioned by name—have been changed to protect their anonymity.) It was not easy for these people to share their feelings and experiences, yet they did so in the hope of helping others. Most of them said that if they could spare even one other person some of the grief and pain they had carried, it would be worth it. May the hopes of our volunteers not be in vain.

Yes, some of the content in this book may stir up feelings of discomfort or unpleasantness. Yet for those who struggle with father hunger, so will any number of everyday stimuli—like seeing a father hug his child, watching a Hallmark card commercial on TV, or overhearing someone else's happy memories. Hope and help exist for those who still carry the scars of a less-than-perfect relationship with their fathers. All of us at Rapha pray that every reader who struggles with father hunger will find the love, peace, and understanding that have thus far eluded them in life's journey.

Robert S. McGee
Founder and President of Rapha
February 1993

PART ONE

What Is Father Hunger?

ONE

Father Hunger Affects Us All

A T AGE TWENTY-SEVEN, Jane is by all appearances a very pleasant and professional young woman. Rather energetic and attractive, she smiles and jokes throughout her interview. Yet as the topic of discussion shifts to difficulties that might be grounded in her past, Jane becomes visibly nervous and uncomfortable. Her voice begins to crack as she tells her story:

> I didn't have a father growing up, and it has become obvious to me how my life has been affected by not having him in the home. My mother and father were divorced, well, they separated when I was two and a half. At that time my father was in the service and my mother said, "He'll come back." But then they divorced and never told me. It was always like I was waiting around for something that was never going to happen.
>
> I was one of those statistical women who sought my father's attention through my dating relationships. I got pregnant before my marriage. I was nineteen. But things have stabilized now. I've been married eight years. I have a home.
>
> Yet during this past year and a half, the big crazies have really started happening. I've been experiencing such an obsession to get attention and affirmation from a man. I feel that it's greater

than myself. It's like sometimes I wonder, *Where is this coming from? Why am I doing this? What are my motives?*

But I think I have a good idea where my obsession comes from. This past year was the first time I'd ever had a job with close proximity to a male boss. He did such a good job of relating to me, and it's like I started to see what I had missed by not having a father. The force of my feelings just took me over the edge. I ended up in a hospital, diagnosed with depression. The final hitting bottom was having to quit my job. One time I had called my boss's answering machine all weekend, wanting him to meet me places. A month or two later I ran away from home one night when my grandparents were supposed to visit, hoping to see him.

Then, just a couple of weeks ago I started following him around again. This time my actions caused my boss to call the police and bring harassment charges and restraining orders against me. *I'm a normal person!* It's simply unbelievable. I don't know where these feelings come from!

You know, I was so small when my father left. I don't think I got past any of those "normal" stages that are supposed to take place between a daughter and a father. It's all just come up recently. All this crazy stuff from my past has been resurfacing. It's very, very painful to deal with.

If you saw Jane, you would probably agree that she is "normal," even friendly and likeable. Yet beneath the surface of many normal-looking people lie deep emotional struggles that keep cropping up in one way or another.

Andrew did grow up with a father, one who was violently abusive. As a result, this thirty-nine-year-old man is unable to remember much about his childhood. Andrew feels frustrated because of this lack of happy memories:

It seems strange, but there are really few details I can remember of what I did as a child. I have little glimpses, but not any complete stories of things we did as kids. I can remember that we moved when I was two and a half. We moved from one town to another; I can remember it very clearly. At about six, I can remember making a go-cart out of an apple crate, learning to ride a bike with my oldest brother running alongside, and jumping off the roof of the garage one time.

The next thing I can recall was when I was eleven or twelve. What happened to those fun years as a kid? Where are all the good times that I'm supposed to sit around with my family of origin and laugh about? Where are all the "remember when" stories?

Another woman zeroes in on her experiences during adolescence. She was neither abandoned nor physically abused, yet continued conflict within the home took its inevitable toll. Although their reactions may not be as dramatic, a tremendous number of both men and women suffer from the lack of communication illustrated by this story.

My mother and father weren't getting along too well and I became my father's "emotional spouse," in a sense. But one time when I was fifteen, he said something that hurt me. I cried and my mother jumped all over him. My dad cut me off at that point. He could never speak to me again. It got so bad that if my father saw me approaching him, he'd turn around and get out of the room. Whenever he saw me coming, he would turn his back and avoid me—or just leave.

I felt completely isolated and rejected. I spent the next two years humiliating myself—begging for affection, begging him to love me, begging him to admit that he had hurt me. But he couldn't. And now I'm hungry for hugs from a man, for attention, for love, for strokes, for kind words. I'm just starving.

STILL HUNGRY FOR A FATHER'S LOVE

These statements are just a small sampling of stories from people who are currently trying to work through a variety of problems in their lives—including depression, lack of self-esteem, an inability to express genuine love toward a spouse. But in interviewing these people, one common element keeps coming up in almost every case: an unfulfilled desire, a gnawing deep in their spirits, a continual craving to experience love from their fathers. The longer this need goes unfulfilled, the more the person suffers.

Some of these people suffer in perpetual hopelessness. Some of their fathers died long ago, or may now be elderly, weak, and unable to express genuine love. Some remain emotionally distant, not knowing any better ways to express love today than they did years ago. Still other fathers continue to struggle with their own personal difficulties and just cannot understand why a grown child would still need to hear the words "I love you." Many of these people have given up hope of *ever* feeling worthwhile, because their fathers are simply incapable of expressing love in any meaningful way.

Whenever adults begin to talk honestly about their prior relationships with their families, this problem of unfulfilled needs almost always surfaces. This feeling of emptiness resulting from the lack of a father's love has been described by others and myself as *father hunger.*

Sometimes I encounter people who are quickly alienated by the use of terms which they label as psychological "buzzwords" or even "psychobabble." They become irritated when friends refer to *co-dependency, dysfunction, addiction,* and obscure clinical terms. Such phrases may very well be overused in certain circles, yet I suspect a more common source of this personal discomfort: some people don't try very hard to understand the concepts defined by these words. It's easy to criticize what one does not understand.

I don't know how anyone can argue with the term *father hunger* as an apt name for this common longing. What better word than hunger can describe the sensation of wanting a father's love? Indeed, the desire goes beyond mere want. It is truly a need. We don't just want our fathers to love us; we *need* them to love us. This kind of emotional hunger acts in many ways just like physical hunger. If we aren't provided with what is best for us, we will soon begin to seek other, less healthy, substitutes. Since hunger is a drive that *must* be met, those who are starving try to cope with father hunger in various ways.

Some women who have never felt secure with a father's love will quickly turn to other men in search of acceptance. They typically begin to identify Dad's rejection or apathy at about the time they reach dating age. Many of them become promiscuous in their eagerness to receive love, first from one guy and then another.

On the other hand, some women think, *I've been hurt by my father, but you can be sure no other man is ever going to hurt me.* Consequently, these undernourished women tend to remain distant whenever someone tries to become friendly. Many turn to the feminist movement where they find "allies" who share their reluctance to seek intimacy with men.

Men experience father hunger just as much as women—perhaps even more. And having been provided with such poor role models, they themselves often find it difficult to respond in loving ways. Until recently, society has traditionally discouraged men from being vulnerable and honestly expressing their emotions. They've been expected to remain strong and silent rather than to freely express pain, grief, or similar feelings. If males do show their feelings, their character may be called into question. "Come on, I know it hurts, but take it like a man."

Today many of them are flocking to the men's movement. They may dress in paint and feathers, beat drums, and affirm each other as they actively seek a deeper level of sensitivity previously denied them. Through these rather expensive sessions, men learn that it is okay to hug each other, cry, be honest with their children and spouses, and do many other things that haven't always been perceived as "manly."

For Christians, father hunger often creates even more serious problems. When the average person in the pew thinks in terms of a father who was unexpressive, absent, workaholic, alcoholic, or even abusive, what is he or she likely to think of God as a heavenly *Father*? How can someone even begin to approach God as a trustworthy father when the memories of "father" cause a vague uneasiness or even intense pain?

How can we ever know God in the way he intended if our own dads haven't done an adequate job in fulfilling God's role for fathers? And since fathers are only human, not one ever succeeds perfectly. Most fail to a significant degree. Some do a dismal job, while others may give up completely for a variety of reasons. The challenge is indeed impossible, apart from the grace of God.

WHY TWO PARENTS?

"But wait," I can hear some of you saying, "with all the divorce in our society today, aren't many people learning to grow up with a single parent—usually without a father? How big a problem can this 'father hunger' be if almost half of us are dealing with divorced parents?"

Again, I would ask you to think of the concept of hunger. If we so choose, we could completely eliminate green vegetables from our diets and substitute milk chocolate instead. That melt-in-your-mouth sweetness would taste so good going down. And it wouldn't kill us. But neither would such a diet provide the kind of nutrition our bodies need for optimum health and well-being.

Similarly, the love of a father provides emotional and spiritual "nutrition." We can learn to do without it. We can substitute other things for it. But we will never feel as healthy as we should, because we haven't been provided with enough of an absolutely necessary ingredient for adequate growth.

Let's consider this issue from another angle. Why do you think God created us with two parents? In his grand design for humankind, God created man and woman to love each other and fulfill each other's needs. And with the command to "be fruitful and multiply," he gave them the joint responsibility of populating the earth. A major element of their parental duties was to pass along God's love to their growing children.

In providing laws to guide society, God took special care to address the parent's responsibility to pass these laws on to the children. As he commanded the nation of Israel:

> Hear, O Israel: The LORD our God, the LORD is one. Love the LORD your God with all your heart and with all your soul and with all your strength. These commandments that I give you today are to be upon your hearts. Impress them on your children. Talk about them when you sit at home and when you walk along the road, when you lie down and when you get up. Tie them as symbols on your hands and bind them on your foreheads. Write them on the doorframes of your houses and on your gates. Dt 6:4-9

Yet how many of today's parents actually carry out this command? The demands of keeping bread on the table alone can be enough to consume their time and dampen their enthusiasm. God intends that we take his commands seriously and that we train our children to do the same.

In Old Testament society, it was the *father's* role to see that his children knew of God's love and protection. This fertile training ground took for granted that families would be close through the years. "Sons are a heritage from the LORD, children a reward from him. Like arrows in the hands of a warrior are sons born in one's youth. Blessed is the man whose quiver is full of them. They will not be put to shame when they contend with their enemies in the gate" (Ps 127:3-5).

Jesus also emphasized the importance of parents—especially fathers—*providing* for their children. "Which of you, if his son asks for bread, will give him a stone? Or if he asks for a fish, will give him a snake? If you, then, though you are evil, know how to give good gifts to your children, how much more will your Father in heaven give good gifts to those who ask him!" (Mt 7:9-11).

On another occasion, the disciples asked Jesus who was the greatest in the kingdom of heaven. The Lord called a little child to come and stand among them. Then he instructed them:

> "I tell you the truth, unless you change and become like little children, you will never enter the kingdom of heaven. Therefore, whoever humbles himself like this child is the greatest in the kingdom of heaven.
>
> And whoever welcomes a little child like this in my name welcomes me. But if anyone causes one of these little ones who believe in me to sin, it would be better for him to have a large millstone hung around his neck and to be drowned in the depths of the sea." Mt 18:3-6

Today's world offers countless examples of fathers who stand in direct contradiction to what God intended. Some of them *do* cause their children to sin—in any number of ways. Some of them *do* respond in a harmful way when their children innocently ask for something. You can hardly read a newspaper without coming across a story of a baby found in a garbage can, a child forced to live in a closet because of crying too much, or any number of other forms of horrible abuse. Too many of today's fathers are habitually domineering, critical, demanding, cruel, violent, or sexually abusive. Some fathers just don't seem to care one way or another what happens to their children.

Probably the majority of fathers fall into the middle ground: those who sincerely care about their children but feel unable to translate that care into genuine expressions of love which touch the heart and soul and spirit of a child. As these children approach adulthood, many have never seen appropriate parenting behavior. And in most cases, the painful consequences are passed along to the next generation.

While many people grow up with absent fathers or fathers who don't come close to fulfilling God's role for them, they find little comfort in the fact that they aren't alone in their suffering. The problem remains very real and very personal. And even though it may be a spiritual issue at the very root, a number of emotional and physical by-products are likely to arise from this deep father hunger.

If you are one of the few who have never experienced the enormous emptiness of father hunger, count yourself blessed indeed. Even so, you regularly cross paths with many people who have been hurt because of painful or inadequate father relationships. Perhaps you live with such a person. Understanding more about this very common source of pain can enable you to relate to others with more understanding and compassion.

If you have experienced father hunger, my first goal is to help you understand *why* you feel the way you do. In doing so, I will ask you to be totally honest with yourself. This will not be a pleasant issue to untangle. Most of the people who contributed their experiences to this book did so through tears or clenched teeth. After laying some groundwork as to why the lack of feeling a father's love can have such a powerful effect, I'll try to provide some practical ways in which you can deal with your loss.

Be forewarned: you aren't going to read this book and be instantly cured of your longing. To be honest, you may feel even worse after you've read it than you do now. When people begin to deal honestly with feelings that have been tucked away for a long while, the experience isn't usually pleasant at first. However, exposing this wound to the open air is the first step toward a more complete and lasting healing. No matter how frightening it may seem at first, you have nothing to lose by being honest with yourself. You can never experience complete freedom or healing as long as you are keeping something hidden.

SPEAKING FROM EXPERIENCE

Since I want you to be honest with me, let me be honest with you. If you're hurting because you didn't experience your father's love, I empathize with you. And I don't mean that I feel for you as a counselor and founder of Rapha feels for a patient. I feel for you because I share your pain. I've been there.

When I think of my own childhood, I recall growing up very poor. I remember taking an old metal bucket and throwing it down a shallow well to get our drinking water. I remember the outhouse on the side of the hill, which was our only bathroom. I remember the white frame house where I grew up. But being poor never hurt. Being ignored and neglected did.

I spent a lot of time alone while I was growing up. My father and my brother were both invalids. Like sponges, they absorbed the attention of the rest of the family. I never remember being touched in an affectionate way. I was comforted a couple of times when I was sick to my stomach, but I never remember being hugged, being petted, or having any kind of loving contact.

As a little boy, I knew I was hurting deep inside, but I had no idea what to do about it. Growing up in rural Oklahoma meant there weren't any other kids my age for miles. So I chose to create my own world—a world where I could entertain myself and imagine others around me. I remember having a hard rubber ball. In spring and summer I would play baseball, envisioning my dream-team around me. In the fall I'd play basketball, throwing that same ball through an old, rusty coffee can with the ends cut out and nailed to the side of the building.

I created my own world to avoid the pain of loneliness. I determined to become self-sufficient, to be able to live without anyone else. I decided that I would relate at a level where I would not get hurt again. I began to keep other people—and God—at a distance.

I grew up, got married, and found myself thrown into the Vietnam War. I was a pilot in an assault helicopter company in the central highlands of Vietnam. I still remember one day very vividly: it was May 10, 1970. I wasn't scheduled to fly that day, so I got up late and was killing time. But I was called on unexpectedly because of an enemy attack in Cambodia.

Another pilot and I, along with ten other "hueys," picked up our troops and took off for Cambodia. The landing zone was tiny—just barely large enough to center the helicopter, kill off its forward speed one hundred fifty feet above ground level, and then hover straight down to let the troops off. The first three helicopters missed and overflew the landing zone. Then it was our turn. We came in over the top, killed off our speed, and began to float down. Immediately we heard small arms fire. All of a sudden I could feel my leg jerk and saw blood begin to stain my flight suit. Eventually we were able to land nearby.

My thoughts that day were so vivid that I can remember them just as clearly as if this had happened a few moments ago. The first thing I thought was, *I just can't believe this is happening to me.* Then I thought, *I didn't want to be over here to start with.* I remember thinking about the fact that I hadn't shot at a single one of those guys yet—though at that particular moment I wished I could.

In retrospect I am amazed at how naïve my thought process was. In the middle of a brutal war, I was feeling offended at having been rejected, even though it was by the enemy! My childhood plan to keep people and pain at a distance had sounded so good. The problem was, it wasn't working. My war experience gave me a somewhat nasty looking scar and a bitter dose of reality. It began to sink in that this Southern Baptist boy who had been to church all his life was not going to be pampered and protected from the hard knocks of life.

After I returned home from Vietnam, I experienced tremendous emotional pain for over two years. And the tragedy was that I continued to try to comfort myself *my* way—just like when I was a little boy with a rubber ball. Once again I was forced to deal with rejection. And every rejection reminded me that as a child I had never experienced the love from my father that I wanted—that I *deserved*. In fact, as I looked back, I became even more resentful. As a child, I had given my father the benefit of the doubt because I knew he had physical problems. But from an adult perspective, I could see that Dad had actually been a very self-centered individual. I realized in retrospect that he could have shown me some affection if he had *wanted* to.

In the last chapter of this book, I'll tell you the rest of my story. At this point, however, be assured that I am personally aware of the suffering that can result when a father cannot or does not adequately express love. I understand. And I also encourage you not to give up, because help is available. But don't be in too big a hurry. Before help can be found, we need to unravel the problem. The first thirteen chapters of this book will give you a clearer perspective of *father hunger.* The last twelve will start you on the road to recovery.

TAKE TIME TO REFLECT

1. Why did you begin to read this book?

2. To what extent would you say you've experienced a "hunger" for your father's love, even if he is now dead or otherwise seems unable to ever provide you with that love?

3. What are some of the questions you hope this book will answer for you?

TWO

The Powerful Influence
of a Father

HAVE YOU EVER STOPPED to wonder what makes you the kind of person you are? Why are you more sensitive to conflict than other people appear to be? Or why do you take control in a crisis situation, while everyone else sits back in stunned silence? Or why do hugs usually make you feel edgy and uncomfortable, when your best friend seems to find a special joy in hugging a family member or another acquaintance?

As adults, we may carry a lot of "emotional baggage" accumulated from our past. We are influenced by a number of variables, some more strongly than others. We can identify many of these influences rather quickly, while others remain hidden and continue to affect us in unexpected ways.

Certainly the *environment* in which we are raised leaves a lasting effect. For example, why do so many people who grew up during the depression era tend to save their money, collect anything that might be of value, and resist throwing anything away? Because these individuals have seen economic prosperity quickly turn into financial ruin. They witnessed parents and other family members suddenly lose their jobs and struggle to get by. That painful legacy continues to affect them. What happened once might happen again. This time, they plan to be ready.

Or consider the difference between a person who grew up in an isolated, rural environment and another who experienced childhood in downtown Manhattan. You don't have to watch long to tell the difference. Their roots become obvious in the way they relate to other people, how they walk down the street, or how they deal with conflict.

People with an urban background are often more willing to initiate a conversation or let you know how they feel. These behaviors were modeled by the adults around them. If you want something from someone, you have to make your presence known. You get attention by turning up the volume—by speaking louder than the traffic, the police sirens, and the person on the other end of the conversation. Country-bred folks, however, tend to be more soft-spoken. They may have spent more time doing isolated chores like milking, planting, cutting hay, canning, and quilting, with considerably fewer opportunities for social interaction so common to those who live in the big city.

We can readily see that a person's environment presents one major factor in shaping the way he or she acts in certain situations. But what other factors can we identify, more human factors?

PERSONALITY, ROLE MODELS, AND PEERS

In addition to environment, basic temperament plays a major role in shaping our attitudes and behavior. Just as God creates each individual with a unique set of fingerprints, he also provides people with a variety of personalities. Many books have been written in an attempt to classify the basic types of personal temperament. For our purposes here, suffice it to say that some people are by nature more outgoing while others are shy. Some are talkative while others hardly say a word. Some are almost always joking around while others are much more straightforward.

Which is the "best" or "correct" personality? Only you can answer that question for yourself. If you feel you're being the person God created you to be, then you need not worry. If you're a serious, sensitive person, that's okay. If you like to laugh, go ahead (even if you're surrounded by more serious-minded types who find it hard to crack a smile). However, if your laughter is designed as a cover-up for inner tensions or serious problems, you need to be honest with yourself. Hiding your genuine feelings is just as wrong as trying to take on someone else's character. You were created as a one-of-a-kind individual. God wants you to cherish the personality he has given you.

We are also strongly influenced by the qualities we see in other people. As children, our heroes are usually larger than life. We start by wanting to fly like Superman or enjoy a perfect life like Barbie. As adolescents we dream of looking like muscle men or gorgeous models. We try to adopt the dress and mannerisms of our favorite rock singers or movie stars.

As we begin to deal with reality, our heroes eventually change. We begin to look more closely at people who have made a difference in the world or in our own lives. We may look up to famous figures such as Martin Luther King, Mother Teresa, John F. Kennedy, or Billy Graham. Or our heroes may include someone we know personally. We might admire the astounding patience of a neighbor who cares for her mentally handicapped child. A boss might demonstrate an enviable talent for dealing with conflict without offending the people involved. A fellow church member might reflect God's love to other people in ways we never thought possible.

All these role models provide glimpses of how our lives *could* be. While we will never *be* those people—and should never try—I see nothing wrong in allowing role models to inspire us to a better way of life. They silently challenge us to move toward a deeper level of commitment and faith.

The people we choose as friends certainly make a difference in our lives as well. Story after story is told of a "nice" guy or girl who gets mixed up with the wrong crowd and ends up getting into serious trouble. Certain relationships can lead us away from God and encourage us to see ourselves in a distorted way. We can always find someone who will tell us what we want to hear, but that person isn't necessarily a friend. We need to find people who will accept us for who we are, yet aren't afraid to be honest with us for our own good.

The goal of choosing friends should be to find people who challenge us to greater levels of maturity. It says in Proverbs, "As iron sharpens iron, so one man sharpens another" (Prv 27:17). The "sharpening" action of another person in our lives can be a wonderful blessing. Since we all have a certain degree of control over the people with whom we spend our time, we should select our friends wisely.

FATHER KNOWS BEST

Of all the influences we will ever encounter—environment, personality, role models, peers, or whatever—nothing usually affects us as strongly as our parents. People can be brought up in harsh environments, experience severe poverty, run around with peers who drink and do drugs, yet overcome all these obstacles and go on to achieve great things. In almost every such case, these people attribute their success to parents who truly cared.

Even one parent who loves and affirms his or her child provides an influence so positive and powerful that it can overwhelm any and all negative influences. Such fortunate children can go out and about with confidence. They know that no matter what happens, they have parents at home who will hug them at the end of the day, protect them, and equip them for the next threatening encounter with the outside world.

Unfortunately, the opposite is also true. When a parent does *not* supply the child with love and self-worth, almost nothing else can ever compensate for that deep emptiness. These impoverished children will keep searching for what's missing through adolescence and into adulthood. But no matter how well they adjust later on, they usually face a lifelong struggle to understand their childhood rejection.

In the eyes of a small child, family essentially constitutes the entire world. Children learn first from observing, and later by asking questions. Much of what they know about priorities, forgiveness, love, trust, truth, and other such values is established as they watch their parents interact with each other and with them.

As the only authority the child knows, parents instill an image in the child's mind of what God must be like. Trusting these human caretakers to act in the child's best interest, most offspring assume their parents are always right. When they grow old enough to discover that significant problems do exist in their families, their first and strongest inclination is to believe that they themselves must be at fault.

While I in no way mean to diminish the powerful impact of mothers, this book focuses more specifically on the role *fathers* play in the lives of their children.[1] The father often occupies a position of power, while the child remains vulnerable and dependent on him to provide the right kinds of influence. We see the scene set for one of three things to happen.

The first possibility is that the father realizes his responsibility and makes the development of his children a top priority. This father spends time with his children, affirming their value both verbally and nonverbally—through affectionate touching, spending time together, tucking the child into bed, and so forth. Such children tend to be emotionally healthy and usually develop a strong sense of self-worth. Their relationships are free of much of the dysfunction with which many people must cope. And these fortunate children often envision an image of God without the usual distortion from paternal shortcomings.

A second possibility is that father and child live in the same home and see each other every day, yet the father is unable or unwilling to express unconditional love for the child. This father may be apathetic or abusive, passive or demanding. But when children don't receive enough love and affirmation, they begin to compensate. Some will continue to seek love from the father; others will begin to look elsewhere. But no matter what the child tries to do, he or she isn't likely to find any way to adequately compensate for the emotional support the father failed to provide.

A third possibility has become far too common: the father is simply seldom around. The high divorce rate has removed Dad from the home in many cases, as well as forced Mom out into the workplace. The child can spend much of the time alone, with no internal family support system. Smaller children tend to assume much of the blame for this kind of situation. Mom and Dad are suddenly out of the picture at the very moment when the child is feeling a lot of internal guilt. When these facts are coupled, you can see the tremendous potential for emotional damage.

THE ABSENT-FATHER SYNDROME

We now speak about this epidemic loss of a father's love and concern as the *absent-father syndrome*. Sometimes a death removes a father from the family, but more often divorce does the dirty deed. This same term can also be applied to fathers who may be *physically* at home, yet remain apathetic toward their children or emotionally withdrawn for long periods of time due to factors such as alcoholism or overly demanding careers.

While interviewing people for this book, we heard story after story of suffering due to the absence of a father during childhood. One of the Rapha counselors commented to me at the end of one of those days, "I wish someone would write a book on *heroic* fathers." This woman went on to describe her own father, a "diligent farmer" whose wife had left him with the farm and seven children. But he loved his kids and made a point of letting them know. The family closeness that he instilled in them has continued throughout their lives.

Her dad had eventually remarried and both he and his second wife had recently died. My colleague smiled warmly as she recalled the sale of her father's estate. No sibling rivalry or bickering marred the occasion. The grown kids agreed to draw numbers for items, and if someone looked sad at not receiving a particular piece of furniture, the brother or sister who got it would most likely give it up. Her story stood in stark contrast to so many that expressed a lack of love. In her case, the love initiated by her father was still going strong.

We will delve into the specific results of the absent-father syndrome in later chapters, but keep in mind that this problem is not easily resolved. Great numbers of adults continually struggle through life with unresolved emotional problems that can be traced back to the lack of a father's love. One young woman expressed her deep sense of loss; her father returned from Vietnam only to leave the family when she was two years old.

> I grew up from the age of two without a father. And before that he was in the service and the Vietnam War, so he wasn't around much anyway. I never had a model for what a "normal" family is. I feel a sense of loss that has very, very much affected my life—my actions, choices, and the ways I relate to others. Whether the father is present and doesn't meet your needs, or whether he's gone and doesn't meet your needs, I think it creates just as much of a loss.

When asked how she tried to cope with this loss, she candidly admitted, "In junior high and high school I would date anybody I could. I even had a couple of teachers take me out to their cars and we'd neck in the car. Something inside me would say, *This is not right. This is not right.* But I would look for any affection I could get. It took a long time for me to get over it, too."

As this young woman points out, the emotional emptiness produced by father hunger can be destructive, powerful, and long lasting. Perhaps you can relate to how she feels. You may even be feeling some despair about such lifelong effects. Since nothing else can adequately replace a father's life, your situation may seem hopeless.

I have seen many people struggle with such hopelessness, yet find a way to overcome it and move on. You will learn much from their courageous stories in the pages ahead. But until you are able to see the problem more clearly, you won't even be able to get started down the road to emotional healing. In the next chapter, let's look more closely at our need for security and comfort. How does that universal longing relate to father hunger?

TAKE TIME TO REFLECT

1. How would you describe the environment in which you grew up?

2. List some words that describe your personality.

3. Who were the important role models in your life? Describe your heroes.

4. How have the people you have chosen as friends influenced your life?

5. Describe your relationship with your parents.

THREE

Our Longing for Security and Comfort

D O YOU REMEMBER being frightened as a child? Perhaps you were scared of the dark; maybe monsters hid under your bed or in the closet; or you may have been afraid of thunder or strange noises outside your window at night. Think back to your earliest memories of being scared. How did you cope with that fear?

If you're like most people, your instinctive response was to call for help or run to one of your parents. You might have run to Mom because she was the one who especially comforted your fears, or perhaps to Dad because he was so much bigger than you. You always counted on one of them to be there when you needed something. As far as you knew, your parents had provided whatever you really needed.

Children view the world from quite a different perspective. For instance, if you ask a little boy to describe his observations after attending a new restaurant, he will offer a point of view from approximately the tops of the tables—his eye-level. Objects and shapes that might seem insignificant to you may loom large and threatening to a child. Yet most children find it inconceivable that any problem could be too big for their fathers to handle. Young children love to ride upon Daddy's shoulders where they catch a glimpse of how much smaller everything appears from higher up.

Children learn very quickly that the world can be a threatening and intimidating place. Even as we grow older, we continually face challenges, risks, setbacks, failures, and sufferings. The sooner we discover that we live in a sinful and imperfect world where things don't always go our way, the better we will be able to cope.

Yet the more we recognize the threats and obstacles surrounding us, the more we feel the need to be assured that everything will ultimately be okay. We want to be comforted. As little children, we hear those "things that go bump in the night" and we run to Mommy or Daddy for a hug. We need a confident reminder that, "You'll be all right. We're here. Don't worry." Although we learn to deal with our insecurities in other ways as the years go by, our inner feelings remain pretty much the same. That little child within can begin shivering in fear of an approaching storm.

COMFORT CRAVINGS

Before we're even aware of what's going on, we develop a craving for comfort. The tiny infant finds nourishment at a mother's breast; a small child cries to be picked up and carried; a youngster wants a Band-aid and a kiss on a scraped knee; the young teen runs home when confronted by the neighborhood bully; the college student calls home for money or for reassurance in the face of a crisis. We all thrive on the love-signals we receive from our parents.

Many children pick up on nonverbal signals to the contrary. One young woman noticed that her dad was usually sitting down, either smoking or drinking with something in his hands, so that she couldn't approach him head-on or give him a hug. Whenever she wanted her dad's attention, she would go around behind him and either scratch his back or try to rub his shoulders. Sometimes he would let her do that for a minute or two, but then he would lean forward and pull away as if to signal her to stop.

One of the most important ways parents communicate love is to show comfort when we're hurt, afraid, lonely, or otherwise insecure. We don't *choose* to want comfort; we can't help but desire it. Comfort is just as necessary as love, food, water, and shelter. If we go too long without receiving it, disastrous results may occur.

The problem is, not all parents provide the comfort their children need. Sadly, I find this especially true of fathers. When a parent denies a child love and comfort, that child can jump to a number of erroneous conclusions.

"I've done something wrong." Children often assume they surely must have done something to provoke a strongly negative reaction from parents. If these all-wise adults refuse to provide comfort, they probably have a good reason. Small children find it nearly impossible to believe their parents capable of doing anything wrong. As a result, children almost always shift the blame to themselves. This is especially noticeable when parents divorce, but is also true in many other situations.

"I must be a bad person." If children cannot identify any *specific* misbehavior that may have caused their parents to withhold love and comfort, the next step is to assume that they must be bad *in general.* Their logic is sound from a childish perspective. Good people deserve to receive love and comfort. Therefore, if they aren't receiving comfort—given the assumption that Mom and Dad would never do anything wrong—then the children believe they must be the guilty parties.

"I guess I'd better take what I can get." The craving for comfort doesn't disappear just because it's ignored. Children who long to be secure in their fathers' love will not lose sight of that primary goal. But they may indeed lower their expectations and adjust their behavior to acquire whatever little bit of affirmation they can.

The Bible has much to say about comfort and about what to do if we fail to receive it. However, Scripture never promises that we will get through life without any *discomfort.* If anything, it warns us to prepare for the worst, as in Psalm 77:1-2: "I cried out to God for help; I cried out to God to hear me. When I was in distress, I sought the Lord; at night I stretched out untiring hands and my soul refused to be comforted."

Scripture also assures tells us that God is "the Father of compassion and the God of all comfort, who comforts us in all our troubles, so that we can comfort those in any trouble with the comfort we ourselves have received from God. For just as the sufferings of Christ flow over into our lives, so also through Christ our comfort over-flows" (2 Cor 1:3-5).

ONE MAN'S STORY

One man who came to Rapha has long sought relief from his childhood memories as the youngest of five boys with a violent, rageaholic, militaristic father. After describing the beatings and sufferings some of his older brothers had received, he said with a deep sense of sadness:

> As far as my own relationship with him, he never came to one of my ball games. He never attended a school play. We never played catch in the yard. I went fishing with him twice, but both times any pleasure of being with him was destroyed by the fact that I didn't fish perfectly. I couldn't use the rod and reel. I didn't know how to bait the hook. I'm not sure how I was ever supposed to learn *how* to do that!... He didn't attend my high school graduation. He didn't attend my junior college graduation. He just wasn't there.... I never heard the words, "I love you"—never.

We asked, "Did your father ever show affection?" He answered:

> From the time I was ten years old I paid for everything I got, from school lunches to new clothes. Dad was very proud of that. As a matter of fact, the very first dollar I earned was when I was six years old. And they saved that dollar. They typed up a little caption to go underneath it—something to the effect that I had earned this dollar when I was six years old for cleaning the garden spot for my next door neighbor. And they typed my name under it, put it on a piece of cardboard, and hung it in a frame in the living room. So they were very proud of the fact that I was industrious. Their affirmation was very performance based. And I think that set the stage for me to try very hard to perform from then on to win my father's approval.

The only other remotely affirming event this man could recall from his relationship with his father occurred several years later:

At fourteen, I traded a shotgun for a car that needed a lot of work done. My father helped me with that. But everything we did was work-related. That's all he took any kind of pride in. Basically, what he did was help me find the right parts to order to rebuild the engine. But it was my responsibility to take it apart, put it back together, and make it run. If I wanted a car, that's what I had to do. And he did tell me that I had done a good job on that—a 1959 Renault Dauphin. But he was never there to say, "You've done a good job," or, "That looks good," or, "I'm proud of you," or "Congratulations."

Dad didn't go to my college graduation and I paid every dime of it. There are probably a lot of fathers today who would be proud of their children just for paying their way through college. But everything I did was expected by him. The only words I received were when I *didn't* meet his expectations. Then I faced chastisement or punishment. I've had to fight very hard to not repeat that with my wife and with my own children. In my management position at work, I also find it very difficult to praise somebody for doing his best, even though it may fall short of my own expectations.

How sad! A whole childhood gone by, and this man could offer only two remotely positive recollections of time spent with his father. Many of us would find little comfort in these particular experiences, yet it was all he could remember. In his perspective, a few words of acknowledgment in response to lots of hard work was all the comfort he had ever come to expect.

COMFORT IS BASED ON TRUST

To a large degree, comfort is based on trust. We typically cannot feel comforted by people about whom we harbor doubts, however justified or unjustified. We expect to be comforted by our parents—until they do something that triggers the thought in our minds: *I'm not sure they can be trusted.* As soon as this doubt enters our consciousness, everything our parents do then becomes suspect. Any further parental attempts at comfort will not be nearly as effective as they would have been before we lost absolute trust in them.

Imagine what happens emotionally when we first discover that our parents—the ones in whom we have placed total confidence—have acted in an untrustworthy manner. They may not have intended to harm us at all. Perhaps they did. Maybe they didn't much care one way or the other. But as small and trusting children, we had counted on them to provide what was best for us. When we finally become able to analyze the situation and synthesize our feelings, we can be appalled at the realization that our parents were not the perfect, loving providers we had assumed.

Since the ensuing emotional maelstrom can be difficult to envision, let's consider a similar situation on a purely physical level. Let's say that you, as a small child, are provided with three well-balanced meals each day. Your parents faithfully serve up this hot and nourishing food without expecting anything in return. But, for some reason, you feel ill after every meal you eat. You certainly don't think to blame your parents. After all, they're working hard to provide and prepare the food especially for you. They make sure you get all you can eat. You simply wish that the food made you feel better. And for all you know as a youngster, maybe everyone feels a little sick every time they eat a meal.

Then, as you become a little older, you begin to hear about physical ailments which can result from various allergies. Out of the blue it dawns on you: *That sounds like the problem I'm having.* At your request, your parents take you to the family doctor for a checkup. "Yes," he confirms, "you are indeed allergic to the foods you have been eating. But I don't understand it. I told your parents years ago that you were allergic to these things."

Imagine how you would feel. All this time you assumed that your parents had your best interests at heart. After all, hadn't they provided all the food you wanted? But when you look at the situation from a slightly older and more mature perspective, the truth can be devastating. Sure, your parents made an effort to provide for your needs—but not much of an effort. They *knew* what was best for you; they just didn't do it.

At that point your trust in them is shattered. You begin to feel a need for comfort. But if you can't trust your own parents, whom *can* you trust? Do you seek comfort from other people—*any* other people—out of desperation? Do you withdraw and determine never to let anyone hurt you again? Do you confront your parents and try to make them love you in the way they should?

People try all of these options, even though none of them usually works very well. No other human bond is as strong as the one between parent and child. When that primary relationship has been betrayed by a parent who doesn't try or doesn't care—for whatever reason—the child is usually left with a void that seems unfillable. Some people search for the rest of their lives for a relationship that will fill that void—peers, bosses, spouses, children, anyone at all. Others quickly give up and determine to live with the void. But the longing for comfort goes on.

As these children grow up trying to cope with such an emotional void, how can they effectively raise their own children? How do they say, with conviction, that, "Everything's going to be all right. Don't worry. I'll take care of you"? How do they break the cycle of hurt that they feel—and that was very likely felt by their parents, grandparents, and on back as far as anyone can remember?

If you have not been experiencing the levels of comfort you think you should, be aware that the condition is not necessarily permanent. Yes, it may have existed for a long time—even for many years. But comfort and security are not unreachable goals. You *can* find comfort, but you must be brutally honest about the past, the present, and the future.

As you work through this process, you will eventually discover that God himself will surround you with the security you so desperately need. The secret of finding comfort lies in your willingness to abandon any attempts to remain comfortable. You will never be able to adequately comfort yourself or be fully comforted by another person. Only when you stop trying will you be able to find peace.

The next chapter deals with a number of ways that society tries to cope with the large numbers of people who are grieving over less-than-perfect parental relationships—especially with fathers. If you're beginning to realize your own feelings of loss as you think of your relationship with your father, the best thing you can do at this point is to keep taking small steps forward. Don't get bogged down. And no matter what looms ahead, keep your eyes open. Don't try to look the other way if you must face something that seems unpleasant. As Jesus promised, "Blessed are those who mourn, for they will be comforted" (Mt 5:4).

TAKE TIME TO REFLECT

1. Was there a sense of security and comfort in your home? Why or why not?

2. Try to recall several times during your childhood when your parents affirmed you. Describe how you felt each time.

3. Do you believe your parents usually had your best interests at heart? Why or why not?

4. How would you rate the level of trust you now feel toward your parents?

5. Do you feel a sense of loss when you think about your relationship with your father? If so, how are you coping with that loss?

FOUR

A Broader Famine in Society

WHEN WE EXPERIENCE a problem, our natural tendency is to keep it to ourselves. Most of us feel reluctant to walk up to neighbors or co-workers and open up about our pain. We suspect that we're alone in our suffering. Since everyone else seems to be getting along just fine, we hesitate to let them know that *we* aren't.

Such a tendency can produce harmful effects. For instance, women have not always been encouraged to talk openly about topics such as rape, abuse, or sexual harassment. Now that we have discovered that such problems are far more widespread than anyone had ever imagined, agencies and shelters have been formed to help victims deal with these intensely personal problems.

Similarly, we went a long time before we realized how widespread the problem of father hunger had become. Many people have gone through their entire lives feeling the pain of severed or unfulfilled relationships with their fathers, yet never knowing how common the problem is. While we may have been unhappy with our own fathers, we assumed that most fathers were good, loving, and fair. After all, we saw these wonderful caring and responsible creatures on television each week.

One woman spoke at length about the suffering she experienced as a young child after her father divorced her mother. Then she said:

I didn't really have a father figure, so I'd pick it up from TV. I watched a lot of TV: *Father Knows Best; Leave It to Beaver; Welcome Back Kotter.* I was drawn to the honesty—where the fathers would screw up with their kids, but they could be honest about it. That appealed to me. I always thought perfection was bad because I could never measure up to it, so I liked seeing fathers be honest about screwing up all the time. But that kind of honesty was never extended to me. And as I listen to other people, I don't think it was offered to them, either. I think of how much easier it would have been if my father could have just been honest. How much easier it would have been to hear, "I love you, but I'm just not perfect."

This woman, like thousands of other people, recognized the disparity between the words and actions of her own father and those of the fictional fathers on TV during the sixties and seventies. But as time passed, she and others gradually realized that this craving for a father's love was not an isolated instance. As more and more people opened up about this unfulfilled longing, others chimed in to reflect similar feelings and experiences.

Large numbers of hurting people have begun to find others who share their deep inner emptiness, who also wish their fathers had shown more genuine affection. The almost universal power of father hunger has been felt in a number of ways—some good and some bad. A number of groups and movements and behaviors have formed partly as a consequence of this void. I would like to highlight a few of them before we take a look at the more personal toll of unfulfilled father hunger.

THE FEMINIST MOVEMENT

The powerful and widespread feminist movement of the late sixties and early seventies helped remedy many longstanding inequalities between men and women in the workplace. Few people could argue with the demand of "equal pay for equal work" or defend the demeaning devaluation of women in professional settings. This just war against sexual discrimination and harassment continues to be waged in the courts.

However, a significant percentage of women seemed to go

beyond the equality aspects of the movement and adopt an anti-male stance. I believe that this attitude resulted in part from the problem of never having had an adequate model of what a mature and loving man should be. Some women had abusive or absent fathers. Others had weak husbands who were simply perpetuating the poor models set by their own fathers in relating to women.

In dealing with a broken relationship with her father, one woman has begun to see how her past decisions have been influenced by her emptiness. She says: "My father relationships have completely tainted everything I do. When my real dad left, I felt alone and rejected. Later my mom remarried, and both she and I ended up going through some fierce, abusive battles with my stepdad. After that relationship didn't work out for me, I didn't go looking for other men. No man was going to control me. By that time, I would face the devil himself before I'd allow a man to control me."

My intent here is not to critique the feminist movement. But according to many of the women themselves, their initial attraction was inspired at least in part by the support of others who faced similarly unpleasant relationships with their fathers.

THE GAY MOVEMENT

On the heels of the feminist movement came the gay rights movement. Many homosexuals who had previously tried to keep their lifestyles a secret began to "come out of the closet." Here again, people give any number of reasons for becoming involved in the practice of homosexuality. But in counseling, many speak about a sense of father neglect.

If they have been rejected by the most important man in their childhood lives, some daughters give up on men altogether. The pain becomes far too great for them to risk further rejection by another man. So when a *female* offers support and affirmation, such a woman feels happy for the closeness. Later, when the sexual advances begin, the woman may be less willing to resist because she doesn't want to give up a loving relationship which perhaps serves as a substitute for the one she never had with her father.

Sons who are not shown love by their fathers may have much the same experience, but many times abuse is prevalent as well. Not only is love absent, but violence is often present. Consequently, the victims respond in other ways that seem "logical" to them. One such response is homosexual activity.

One of five male children who had all suffered violent abuse at the hands of their father had come to Rapha for counseling. Now a married adult with children of his own, he was giving in to recurring exhibitionism toward young children on playgrounds and school buses. Unable to control his impulses, this man feared it was about to destroy his marriage. As he talked about his brothers, he described numerous other problems—including homosexuality:

> Of the five of us, I and one other brother have ended up in counseling. My oldest brother has become a recluse. He bought a mobile home, totally isolated himself from everybody, and no one in the family has heard anything from him in the past four years. My next oldest brother became an alcoholic, brutally beating his wife and children. The next two are twins, both of whom were homosexuals. One is… reformed, I guess would be the word for it. The other is practicing. Both are married. One of them struggled with it and seems to have overcome it with counseling. The other remains married, but he would definitely prefer to be with other men. In my situation, I've developed some sexual addictions, including exhibitionism and excessive masturbation. There is a driven side to me that says: *I've got to wound as many people as I can.*

Some people seem to choose homosexuality as an alternative source of love to replace a poor father relationship. Others gravitate toward it out of a sense of emotional desperation. Still others feel they have no choice. Consider another man's experience:

> There was no love in the home where I grew up. I had been sexually abused since I was nine years old. By the time I was fifteen, I'd gotten thrown out onto the street. I hate to admit this, but I became the victim of the homosexual element in the area. You know, when you're walking down the street and you don't have a bed… you don't have anything to eat…. it's easy to respond to someone who says, "Hey, you want a ride?" You don't know what you're getting into, but all of a sudden you're in trouble.

Certainly not all incidents of homosexuality can be attributed to fathers who did a lousy job of helping daughters feel feminine and sons feel masculine. But many cases *can* be. And when people can't find find love and acceptance from a father, they will look somewhere else.

SEXUAL PROMISCUITY

As we discussed earlier, much of the sexual activity outside of marriage connects in some way to a continuing need to fill the void left from not experiencing enough of a father's love. Countless women relate how feeling rejected or ignored by their fathers led to their becoming sexually active as soon as they were old enough to date.

To make matters worse, such behavior is now generally condoned by a society rushing headlong into sexual liberation. As long as "safe sex" is practiced, having an intimate relationship outside of marriage is no longer deemed immoral. However, the safety of the sex act has little to do with finding the fulfillment so obviously missing in a person's life. One woman explained how she had never felt that her father truly cared about her. Then she went into a little more detail as to how her entire family had been affected:

There were three girls in my family. The oldest sister never had a date the whole time she was in high school—never did anything with any man. She was a studious, straight-A student. Then she went away to college, went totally wild, found a boyfriend she became totally obsessed with, got pregnant, got married, and eventually lost the baby.

I had a lot of different boy interests, most of whom I considered serious. From the very beginning, I almost always had a steady boyfriend—one who wasn't going to leave me. My very first boyfriend lasted a year. The next one was a three-year relationship. Then I moved on. Before I'd break up with one, I always had another one lined up. By the time I met my present husband, I had experienced a lot of sexual and relational dysfunction. I felt that virginity was a laughable affair.

I became sexually active with him, got pregnant *before* I got married, and the shame hit my family again. I had seen how much it hurt my parents when the same thing happened to my sister. Yet the compulsion, the need to be accepted and *with* somebody—coupled with the way people have relationships today—when you add those two together, you really have a no-win situation. Anyway, we got married.

Then along came my younger sister, who was supposed to be Daddy's little baby who would *never* do such a thing to him. She was going to be wearing white and have him walk her down the aisle in a traditional wedding, and so forth. And pardon me, but she slept with more people than I could keep up with. My sister and I both clung to one particular guy, but while my other sister has never become pregnant, we couldn't name the list of guys she's been involved with.

I think a lot of sexual dysfunction is tied into the longing for a father's love. With pornography, free sex, passing out condoms, and everything else in our society, the clinging need you feel can easily be fed... which leads to unhealthy relationships... which leads to divorce.

While the problems we face with our fathers concern one-on-one relationships, the prevailing moods and mores of society lend themselves to increased promiscuity. For some, the search for a father's love is carried on from person... to person... to person.

NEIGHBORHOOD GANGS

One of a father's primary responsibilities is to model masculinity to his sons and daughters. Young girls need to know what real men are like to be able to establish strong relationships and reject men who are abusive, overly self-centered, or otherwise potentially threatening. Young boys need to witness first-hand the broad range of characteristics needed to be a good husband and father—or simply, a real man.

When fathers are absent or uninvolved, too often the sons create their own concepts of what manhood should be. Many times they overstress qualities such as strength and protection, while missing other traits that are equally important, such as tenderness, submission to authority, or humility.

We see one result of this shortsightedness in the increased prevalence of gangs. Once limited to the streets and alleys of large cities, the gang problem is rapidly spreading to suburbs and smaller towns. The members emphasize toughness, as displayed in fighting, shooting, drug use, drinking, and similar behaviors. Some gangs require tattoos on every member as a form of identification.

In a very distorted way, these bands of young people are trying to create their own version of unconditional love. Having never experienced it from parents—especially fathers—they form their own brotherhoods. While true love does not actually hold them together, a particular combination of colors and a blind sense of loyalty does. Gang commitments are taken very seriously. After a person becomes part of the gang, withdrawing his membership becomes very difficult. In some cases the member who wants to leave must submit to a violent (and sometimes fatal) beating by the other members *of his own gang*.

DIVORCE

Many men and women enter into marriage desperately looking for something. While some search in one promiscuous sexual relationship after another, others focus their attention on one special person they think can make a significant difference in their lives. They expect this person to change them in some way, or else they expect to change that person into whatever they most desire. Many people—both men and women—somehow expect to find or manufacture in a spouse the love and attention they never received from a father.

In many cases, the needs of both husband and wife are simply too huge for one other person to satisfy. After a few months or years of struggling with incompatibility, divorce seems to be the logical answer—even though neither person necessarily clearly perceives the real problem.

The way some people approach marriage can be compared to trading cars. If you have a car that I want, I'm going to do everything I can to "sell you" on my car. I'll polish it up, vacuum the interior, dab paint over the rust spots, and fill it up with gas. But meanwhile, *you're doing the same thing with your car.* When we meet, we might look at each other's shiny and clean vehicle and decide to trade. But unless we take an educated look at the condition of the engine, transmission, tires, and so forth, we don't really know what we're getting in return.

A bride and groom are both very likely to be "clean and polished" for each other. But the "test run" during the first year of marriage may turn up a lot of unexpected, previously hidden problems. When the spouse turns out to be no better at meeting those very deep needs than Dad was, divorce more and more frequently becomes the end result.

THE MEN'S MOVEMENT

One of the most recent responses of society to the issue of father hunger centers around the men's movement. Most people credit Robert Bly as the founder, a sixty-five-year-old poet and author of *Iron John*,[1] which adapts one of Grimm's fairy tales as an allegory for stages of male growth. Bly himself had an alcoholic father. According to a recent *Newsweek* cover story, "Bly's is a voice in the desert of America's backyards, calling for the missing father—the father whose indifference, abuse, or alcoholism has permanently wounded his sons."[2]

As men begin to identify with the feelings and situations described by Bly and others, we have witnessed the growing popularity of retreats where men can assemble for weekends to reestablish a sense of what it means to be a man. Some re-enact rituals of the Sioux and Chippewa Indians or the ceremonies previously designed for African tribal gods. Drums are especially popular, perhaps because they are more primal than anything you would find at your average seminar or church meeting.

Ritual sweat lodges also play a major role in social interaction at such retreats. The goals center around men being with other men, learning together how to be *real* men. They search for a deeper level of manhood through drumming, sweating, burning of sage, chanting, and communicating with each other. Some are quick to attest to the effectiveness of such methods. They go home able to relate more intimately with their wives and children and thankful for all their new discoveries.

To others, the whole concept seems silly. They doubt any long-range benefits can come from a weekend of such primitive activities. It is yet to be seen if the men's movement will continue to grow stronger, or eventually evaporate like the steam from one of its sweat lodges.

THE RECOVERY MOVEMENT

With far less showmanship than the men's movement and far less publicity than the feminist movement, the recovery movement has steadily gained momentum during recent years. Small groups of people throughout the country attend meetings at least once a week to identify and confront problems that have been plaguing them for years.

Many of these recovery groups use the twelve-step approach to recovery, adapted from Alcoholics Anonymous, to deal with their dysfunctions. They gather and commit themselves to honesty, vulnerability, and accountability. They begin each meeting by publicly confessing their addictions or problems: "I'm the adult child of an alcoholic," or "I'm an incest survivor," or "I'm a compulsive overeater," or "I come from a codependent family," or whatever.

It may be scary to think of sharing your past so openly with a group of strangers, but special encouragement can be gained from realizing that you're not alone in your suffering. A healing balm of comfort seems to flow from hearing the personal testimonies of people who were previously incapacitated by the same problem you still have, yet who now seem well on their way to emotional health.

As we consider the movements and behaviors rooted, to some degree, in father hunger, we begin to realize the large number of people involved. Many, many people are still suffering because of hurts they experienced as children. Far too many fathers desert, degrade, or demand too much from their kids. The intense grief that results may never be totally relieved. Some of these wounded people search in the wrong places or take on behaviors that may provide added hurt rather than lasting help. But at least they're looking and trying something. How many suffer in silence?

How about you? Does this issue of father hunger cause any emotional twinges within you? If so, that's all well and good. If father hunger is a problem in your life, the sooner you acknowledge it and begin to deal with it, the better. Or perhaps you suspect that you yourself are suffering serious consequences because of a loved one's father hunger. In the next section of this book, we will become more specific in helping you evaluate your own background and identify any symptoms of father neglect. Once you have dealt with this issue in your own life, you will be in a much stronger position to help someone you love know how to travel this rocky road to wholeness.

While society may try to deal with such problems with a broad brushstroke, *you* will personally feel the pain until you decide to do something about it in your own life. In the pages that follow, you will learn how to pinpoint specific sources of discomfort in order to relieve the hurt and hunger in your heart. Remember, you are not alone. Many have gone before you, and God goes with you.

TAKE TIME TO REFLECT

1. Do any of the following TV fathers resemble your own dad? Which television family would you have chosen for your own?
   J.R. Ewing or Bobby Ewing, *Dallas*
   Jim Anderson, *Father Knows Best*
   Cliff Huxtable, *The Cosby Show*
   Andy Taylor, *Andy Griffith*
   Mike Brady, *The Brady Bunch*
   Archie Bunker, *All in the Family*
   John Walton, *The Waltons*
   Steve Douglas, *My Three Sons*
   Ben Cartwright, *Bonanza*
   Al Bundy, *Married with Children*
   Homer Simpson, *The Simpsons*

2. Which, if any, of the movements, groups, or other consequences of father hunger have you personally experienced?

3. To what extent have you felt alone in your suffering as a result of father hunger?

PART TWO

When Father Hunger Goes Unfulfilled

FIVE

No Father Is Perfect

NO FATHER IS PERFECT, a fact which becomes undeniable after talking to a large number of people. And with a few fortunate exceptions, certain specific shortcomings of our fathers have affected most of us in negative ways. The extent of that damage varies widely. Some people have been slightly affected and recover rather quickly. But the majority of those who do suffer father hunger usually struggle for years in trying to find the love and affirmation that their fathers should have provided, but didn't.

Many of the people who come to Rapha for help have perhaps experienced the worst effects of fatherhood. Not everyone goes through the severe trauma of abuse, abandonment, or gross neglect. But many fathers may nibble around the edges of these faults, perhaps leaving tiny bite marks in the spirits of their children rather than gaping holes of emptiness. Every father brings his own pain to the job of parenting, a fact of reality which children are ill equipped to understand.

You may not be starving for a father's love, but still experience a dull ache because you haven't been quite satisfied. Even though your father may not have been especially gifted at offering intimate acceptance, affirmation, and encouragement, you may nonetheless have many more happy memories than our volunteers are able to share. You may not need to purge yourself of a lot of anger or make blanket statements about your father's utter failure. Thank God if this is the case. But I would encourage you to read through these descriptions to see if they shed any light on the possible connection between father hunger and the way you experience life.

In later chapters we will discuss the ideal qualities and characteristics of fathers. First, let's take time to look at the various realities. Frankly, of all the people we interviewed, almost no one was completely happy with the childhood relationship formed with his or her father. While no two fathers are exactly alike, our interviewees often mentioned certain common "types" of father figures. Of course, a father might fall into more than one of the following stereotypes. As you read through these groupings, think about whether any of them may apply to your own father and to what degree.

THE ABUSIVE FATHER

The abusive father can be the easiest type to identify. We may have questions about whether or not a father is truly a perfectionist or a workaholic, but physical abuse tends to be more obvious. Some children, however, are disciplined only when the father flies into an occasional rage. They can fail to recognize repeated beatings or beltings as abusive until they look back from an adult perspective at their father's out-of-control behavior.

Other fathers heap on such vile verbal abuse that the toll exacted can at times be even more gruesome and scarring than physical abuse. The severity of physical or verbal abuse that children must endure seems difficult to comprehend at times. Many of these victims live in constant fear of what will happen next. One man recalls the horrors that he and his brothers endured:

> My father had been a drill sergeant during World War II. As children, we had bed checks. We were given instructions (or rather, commands) only once. There was no room for error, whether or not we understood them. We were never allowed to question. If you didn't follow through on the command immediately, the punishment was quick to follow.
>
> Most of the punishment was brutal. I remember how my father chased my oldest brother through the house with his Florsheim shoe. When he got him cornered, he beat him with

the shoe until my brother collapsed on the floor. I can remember holes in the walls and doors ripped from the hinges. Dad made a nine-foot-long bullwhip out of leather. He wove it himself. That's what he usually used for punishment if he could get his hands on it. Typically, punishment came swiftly and immediately. The bullwhip was the ultimate. That was his weapon of choice to punish us.

Later, as part of his therapy, this particular man was asked to write a letter to his father, even though the father had since died. The following excerpt shows how this adult child was still trying to work through these incidents of abuse many years later.

Dear Dad,

There was never any relationship between you and any of us. Were we so bad that you had to drive us all away? Did you see a reflection of yourself? Did you hate yourself so much that you wanted to destroy us? Where did you get the idea that beating children would shape them for successful lives? I will never forget the beatings—the nights that you came upstairs and beat us in the dark with no regard to where the licks fell. A bullwhip for children seems so extreme to me.

Just so you will know, I'm the one who stole that whip. I buried it in the woods so you could never use it again. I know the spot and I could take you there. Many times I went back to that big tree and dug it up, just to make sure it was still there. By now, it's rotting in the ground, just like you.

How badly I craved your love, yet it's clear to me you never had the capacity to love. I never knew your parents, but they sure produced some screwed-up kids. You always tried to make us proud that we were Jacksons. Well, if being a Jackson means I have to be like you, then no thanks. I would rather go through life nameless.

For a long time, there were no memories of childhood for me. Now I clearly remember the arguments, the thrown objects, the holes in the walls, and the doors that were ripped from their hinges. I remember you chasing J.W. and beating him with your Florsheim shoe until he dropped, unable to defend himself. I remember you giving him until the count of three to run until you shot him with the pellet gun. He still has the pellet embedded in his leg.

I remember being chased in the yard while you beat me with the belt, using the buckle end to strike me over and over again. The temper tantrums I used to have only caused you to whip me with the whip made by your own hands. What kind of a monster could braid a nine-foot long whip to discipline his children?...

I wondered for quite some time why I cried at your funeral. There was a sadness that I would never have an opportunity to develop a relationship with you. But greater than that sadness was the joy that you were finally out of my life. Goodbye, Dad, and may our paths never cross again.

Abusive fathers confuse children so much that some of them reach the point of simply wanting the father dead. The anticipation of further abuse becomes almost too much to bear. In the previous case, fear drove this thirteen-year old boy to steal the dreaded bullwhip. Obviously, if the father had ever found out what his son had done, the consequences would have been unthinkable.

Yet even such an intense level of fear and loathing does not erase the longing for a close paternal relationship. Abused children still crave affirmation. While they may wish their domineering, unreasonable fathers were dead, at the same time they wish that some miracle would suddenly make the abusive fathers recognize the worth of their children and begin to express love.

Abuse is almost always repeated over and over. You aren't likely to meet many people who were abused once, and then their parents somehow decided to stop. Once it begins, it usually continues. As the child's craving for love continues to go unmet, and as the abuser inflicts pain time and time again, a strange thing happens. The established pattern seems to take on a life of its own, repeating itself over and over.

The abused victim, in many cases, grows up to be an abuser of his or her own children. Logic would predict that anyone forced to endure such ongoing abuse would never make another person face the same kind of pain. But that's one of the most disastrous effects of father hunger. If the person fails to seek professional help after being abused as a child, it's all too easy for that individual to repeat the exact same patterns. The adult role modeled by an abusive father often becomes too strong to overcome. Generation after generation will often suffer the tragedy of abuse.

THE ABSENT FATHER

Some children have very little concept of a father's role. Today's high percentage of divorce means that many children miss out on having a father present during their earliest years. In other cases, the father dies and the children remain in the care of the widowed mother. The reason for the father's absence doesn't matter so much to the child. Either way, he or she will be strongly affected by a pervasive sense of father loss.

A divorced woman can continue to carry a great deal of resentment toward her ex-husband. Whether a conscious effort or not, some mothers attempt to enlist their children as allies in this ongoing war. Anything that goes wrong is somehow blamed on the scapegoat father who is no longer there to defend himself. As the children mature, they often discover that their fathers aren't the monsters their mothers may have portrayed them to be.

Fathers often believe that young girls are primarily the responsibility of their mothers. When their wives become overly aggressive, husbands tend to look for avenues of escape—sometimes by divorce, sometimes by drinking, sometimes by finding work or other "priorities." And while the fathers may find temporary relief from domineering wives, daughters can be left to receive the full fury of those same powerful women. The children in such cases feel not only the loss of the father's love and support, but a sense of abandonment as well.

THE WORKAHOLIC FATHER

When a father is absent due to death or divorce, the child's pain is significant. Yet the finality of the situation often triggers a kind of coping mechanism. When a child comes to realize that Dad is never going to be around again, he or she begins to deal with feelings of loss. However, some fathers repeatedly *choose* to be absent—to put other priorities ahead of their own children.

In such cases, the child often becomes emotionally stuck—never wanting to give up on having a good relationship with Dad, yet feeling incapable of doing anything on his or her own. If Dad works seventy-hour weeks and plays golf with business associates on the weekends, he rarely has much time to spend at home. And even if the child manages to catch him in a one-on-one situation, the father is usually too exhausted to devote any significant attention to the love-starved son or daughter.

With the father still present from time to time, the child never wants to give up hope that *someday* Dad will put him or her above his other priorities. Yet again and again the child faces harsh disappointment when Dad "just doesn't have the time." Some fathers further complicate the situation by substituting money or gifts for time and genuine love. The child is led to think that the token gifts offer proof of love, but such a definition of "love" is quite distorted.

THE PASSIVE FATHER

Some fathers come home from work every night, live under the same roof as their wives and children, and seem to have plenty of free time. Yet if the mother remains dominant, these apathetic types offer little more to their children than absent fathers do. While physically present, they fail to model what an effective father should be.

Knowing their wives easily become jealous and then vindictive, some men leave it to Mom to tuck the children into bed, to hear the stories of what happened at school that day, and to otherwise show love and affirmation. Other fathers simply choose not to get involved with their children, for whatever reason. Such fathers have little if any idea of how much their children are likely to be affected by their lack of involvement.

While some father neglect is active ("My father never wanted to have anything to do with me!"), I believe passive neglect exacts an even greater toll ("My dad worked sixteen hours a day; he was a good man, sure, but..."). If a father wasn't attentive—whatever the reason—the child feels neglected. As an adult, he or she may rationalize why the father failed to communicate, but the feelings of that lonely child continue to be carted around. Without consciously recognizing it, the person becomes a victim and adopts some of the symptoms described in chapter eight.

THE ILL FATHER

In a small percentage of cases, the father in the family suffers some kind of mentally or physically incapacitating illness. As I have already shared in the first chapter, my own father fell into this category. As an invalid, Dad received a lot of attention. I certainly didn't begrudge his being "in the spotlight," so to speak, but I did feel badly about being virtually ignored by all the same people who swarmed around to help my father. I constantly felt alone.

I am astonished how often children with ill parents are left to cope with the problem on their own and figure out some way to help themselves. In the interviews we conducted, we found *no one* who had been taken aside and told why one parent would sometimes act a little strange. Even if the father could point to definitive medical reason why he might not be able to show proper love and affection for his family, that fact was never clearly communicated to the children.

These children were instead left in the dark, wondering why some fathers laughed and hugged and carried their kids on their shoulders, while their own dads were emotionless, violent, or otherwise unable to care for them. Most were old enough to have handled the truth, but other adults chose to withhold the truth. Imagine the scene as it must have appeared to this woman when she was a young girl:

When I think of my dad, I think of him as "nervous." He changed *so* many times. He could be one hundred sixty pounds one month, and within two months he could be two hundred and something. Then he could drop right back to his original weight. It was just incredible.

He was in and out of VA hospitals. In three months, then out. In and out. In. Out. Because of his medication, he was pretty strange most of the time. He'd either sleep for long periods of time, or he'd be agitated and nervous.

When I was younger—nine or ten—Dad would terrorize us.

He'd go outside and try to spook us—knock on the windows, cut the phone lines, and do a lot of strange things that would really scare us. One night my sister and I kept hearing a lot of noises outside. Dad had been away for a day or two, but we assumed this was him. (We had experienced this kind of thing before.)

It got quiet and we thought he had gone. But when my sister finally raised the shade, he *wasn't* gone. Dad's face was in the window. It was a horrible face. He was frothing at the mouth, and then he started clawing at the window like he was trying to get in. We put the shade back down and ran in to my Mom, who called the police.

My father was wild... like an animal. When the police got there it took several of them to catch him and get him into the house.... He kept saying he was in hell. I don't know why, but I went into the other room to see him. My mom was trying to shove me back into my room, but for some reason I had to go out there. My dad saw me, and he said my name, and he asked me what I was doing in hell with him. With that, the police took me into my bedroom, and my sister and I watched from the window as they took him away.

The doctors eventually diagnosed this man as suffering from paranoid schizophrenia. When we asked this grown woman if she understood that her dad had a physical problem, she replied that it was simply never talked about. She was left feeling like a freak, unable to have friends over, living in constant fear—but never knowing why her father acted the way he did.

A young child has no other databank upon which to draw in defining a "normal" father or "normal" family life. His or her own home makes up the whole world. Surely by the time this woman had turned nine or ten, it would have been wise for her mother to discuss the father's problem in an open and honest manner. Certainly this approach could have done no more harm than allowing the children to grow up with the problem "never talked about."

THE MANIPULATIVE OR PERFECTIONIST FATHER

A medical illness at least provides some excuse for eccentric behavior. What happens when a father intentionally manipulates his wife and children into doing what he wants? Stuck in a mode of controlling others and running the show, some men seem unable to show any signs of compassion or vulnerability. In fact, they may deem such characteristics as unmanly. Even with their own families, they are unable to let down their guard.

Perhaps these fathers feel what they are doing is best for their children. Maybe they're afraid to reveal any glimpses of who they really are. Whatever the reason, the effects on the children can be quite harmful. When asked to recall anything she remembered about her father, these were the first words out of one woman's mouth:

Well, he was a very harsh, controlling man. He was very manipulative. He withheld affection and approval as a means of controlling me. I never ever remember doing anything in my life that pleased my father. I never did anything that elicited approval or affirmation from him. He taught me fear—to fear men and the power and control they had over me. I'm speaking of my father's mental and emotional control. I was not physically abused. But I still have a great fear of relationships with men. I don't have a good marriage.

Many children grow up in homes where nothing they do is ever good enough. In these cases, it's not so much that the father is trying to manipulate the child. Rather, the perfectionistic father hopes to be able to bask in the glory of the child's abilities or accomplishments. This type of father almost seems to detach himself from any kind of parent/child relationship. Instead, he sees his child through the eyes of others. If the child exhibits well-behaved and talented behavior, it reflects well on him. If the child indulges in wild antics, the father's effectiveness as a parent might be questioned.

What happens when the child realizes that Dad cares more about what strangers think than about what is best for his own child? One woman writes about her childhood: "I kept trying to be the kind of person I thought my father wanted me to be. He would set a lot of really unreasonable standards for me. And when I would finally... by just groaning and grunting... finally achieve some of those standards, he would change them. I never succeeded."

It's not uncommon to find pastors who fall into this category. The following woman expresses the sentiment of a lot of "preacher's kids":

I come from a dysfunctional, evangelical family. My father was a pastor. My mom was the central figure in my life at first. But we made a big move when I was eight years old and my mom had to go to work. My father had his study at home, so at that point *he* became the central figure in my life. He began to play a *huge* role in my life. He is the one who taught me how to cook, how to clean house. He told me about sex. He told me about my menstrual cycle. He became dominant. And he really put me in a performance-oriented status—*big time*. I had to be the good minister's daughter.

If I were to sing a solo in church, he'd go with me the night before to rehearse it. He'd tell me, "Look at everybody. Don't just look at one thing. And sing the words distinctly." He was like my voice coach. He had had no training, but he was making sure I would do the best job possible. So by the time I got up there, I was so afraid that I would shake.

My dad had a powerful influence on me. It was very hard for me when he was taken by a stroke at the age of fifty. (I was nineteen at the time.) Then I took on my mother. When he had the stroke, he told me, "If I die, I want you to take care of your Mom." This was just six months after I got married, but for the next nineteen years I took care of my mother—in my home—because my dad had expected me to. I always tried to do what he wanted.

WHO WOULD YOU CHOOSE?

In gathering information for this book, it became almost comical whenever we would assemble a group. As soon as they began talking about their fathers, most of them would express a longing to have had some *other* kind of father.

Those with picky, perfectionist fathers would tend to envy those whose fathers left them alone most of the time. Those with passive fathers longed for more involvement—even if it would have meant trying to meet certain performance standards. The people who had grown up under the harshness of an abusive father would frequently speak of their secret desire for him to die, if that's what it took to free them from their living hell. And many of those with absent fathers had gone through their whole lives wishing for *anyone* who would have assumed a fatherly role in their lives.

When children become confused and misled by fathers who fail to show enough love and affection, they will tend to look in other areas for clues as to how they should respond. The first logical place for them to look is at how Dad gets along with Mom. The next chapter will deal with how we tend to define intimacy based on the husband/wife relationship.

TAKE TIME TO REFLECT

1. What aspects of your relationship with your father dissatisfy you the most?

2. Does your father fall into any of the categories mentioned above (abusive, absent, workaholic, passive, ill, manipulative, perfectionist)? If so, in what ways?

3. List some specific ways in which your father failed to show you adequate love and affection.

SIX

What We Learn by Watching Our Parents

WE LIVE IN AN AGE of awesome exploration. Rockets carry multimillion-dollar telescopes into space to reveal celestial bodies as yet unseen. Electron microscopes magnify the smallest details of cells—down to the tiniest atom. And yet my vote for the most amazing instrument of discovery of all is the eye of a young child. Nothing seems to evade that perceptive gaze.

No matter how hard parents may try to hide certain facts or behaviors, their children usually take notice. But what the eye sees, the immature mind does not necessarily comprehend. Children see *what* their parents do, yet usually without any idea as to *why*. So they reach their own conclusions, ones which may be right or wrong.

Parents constantly teach by example, for better or worse. Many visual lessons contradict the verbal instructions given to the child. This disparity, of course, drives home another point: it must be okay to say one thing and do something completely different. If the father models commendable behavior, the child is likely to learn something positive. If the father acts in a corrupt way, the child still learns something—but probably not what the parent had hoped.

Perhaps no lessons come through as clearly as those we learn by watching how our parents relate to each other. How they each relate to us constitutes the two strongest relationships we know

(Mom-and-me and Dad-and-me), but certainly what we witness between them reflects the next most important relationship we know (Mom-and-Dad). As we watch our parents interact, we unavoidably come to believe certain things are true. Let's examine a number of these *either/or* conclusions we may reach by observing our parents' interactions.

WE LEARN EITHER RESPECT OR CONTEMPT FOR THE OPPOSITE GENDER

One of the first things children learn is how men should treat women and how women should treat men. Again, what we learn may not be at all correct, but as young children we know no better. We interpret whatever Mom and Dad do as true and right. As older children, we may rebel at some of the behaviors we don't condone. But youngsters simply watch and learn and absorb like little sponges, even though they may be uncomfortable as they do.

Some of the behavior we observe can be quite subtle. We might notice condemning glances, overhear comments made to other friends or relatives, or detect other signs that Mom and Dad aren't really as fond of each other as we had believed. Other actions shout out painfully clear messages. One man gives an example of this latter category:

My mother was treated more like one of the children. When they married, my father was twenty-three and my mother fourteen. He used to laugh and say, "Marry them young and raise them like you want them to be." Mom was never given a voice or opportunity to give any input into the decisions he made. When she discovered she couldn't talk to my father, she would talk to me. I became like a surrogate parent to Mom. I was only ten or eleven when she started coming to me to talk about her problems: how poor everything was—from their sexual life, to finances, to how cruelly she was treated.

Sometimes one parent gets hurt by the other and sets out to intentionally sway the opinions of the child. Frequently this goes beyond the other parent in particular, to the other gender as a whole. The following woman tells what she was taught by her mother in the wake of a bitter divorce:

> When my father left, I had no male role models. Listening to what my mother had to say about men, I learned they were chumps. They were fools. They do nothing but lie. They only want one thing from you, and if they can't have it, then you're not terribly important to them. They don't respect you if you do; they don't respect you if you don't. So it's a no-win situation. I didn't date at all through high school. I didn't go to my senior prom. I finished up my school credits and graduated six months early so I could avoid that whole spring celebration. I just couldn't handle it.

Such stories echo the sentiments of one of my associates here at Rapha who says, "I not only suffered from *'father hunger.'* In my dad's absence, I also suffered from *'mother smother.'*" Perhaps nothing else shapes our attitudes toward members of the opposite sex more than observing how our parents relate to each other.

WE LEARN EITHER INTIMACY OR EMOTIONAL DISTANCE

If you saw your parents hug and kiss, hold hands, and show gratitude for each other in lots of little ways, you should always count yourself fortunate. Not many people enjoy that privilege. And when we don't see intimacy modeled by our parents, we usually find it very difficult to conceptualize emotional closeness. In lieu of true intimacy, we create our own ways of interacting.

One woman describes how her father had been brought up in a European home, with a heavy emphasis on the importance of sons. Women were, according to his way of thinking, secondary and more functional. Besides producing problems for her as a daughter, she saw clearly how this subtle message affected the way her parents related to each other.

> My mother worked from the time I was in kindergarten until I graduated from high school. Her relationship with my father was

kind of passive. She worked to help supplement my father's income and support us, so we would have a good way of life. She had her money, and he had his money, and I don't think their nickels ever touched. They felt very free to ask one another for financial help, but it was always paid back. And that's kind of the way their whole relationship was. They gave back and forth to one another, but they carried their own separate wallets... and responsibilities.

Put yourself in the place of this woman. If you never observed any emotional fondness expressed between your mother and father, and if you knew your father would never value you in the same way he bestowed favor on his sons, what could you ever know about intimacy? As you entered into your own marriage, would you be able to open up completely and be intimate with your spouse? A tremendously high number of people from such households try... and fail.

WE LEARN EITHER SACRIFICE OR SELFISHNESS

Mothers and fathers who truly care for their children willingly make whatever sacrifices may be necessary. And while the kids never take note of everything the parents do, they certainly do see a lot. They also see when one parent sacrifices for the other—or chooses not to. When Mom and Dad model an appropriate level of sacrifice, the child usually grows out of the selfish stage of childhood more quickly. But when sacrifice remains the exception rather than the rule, the child may never outgrow that selfish mode.

When one or both parents continue to cling to personal desires rather than do whatever seems best for the spouse or family, the entire family suffers because of that choice. This man describes a situation where each of his parents seemed to expect too much of the other. Consequently, they never worked out an acceptable compromise:

When my dad married my mom, she had high expectations because she had been brought up "on the other side of the tracks." My mother gave up a lot, hoping that marriage would take care of all her needs. You see, Dad had been previously married and divorced. Mom was Catholic, and when she married a divorced man she was written out of her father's will.

It was hard on us kids because she and Dad always seemed to be in an argument—about money, about some social event that was coming up, or just the fact that Mom was stuck in the house all day with a bunch of children. My mother had grown up in the city, but when I was small we all moved to the country with the cows and the corn. She felt like a prisoner. She was used to a place with sidewalks and stores just a few blocks away and being able to walk around and socialize with people. When all she had was dirt roads, she couldn't do that anymore.

We grew up under the grey cloud of Mom's broken heart and disappointment with her life and the choices she had made. She had high expectations of my father which he was just not able to meet. He tried early on to please her, but experienced only fruitlessness in his efforts. So Dad learned to live with the conflict instead. And he always had some other place to go if things got too bad—to a relative's or a friend's. I always felt bad for my dad. I knew he was feeling a lot of hurt, but just wasn't able to get it out. You could never approach him.

This husband couldn't open up to his wife, and the wife couldn't be satisfied with the best her husband could do. Meanwhile, the children were growing up without the attention they deserved from either parent. Each one of these adult caretakers could have modeled a sacrificial attitude, but both chose to stick to their own way of doing things—which they had most likely learned from *their* parents.

WE LEARN EITHER TRUTH OR HYPOCRISY

A couple can fool a lot of people in regard to the strength and stability of their relationship. For example, they can be fussing and fuming at home twenty minutes before church starts, but quickly don their Sunday-morning smiles as they leave the house and no one would ever suspect. But the children see. They notice. And they are a lot smarter than most parents give them credit for. One woman states clearly the mixed messages she received from her parents:

As a kid, my mother tried to make excuses for my father. She would tell me, "He is your father. You have to love and respect him. He cares about you. He provides for you." But then when *she* would argue with him, all I would hear was, "He's a jerk. He's no good. This is a stupid marriage. He never talks to me. I'm miserable."

So I heard a double message all the time. As a child I knew, *Okay, this is the truth. But this other way is how we're going to live, which is the lie.* There was the appearance we were supposed to keep up for others, and then there was the way we actually were. But we would never *talk* about it; it was just the understood rule of the house.

My mother just took it upon herself to be the fixer, the smoother-outer, the middleman. At the same time, she was an emotional wreck who used me as her main emotional support instead of the other way around. I felt like I was mothering my mother, providing the support relationship for her that my dad was not.

But at the same time Mom was *saying,* "He really means well," or, "Daddy just had a really hard day," or, "Dad didn't have it easy when he was growing up and he's trying to provide better for you." So it was like, *This is all a big joke, but okay, I'll accept it.*

When we got into our high school years, things started getting too much for my parents to handle.... Conflicts would come up and they didn't do a very good job of dealing with them. There came a point where Mom just said, "Forget him. Don't ask your father any more. You do what I say." She would outright lie to him and then take the responsibility and worry all night in case something should happen to us. He wouldn't know where we *really* were, but she did—things like that. We started to play the game. It was a big lie. Our whole life was just a big lie.

When children become entangled in the lies and conflicts of their parents, life is never easy. To begin with, the immediate situation becomes increasingly difficult. They don't want to get either one of their parents in trouble with the other, so they find themselves trying to keep up with and perpetuate the lies that the spouses are telling each other. But the long-lasting result can be even more detrimental: the children become pretty good at lying in their own relationships.

WE LEARN EITHER CONSISTENCY OR "ANYTHING GOES"

Perhaps nothing confuses a child as much as being treated differently for the same action. This is true of both positive and negative behaviors. Suppose a son goes out of his way to do something to impress his parents—completing a dreaded chore or creating a detailed painting, for instance. If he is rewarded with praise, he is likely to enjoy the feeling and do it again. But if the parents for some reason don't even acknowledge his efforts the next time, he becomes perplexed. Did he not do as well this time? Must he do something even more spectacular in order to get their attention?

The same principle holds true when a child misbehaves. Most youngsters go through periods of testing, seeing how much they can get away with. Let's suppose a young daughter decorates the walls of her bedroom with colorful crayon drawings, even though she knows her parents disapprove of this particular expression of creativity. When she steps over the lines of acceptable behavior, she expects to be disciplined. However, if this girl is spanked one time, ignored another time, and given a light talking to the next, she doesn't know how to interpret the difference in reactions stemming from the same behavior.

Meanwhile, fathers and mothers are always going through a variety of ups and downs in their own lives. Some days go pretty well; some days they constantly fight with each other; some days they feel burdened down financially or emotionally. Perhaps they can point to very reasonable excuses why they sometimes respond differently to their children. But the child never knows this. All he or she sees is the lack of consistency, which can be very puzzling indeed.

If parents do not model consistency for their children, where will they learn it? If our parents fail to demonstrate the kind of unconditional love that transcends their own immediate feelings, how are *we* supposed to feel? When we become parents ourselves, are we suddenly going to behave consistently with our own children?

I know from personal experience how very difficult it can be for parents to look past their own immediate concerns when a child needs their attention, but such occasions provide one of the best opportunities they will ever have to show their love. If a child begins to realize that he or she is more important than anything else in a parent's life, that child is far along the way to developing confidence and self-worth. If not, that person will inevitably face some emotional struggles down the line.

One woman tells of having a mentally ill mother. Her father eventually began to drink in an attempt to cope with the situation. He became an alcoholic. The woman explains:

> I feel like I was a victim in my later teen years because my father did not protect me and my sisters from my mother. She was verbally and physically abusive. He was an absentee father, in a way, and couldn't deal with her himself. His drinking was his way of escaping.
>
> I at least know *why* my father did what he did. I knew his drinking was his way of dealing with her. I never really understood my *mother's* behavior. There came a point when I realized she was mentally ill, but I still couldn't understand her behavior because she could be rational a lot of the time. But because of her particular illness, there was such inconsistency that you never knew what was going to happen next. I couldn't make any sense of this until much later.

As a child, this woman understood her father's behavior more clearly than her mother's. Her father at least acted in a consistent way, while her mother—due to her mental illness—remained totally unpredictable. Children naturally deal much better with consistent behavior. Of course, *positive* consistent behavior should be our goal as parents.

WE LEARN EITHER COMMUNICATION OR SECRECY

As we have already seen, children aren't necessarily fooled when parents try to keep secrets from each other. In fact, kids seem uncommonly adept at picking up on the ways their parents avoid communicating. One of the most destructive lessons they learn is how to cover up one lie by telling another. Keeping such "family secrets" can eventually make it impossible to communicate truthfully with anyone. Here is one example:

> When I was about twelve, my dad came home with a black eye and a bloody lip. My mom told us to leave the room, but we lis-

tened at the top of the stairs and found out that he had had an affair. The other woman's husband had just beat him up.

My parents never divorced; they never separated. They're still together, and my dad recently retired. They just shut out that incident. They just closed up, but I don't know how they got through it. I guess in the generation when they grew up, you just dealt with what you were dealt. You didn't talk about it. It just happened, and you went on.

But things were never the same after that for either my parents or us as kids. In my high school years I lost respect for both my parents and became very sexually promiscuous. I felt that my mom didn't even have a say in what I did because she didn't stand up and do something about what Dad had done to her. My father will not claim he's an alcoholic, but he did drink in the later years. I think it was basically after the affair was found out. He just went downhill.

My other brothers and sisters tried to block out the memory, just like Mom and Dad did. They don't really think it's a part of their lives. Maybe they don't remember or want to deal with it. But I just thank God that I'm the person I am and that I was eventually able to seek out his help and give everything up to him.

The failure of a husband and wife to communicate openly and honestly prevents growth in their own relationship. It also renders them unable to be truthful with others. And it causes their own children to keep secrets as well—secrets that at times can be quite harmful to their emotional and spiritual maturity.

WE LEARN EITHER TAKING RESPONSIBILITY OR ASSIGNING BLAME

When parents blame each other for problems in the family, the children are usually taking mental dictation. Then they use these same excuses for their own problems later in life. The more frequently they hear, "It's all your fault," the more children will learn to blame others for their own failures. On the other hand, if they hear, "I'm sorry; I should have known better," they see how simple it can be to take responsibility for one's own life and actions.

Perhaps nowhere can we see the assignment of blame more active than in divorce proceedings. The spouse who wins custody of the children seeks their support, and may even go out of the way to cast the other spouse in a bad light. While such a tactic may work in the short run, children can often be quite resentful if they find out the truth as they get older. By that time the children have frequently developed incorrect assumptions about the opposite gender in general. Here is how one woman describes this kind of scenario:

> As I've been trying to work through my own problems in order to be a better mother, I'm beginning to see more clearly some of the things *my* mother did. My father left us when I was young, and I grew up with a lot of anger and assumptions toward my father that I discovered had been planted by my mother.
>
> They had been married after knowing each other only a few weeks. Mom had carried unrealistic needs into her marriage and my father hadn't been able to fulfill them, so she dominated him. Then, when a daughter came along, she couldn't bear to see him give me so much attention and it destroyed their relationship. They were having problems on a husband/wife level, and my mother needed so badly for others to see Dad the way *she* saw him that all she could do was put him down. After a while he didn't know how to handle it, so he ran. It was all my father knew to do. It was get out or be destroyed.

Parents need people who will listen to and support them during times of divorce and other crises. But they should find peers who can offer unbiased opinions rather than involving their children who feel emotionally shattered as well.

WE LEARN EITHER SELF-CONFIDENCE OR GUILT

Few things a father can do to a child are as devastating as instilling a sense of guilt, whether or not it is done intentionally. Children need lots of assurance from fathers and mothers—at every age—in order to develop a healthy feeling of self-confidence.

If children aren't affirmed, they often develop a sense of doubt about themselves instead. It doesn't take much carelessness on the part of parents before children begin to take upon themselves the blame for everything that goes wrong in the family and feel tremendous guilt. When parents get caught up in fighting between themselves, the child frequently misses out on receiving support from either one of them, much less both.

One woman speaks of watching her father degenerate into active alcoholism. As he started to drink more and more, he first stopped spending time with her as he had done before. Later on, her father started beating her mother. She says:

> I started going to my room whenever Dad was home. I was not physically abused, but my mother was. What scared me most was I knew that when he was upset at us kids, he would abuse my mother. That was an awful feeling for a child to have: *Whoa! Wait a minute! I caused this!*
>
> I was the oldest of four brothers and sisters, and the others had already left home. I thought I had no choice but to stay and become a protector of my mother, even though I felt abandoned. I was left to deal with the worst years of Dad's alcoholism. I would ask my mother, "How can you live with him? He's awful. He's evil. He's mean. Why are you staying with him?" And she always gave me the same answer: "Your father is a good man."

This woman, an adult child of an alcoholic, was still feeling guilty for something over which she had absolutely no control. But where was she to find that all-important sense of self-confidence? Not from her father, certainly, who continued to turn to alcohol for support. And not from her mother, who continued to stay with and defend the man who physically abused her on a regular basis. Here again we see how the model provided by parents exerts tremendous influence on young people.

AN ADDED COMPLICATION

As we look back at childhood from an adult perspective, we may find it easier to connect certain events or patterns. We may realize, "So that's where I developed my selfish tendencies, my attitudes toward the opposite gender, and so forth." As adults we may be better able to see that many of our childish definitions were actually based on *misperception*.

For example, what we may have defined as genuine "intimacy" between Dad and Mom might actually have been a severely co-dependent relationship. Mom's "unconditional love" in regard to Dad's drinking might really have been "enabling" his alcoholism, allowing him to continue a problem for which he needed to become accountable. The "respect" we developed for Dad might be a lot closer, in truth, to fear of an authoritarian tyrant. Even though we think we know the truth, we may actually be way off base.

Chapter sixteen will deal with reevaluating some of your key definitions. At this point just be aware that even though you *think* you might have learned, for example, sacrifice rather than selfishness, you may eventually discover that your parents were actually modeling some pretty selfish motivations. And the misperceptions we develop as children can stay with us for a long time to muddy up the waters of our adult relationships.

The nobler concepts of life—such as love, trust, maturity, and teamwork—are difficult enough for children to learn. And it can be next to impossible if these values are never modeled by their parents. Fathers and mothers attempt to gloss over a lot of their less admirable qualities by quipping, "Do as I say and not as I do." Experience proves this to be an unworkable philosophy in most homes. You'd better believe that most young people are going to do exactly what they see their parents do. If you doubt this to be true, you can probably list several of your own qualities, good or bad, that you picked up from your own parents. Your children will do the same.

Fathers and mothers are teachers. The teaching portion of the job description is not optional; it's automatic. It comes with the territory, as the saying goes. The past now lies behind us. But if you are a parent, you can still make adjustments in how and what you teach your own children. As challenging as it might be, you need to spend some time thinking about what your parents taught you—and how you truly feel about some of those lessons.

TAKE TIME TO REFLECT

1. What did you learn by watching your parents?

2. List some words that describe how you feel about the behaviors and attitudes that you have learned or inherited from your parents.

3. Would you say that your father:
   - respected women or had contempt for women?
   - expressed intimacy or was emotionally distant?
   - sacrificed for you or clung to personal desires?
   - was truthful or hypocritical?
   - was consistent or inconsistent?
   - communicated well or kept secrets?
   - accepted responsibility or constantly blamed others?
   - built your self-confidence or instilled in you a sense of guilt?

4. What behaviors and attitudes are you most concerned about passing on or not passing on to your children?

SEVEN

How Can Trust in a Father Be Lost?

W HEN A MARRIED COUPLE first has a child, the family has a lot going for it. A bond forms between parent and child—one that can never be completely severed. The father need do nothing to earn the trust of his son or daughter. He already has it! It's automatic. Yet, as the child grows older, that inborn trust becomes fragile. Trust that isn't regularly reinforced by the parent tends to dissipate quickly. And any number of factors might initiate an even quicker demise of the child's trust in his or her father.

Remember that children first assume that fathers are always right. They always tell the truth. They always have the child's best interests in mind. They do not make mistakes. At least, this is what the child thinks. Eventually we all discover that fathers are not perfect. They do make mistakes. But even so, children still trust fathers to look after them. In fact, children often go out of their way to excuse much of a father's irresponsible behavior because they truly believe Dad to be someone quite special.

But if a father continues to behave in ways contradictory to that belief, the child will eventually lose trust in him. As we saw in the last chapter, the child observes parental behavior which predominately teaches either one lesson or just the opposite. Fathers either make a child feel mostly affirmed, loved, valued, and self-confident, or they act selfishly and cause the child to suffer unnecessarily. In the latter case, that bond of trust that once seemed invincible begins to dry up and crumble, leaving the child feeling alone, unloved, and afraid.

The erosion of trust is usually a gradual shift that takes place over a lengthy period of time. Even after children come to the realization that their fathers are only human, they are still quick to forgive when Dad makes an honest mistake or occasionally treats them unfairly. The father/child bond remains strong—especially if the parent does something to compensate for the injustice. This might mean simply saying, "I'm sorry," or affirming, "I love you." But if the father *doesn't* show genuine love and affection, the child eventually begins to notice. The day will come when the child loses his or her willingness to forgive.

A single event frequently becomes "the straw that breaks the camel's back." A woman might say, "I lost trust in my father the day he called me a slut in front of my friends." In actuality, the process began long before. But she keys in on that one event in her memory as her justification for giving up on him, for no longer trying so hard to maintain a good relationship with her father. And from that point on, the father—who had probably taken for granted the trust of his daughter—will find it next to impossible to regain the trust which has been lost.

The concept of trust can be hard to grasp. A trapeze act provides a helpful analogy. Imagine the trust required for a trapeze artist to let go of one sure support in order to connect with a catcher instead. Much can go wrong: the timing of the transfer, the security of the grip, the total concentration required on the part of the catcher, and so forth. When someone falls, we gasp at the tragedy—with luck averted by a safety net below. But when the essential elements of trust and competence work together to pull off a successful transfer, it is a thing of beauty to behold.

In understanding this bond of paternal trust, picture the father as the one who is supposed to be there to do the catching. Picture the child as the one who feels "up in the air" about some issue, all alone and clinging to any bit of truth or support to be found. The child needs to let go and connect with the father. But in order for the transfer to be successful, the child first has to be willing to let go of whatever he or she is clutching. (A common problem among teenagers is that they cling more tightly to a potentially harmful peer group than they do family ties.)

If father and child come together and firmly connect, the child feels safe and the father feels fulfilled. But if the father isn't there, the child either continues to be "up in the air," or else suffers a slow and painful fall—either way, all alone.

The following true stories help us to see how people can lose trust in their fathers. When pressed, these individuals could list a number of offenses that they had tolerated up to a certain point. But the time finally came when trust was completely eroded—much like the catastrophic breaking of a dam. In each case, this loss had long-lasting effects.

TRUST CAN BE LOST BECAUSE OF WHAT WE HEAR

Teasing young children seems to be part of almost every family relationship. Dad says something like, "If you keep making that face, it's going to freeze that way." And the daughter says, "Oh, Daddy, you're so silly." And the light-hearted exchange seems to somehow bring the two of them closer together.

But a father's words can assume much more power and influence than he might suspect. Teasing can easily go too far. Many of our volunteers shared stories of how a father's words proved to be a primary factor in their loss of trust. At some point they seem to have made a mental transition from, "He teases me, so he must love me," to, "He teases me, so he doesn't think much of me."

If the father is continually affirming his love, hugging his kids, and showing his concern in other ways, I don't believe that most children will hold them responsible for one careless statement here or there or carrying teasing too far every once in a while. But if those actions are absent from the relationship, a few careless words can explode like verbal atomic bombs right on top of the emotional stability of the child. Consider the experience of this older woman:

One of my earliest recollections of my dad was his taking me to the park on Sunday mornings after my brother was born. I suppose he was giving my mom some peace and quiet because I was just a toddler at the time. It's probably the only time I remember really feeling cherished or loved by my father. The name of the park was Wade Park, and it contained a little pond. When the weather was warm, he'd let me take off my shoes and socks and wade in it.

Then he started telling everybody a story that, "Sally thinks the place is called Wade Park because she gets to wade when she goes there." It was a put-down, like, "You dumb kid!" And immediately the park stopped being special.

This may seem like a child's memory blowing something up a lot bigger than it was. But it just seems like he spent an awful lot of his time shaming—or I perceived it as shaming me—telling other people, "She thinks it's called Wade Park because you wade there." It made me feel bad inside.

That's the first time I remember really being uncomfortable, feeling shamed and rejected by my dad, like he had to tell this story to make me look bad. It was sort of the pattern that our whole relationship followed. He took great pleasure in finding my slightest flaw and blowing it up out of proportion.

Even after I was married and had children of my own he would tell my children about some of the things he considered failures in my early life. He was still ridiculing me and mocking me—to my own children! It was something I never got over. It came from that first recollection, which became the pattern that continued as long as he was alive.

Our fathers have the power to devastate us with careless comments, whether they intend to hurt us or not. And when a child becomes uncomfortable with a father's teasing, or reaches the point where he or she can never know what will come out of his mouth next, it is almost impossible to continue to trust him.

TRUST CAN BE LOST BECAUSE OF WHAT WE SEE

One of our volunteers spoke of how cruel and abusive her father had been, certainly providing no reason to trust him. As she told story after story of how dreadful her young life had been, it became clear that she didn't even have to listen to her father to know he couldn't be trusted. Some of the most striking portions of her story involved the things she witnessed her father doing:

When I was still very young, I remember I could hardly finish— or even begin—my meal if my father was there. He would always do very gross things at the table that would cause me to run to my room.

He would do things with food—eat it in strange ways and make rude comments. Like he would take horseradish and put it in our potatoes and not tell us. Then we'd take a bite and realize what was going on, but he still made us eat them. And he wouldn't let us drink anything. I still have a hard time eating to this day. It's like everything sticks at the top of my throat. It finally goes down, but I'm a really slow eater. And it's from *that*. My stomach was always upset. It's like I was crying inside, and trying to eat because I was *made* to.

He would also sit my sister and me down on the sofa and he would pull up the hassock across from us. He would take any kind of food that was crunchy (like an apple or a carrot, or potato chips, especially) and he'd sit there and eat the whole thing very grossly and make us sit still. We weren't allowed to move. To this day my sister and I just flip out when any of our family members eat crunchy food. I don't know if I'll ever get over that. Mom says that's how he got attention.

My sister had a different personality than I did, and she did better around him. I couldn't stand the internal conflict he caused. To me it was gross, and he was just being mean and cruel in what he was doing.

This father got attention by his offensive, outlandish behavior. But he never gained the trust of his own children. A more common example was shared by a woman who watched her father succumb to the effects of alcoholism as she was growing up:

I remember real positive experiences with my father up until about age five. Then his alcoholism began to progress. I couldn't understand who this man was becoming. He wasn't the daddy I knew as a little girl. It always seemed to others that he was there for me. He would come to my school functions; he always encouraged me in school. (That's how I got my approval from my father—by excelling at school. When I'd get straight A's, I was Daddy's little girl.) I also became his best buddy in sports. I loved his teams. I would watch games with him, and I realize how superficial that was, but it was the only relationship I could have with him.

Yet I would see this man turn into a monster with me or with my mother during a physical fight. I would see him change, and it really caused me to be confused as a small child. I then became very bitter. I determined in my heart that I was never going to be dependent on a man. No way! I would be my own person. I would do my own thing. I could not trust men. I made life-changing decisions that were not healthy for me based on what I witnessed in my father.

Like a father's careless words, his actions also carry the potential for the emotional destruction of his child. Trust cannot grow in a climate of fear. Whenever a child fears what the father is going to do next, the relationship has reached a point of crisis. Working out whatever problems do exist becomes much more difficult from this point onward.

TRUST CAN BE LOST
IF THE FATHER INTENTIONALLY BREAKS THE BOND

So far we have been talking about situations where the child reaches a breaking point and determines that he or she no longer trusts Dad. The father's actions were not necessarily intended to destroy the child's trust or cause a permanent rift in the relationship. Yet because of the child's interpretation of those actions, a loss of trust became the end result.

Sometimes, however, the father actually initiates the break in the relationship. He becomes the first to stop trusting. And how can a child trust a father who puts no trust in him or her? Trust must be voluntary. It cannot be demanded or achieved through manipulation. One woman provides a powerful case in point:

I had always tried to do whatever it took to please my father. But he never approved of dancing, and one of our big parting of the ways came when I decided to go to the prom my junior year. It was the only time I think I looked beautiful. Most of the time I thought I looked like trash. But I was beautiful that night, and my father wouldn't even look at me because I was going to prom. I wasn't doing what *he* wanted.

Up until that time I had kept myself a virgin, but after that he started making nasty comments about my going to proms, dancing, and doing other things that "loose women" do. So I thought, *That's fine. What am I worried about? Why not just let go?* And I proceeded to go the other way. It was like his love for me turned a corner that day. I had never before realized how much our relationship depended on my doing what he wanted.

Had this father been able to trust his daughter in spite of their disagreements, their relationship might have continued to be relatively strong throughout her teenage years. A father hopes and expects that his children will continue to trust him even though he might do things that are contrary to their desires. And by the time a son or daughter reaches the age of sixteen, he or she will expect a father to trust back. But if the father doesn't trust the child, the child cannot trust the father.

Of course, no breach of trust compares to that of sexual abuse. When a child depends on a father for love and protection, serious emotional damage ensues if that father betrays the child's trust in favor of his own perverse gratification. Unfortunately, sexual abuse is a tragic fact in far too many homes.

One woman described her own version of this pitiful plight. Her mother died when she was eight. Her father didn't want her or her brother, so they were passed from home to home. She described feeling insecure, rejected, unloved, unwanted, and mad at the world. At eight years old, she was forced to be "a mother hen" to her younger brother. Just when it looked as if they would be placed in an orphanage, they were adopted on Christmas Eve, 1963.

She describes her feelings: "What a wonderful time it was for us! My new mother had recently become a Christian, and soon I put my faith in Jesus as well. My new dad wasn't a Christian, but he was a family man. He was a truck driver, yet always made sure he spent time with us. He took us to parks, zoos, amusement parks, out to eat, for Sunday rides in the country, and so forth. The first two years with my new family were great."

However, when she was ten, the girl's adoptive father began to drink more. The enjoyable family times stopped and he became more violent and physically abusive toward his wife. After he got fired from his job, the mother had to go to work. A grandmother moved in to babysit the children.

One Saturday evening the father was home watching television.

The mother was out, the brother was spending the night at a friend's house, and the grandmother was in her room listening to the radio with the door closed. The young girl decided to take a bath. As a grown woman, she recalls what happened next in graphic detail. This man whom she had come to trust and admire entered the bathroom and forced her to do a series of things that culminated in sexual intercourse.

Her words cannot even begin to convey the enormous emotional impact of this event on a ten-year-old child: "I wanted to scream and ask for help, but my grandmother couldn't hear what was going on. I wanted to crawl and then run away. I was threatened that if I ever told what had happened, I would not be alive long enough to tell anyone else. I wanted to die. Better yet, I wanted *him* to die."

The sexual abuse continued for about a year, until her wish came true. The adoptive father finally got another job. After working a double shift, he spent one evening in a bar and died on the way home when he fell asleep at the wheel and hit a telephone pole. Needless to say, this woman finds it hard to trust anyone—even twenty-six years later: "I find that trusting people is very difficult. I have a hard time trusting men in particular. I do not like to be alone in a car or room with them, not even in my own house. Someone else—a child or another adult woman—needs to be present before I'll ask anyone in."

When a father breaks the bond of trust with his child—especially through something as hideous as sexual abuse—the child may never trust again.

TRUST CAN BE LOST
WHEN OUR PERSPECTIVE CHANGES

Some people never lose trust in their father based on his words, actions, or criticism. They go through life thinking their relationships are solid. They think highly of their fathers and praise them to the hilt.

But sometimes their opinions are faulty. Certain people can't admit that a father has faults, that he didn't actually provide as much love and affirmation as they desired. They begin to make excuses for their fathers and go on seeing them only in the most positive light. They refuse to see their relationships with their fathers for what they really are: a one-way street. They trust their fathers, even though these men aren't necessarily trustworthy people.

Some people can live their entire lives and never realize the truth. Others are more fortunate. Something happens—perhaps an event completely unrelated to fathers or families—and they suddenly begin to see their fathers from quite a different perspective. In retrospect, they discover their fathers weren't quite the saints they had been painting them to be all these years. Here is one woman's revelation:

> I always thought my dad was just the greatest man on earth. But two years ago that picture of him was shattered when I began to go to a recovery group and look for reasons why I overeat. I began to recall a lot of negative events—a lot of things I hadn't remembered before. I still try to think of my dad as positive, but now I'm very angry at him and almost can't stand to be around him. I don't know why.
>
> He *was* a very gentle man—he's a very angry man now. I want to attribute it to old age, but I don't think that's it. Maybe it's because of the viewpoint that I now have and the other things that I'm seeing—the negative things that he didn't do for me emotionally. He's very cynical, very critical, very perfectionistic.
>
> I always admired my dad, and I still do, for his hard-working attitude. He's a man of integrity and character, and I've taken on those traits. They have become super-important to me. Yet I see myself as a victim in that I take them to perfectionism and with a critical attitude if others don't do things the way I do. I had to please my dad. I had to do things the way *he* wanted them, and I see for myself how it is now destroying some relationships. My mom sees that's one of the things that made our family very unhealthy. I always thought that was commendable. I now know it was wrong.

WHAT HAPPENS WHEN WE LOSE TRUST?

When people discover that they have placed their trust in a father who was not actually trustworthy, they can find it extremely difficult to trust anyone else. Putting your faith in anyone who eventually lets you down proves painful enough. But what if that person happens to be your father? And what if you've already spent months and years trying to convince yourself that he is still trustworthy?

Having trust destroyed in this kind of relationship usually produces extreme reluctance to ever trust anyone again. We start by "trusting too much," even though we might not have an accurate definition of trust. Then we get to a point where we can't take it anymore and we stop trusting other people altogether.

If left unresolved, a broken trust relationship with a father can absolutely devastate a relationship with a spouse as well as hinder strong relationships with children. It can keep a person from opening up with others at work. No future relationship will ever be as strong as it *could* be if the person's father proved to be unworthy of trust.

After trying to cope with such an emotional void in childhood, how can hungry parents adequately raise their own children? How do they say with conviction that, "Everything is going to be all right. Don't worry. I'll take care of you"? How do they break the cycle of hurt that they feel—and that was very likely felt by their parents, grandparents, and on back as far as anyone can remember?

We will address these haunting questions in the third part of this book as we begin to work our way through a healing process. But first, we need to understand more about how children tend to cope with the painful realities of their lives. Meanwhile, if certain recollections are coming to mind, don't push them back down into the recesses of your memory. Write them down. We will begin to deal with them shortly.

TAKE TIME TO REFLECT

1. On the continuum below, circle the level of trust you feel toward your father.

1	2	3	4	5	6	7	8	9	10
Distrust									Trust

2. If you circled a level below six, describe some ways that trust was lost because of your father's words or actions. If you circled a level above six, describe some ways that trust was reinforced by your father's words or actions.

3. How has your relationship with your father affected your ability to trust others?

EIGHT

The Child as Victim

WE HAVE ALREADY CONSID-
ERED many of the serious
complications which can arise from not receiving what we needed
from our fathers. Obviously, we would all prefer to have a father
who took good care of us, who was available, who made us feel
important, who took initiative in building an intimate relationship
with us, and who assured us that we were unconditionally loved and
accepted. Many of us, however, realize that we will never have this
kind of father.

If our hunger for a father's love has not been satisfied, we will
struggle to resolve the discrepancy between what we needed and
what we actually received. Can't we just forgive those who failed us
and get on with our lives? If we move away to school or leave home
to get married, isn't it enough to find other people who will boost
our sagging levels of self-esteem?

Unfortunately, it's not that simple. People who grow up starved
for enough fatherly love become victims in the same sense that
someone might be victimized by an anonymous mugger or by a
faceless cancer. The person who encounters such a trauma eventually develops discernable patterns of behavior. Unless the root problem is uncovered and dealt with, these reactions may continue
throughout the victim's life.

Because we are not usually very good at recognizing harmful patterns, many people may be victims without realizing it. Have you
ever seen a rock that has been cut in half and then polished? As you
start at the outer edge and begin to work your way toward the cen-

ter, you can see how each layer formed in the same shape as the previous one. When you get to the core of the stone, you're likely to find the imperfection that initiated these three-dimensional patterns.

Similarly, we act in certain ways as small children when we don't feel loved as we should. These coping behaviors are likely to be repeated again and again, applied to relationships with peers and spouses, and eventually passed along to our own children. Even though we may never consciously *choose* to do so, we become victims who act defensively.

VICTIMIZED BY DEGREES

Many victims become so by degrees—due to a series of events, none of which seem very dramatic at the time. Mary tells of having been accidentally dropped head-first into a kitchen trash can as a child. Her parents certainly didn't mean to do this or intend to harm her in any way. However, when they saw Mary wasn't hurt, they didn't comfort her right away. Instead, they ran to get a camera.

This one event was not that traumatic in itself. In fact, Mary didn't even remember it until she was going through a scrapbook, saw the picture, and heard the incident humorously retold by her mother. Yet she recalls numerous other times when her parents didn't show the attention she thought she deserved. One example occurred when Mary was dressed in cap and gown ready to attend her college graduation exercises at the university just thirty minutes away from where her parents lived. Her mother was in the backyard, digging in her flower garden, and simply decided at the last minute not to attend. However, the next year when their son graduated, the parents drove across several states to attend the ceremony.

Now an adult, Mary still struggles with her confidence and self-image. She finds it hard to feel loved by others. A painful pattern had been set into motion at an early age. Mary would find herself in a situation where she needed someone's support but she wouldn't get it. Then she would struggle to determine what it was about her that prevented her from receiving the love she needed. Eventually she learned to avoid getting into situations where she would need love from others—or so she thought.

Another man recalls being continually put down because his

grades were never quite as good as his sister's. His sister received lavish praise, while he was made to feel inadequate. His parents should have realized that grades aren't the only criterion by which to evaluate a person, but they did nothing else to encourage and affirm him. Consequently, this man still tends to rate his self-worth based on his performance. If he doesn't give the best presentation at work, he concludes that he's no good as an employee. If he can't spend as much time with his children as the neighbors spend with their kids, then he assumes he's a lousy father. This man has become a victim.

Sometimes people cannot even recall or identify childhood situations that left them feeling traumatized or victimized. But through an insidious series of events—often due to parental insensitivity—they don't receive the encouragement they need to become emotionally healthy adults. They learn to compensate and get by, but they suffer in many ways because their perspective has been seriously warped.

Many victims are quick to defend their parents. At the least suggestion to the contrary, a man might argue, "Why, sure my father loved me. Oh, he had to be gone a lot because of his work, but I know he cared for me." If he goes on to describe his home life in more detail, you might realize that his father was almost never home. In effect, this child had grown up abandoned by his father, yet continues to defend him vehemently.

What happens to such people? They often feel a great deal of anger toward their fathers. As a child gets old enough to realize that the parent could choose to be around if he wanted to, resentment begins to build. Yet the overwhelming need to be loved by that person remains strong. As a result, defenses are created. The victim rationalizes the situation and makes excuses that sound good to other people. Anger is internalized as this child continues to crave a father's love.

Others may be victims of some traumatic event. Many people can tell of irrational, horrendous abuses at the hands of their parents. And this type of abuse typically becomes a pattern, as we discussed in chapter five. Again, no one by nature wants to admit being abused by his or her own parents. Victims will spend much of their lives searching for a reason when none exists, other than the ugly truth: the parent failed to show genuine love for the child.

Current research tells us that as many as twenty to thirty-five percent of adult women have been sexually abused. The number may be even higher. It's not uncommon for people to completely block out such incidents from conscious awareness. But later in life, stress may begin to trigger those painful memories. Or a parent whose child reaches the age at which he or she was abused may suddenly recall these incidents.

EFFECTS OF VICTIMIZATION

Whether insidious or traumatic, unprovoked and unloving actions by parents victimize children in ways they may or may not realize. You may feel in doubt as to whether you fall into this category. If so, consider the following characteristics typical of victimization. If several of these descriptions apply to you, chances are that you have been victimized in some way in the past—whether you are consciously aware of it or not. The twelve symptoms listed below are indicative of any kind of victim. Yet if the root problem is father neglect or abuse, it should become obvious how these symptoms might develop.

When confronted with this list, some people say, "Yes! Most of these things are true of me. But my father never did anything to make me feel like a victim. He never abused me and I can't point to any specific traumatic event. What's wrong with me?" Perhaps your victimization is grounded in something other than father hunger. In any case, trust God to bring healing out of your continued prayer and reflection even if you never know what caused your difficulties.

Later chapters will provide some positive steps for victims to take. But for now, reflect on the characteristics of victims listed here and see if they might apply to you or to someone close to you. Only as you evaluate your situation with brutal honesty will you begin to glimpse the light of freedom.

Fragility. Victims are very sensitive to being offended. When someone upsets them, it is difficult for them to maintain any kind of perspective. If you try to befriend one of these people, you will have to behave almost perfectly.

But don't mistake *fragility* for *weakness.* Victims, having lost out on controlling the injustices of the past, tend to become very controlling people. Think in terms of a three-hundred-pound professional football lineman carrying a tiny porcelain figurine. The fragile figurine has been protected to the extent that no one is likely to get close enough to break it. Anyone who tries stands to get hurt.

Or suppose you're trying to help a large dog who has gotten stuck in an animal trap. Even though usually docile, the injured dog could react and hurt you without meaning to. Similarly, an emotionally wounded person feels a great deal of internal pain and is likely to lash out at anyone who comes too close. Though fragile, such individuals can still do a lot a damage if you aren't careful.

Extremes in perception. Victims tend to view people as either evil or wonderful—one extreme or the other. And the perception is likely to shift quickly from one to the other—usually from wonderful to evil rather than the reverse. These people have tried for so long to justify in their own minds the ones who hurt them that there remains no middle ground. Small offenses against these victims quickly become magnified all out of proportion. Hostile feelings toward past abusers are often unjustly projected onto present relationships. It is very difficult for victims to allow their peers to be simply normal people with normal problems.

Feeling misunderstood. Victims grow up with others refusing to listen to their valid complaints about the pain they feel. When the pain becomes too intense for them to carry alone, they may reluctantly seek help from others. Ever since being hurt as small children, victims desperately seek comfort and security, but they cannot fill that need simply by talking to another person.

If these people grew up malnourished by a father's love, no other person will ever completely fill that void. Besides, victims commonly feel that too much has happened to them for anyone else to ever understand completely. If and when they try to open up, they never feel that others truly comprehend what they are saying.

Tremendous rage. Anger and rage are not simply a straight-line continuum of the same feeling. I think of *anger* as being somewhat object-oriented. If I'm angry at something, there's usually a specific reason. But *rage* is more of a continual state—*anger looking for direction*. Victims have not usually been allowed to express anger, so the feeling sort of ferments within them until rage builds.

Many people cannot even identify the source of their rage. And since the feelings seem so incessant and it is difficult to cope with anger *all* the time, these people tend to repress the feelings and try to get on with life. But in such a state, the least offense might trigger all those inner emotions. Rage can result. A common by-product of this process is shame. Victims don't want to lose control, but just can't help it. When it happens, they feel ashamed.

Lack of trust or commitment. Trusting someone else requires a certain level of vulnerability. You must let down your own defenses in order for someone else to get to know you better. But victims who have attempted this in the past have often been betrayed. When they have opened themselves up to someone else, they have been hurt rather than befriended. Consequently, they've erected a "wall" between themselves and others. Some victims may not even be aware that the wall exists; others are simply too afraid to make themselves vulnerable.

Some people can really fool you. Someone may appear to be the most open, transparent, social creature you've ever met. But if you're very observant, you may see this person reach a certain level of openness and then suddenly shut down. As an inveterate people-watcher, I see numerous people who seem to be warm, outgoing, and gracious—but I have to wonder what they're like in the privacy of their own homes.

A husband who happens to be a wonderful conversationalist with every other woman he knows may end up divorced because he has completely stopped talking to his wife at home. This lack of trust often creates havoc in a second marriage. A person has learned to be open and to appear trusting—but only to a certain degree. When expected to communicate on a deeper level, he or she is incapable of doing so.

Some people enter into relationships much too quickly to be realistic or healthy. They know they cannot genuinely make themselves vulnerable to others, so they try to force themselves to do so. They might be introduced to someone, and an hour later be acting as if that new acquaintance were a lifelong friend by making requests of or doing things well beyond the expectations of a casual relationship.

This "pseudo-vulnerability" is intended to draw a similar response out of the other person. Victims so much want to be included in someone else's life that they will (for a short time) seem to drop the wall that surrounds them. The other person may enjoy the attention for a short while, but soon bolts when it becomes clear how much the victim demands. Why? Because such an intense relationship was never agreed upon.

Solid relationships are built one piece at a time, little by little, with one person keeping in pace with the other. People who try to rush the process are almost always disappointed in their relationships and angry at those who don't relate well to them.

Lack of thankfulness. It's not that a victim is never thankful for anything, but the gratitude rarely lasts long. If you do something for such a person today, he or she may express genuine thanks. But by tomorrow, that grateful feeling is likely to have faded. A victim's life is immensely influenced by negative thinking. Thankfulness may overcome the negativity for a short time, but soon the much greater level of negativity again takes control. Victims commonly feel short-changed in life. They know they don't have the same thankful spirit they witness in others. And for now, there's no easy way for them to acquire it.

Demand for entitlement. We all have some innate sense that life should be pleasant, at least to some degree. Those who receive more joy out of life than others tend to think they deserve more. For victims, this becomes another defense against the inner "black hole" of negativity. When these people marry, they expect their spouses to help them overcome those powerful, negative emotions. ("Since my parents weren't as good as they should have been, I deserve a partner who will help me out.")

Assignment of blame to others. Victims are typically very guilt-prone, but accepting the blame for something is especially painful because of the hurt they already carry within them. They are like a person with a broken rib who gets slapped on the back. The blow certainly shouldn't have hurt, yet the pre-existing injury intensifies its effect. To counteract this oversensitivity, victims are quick to find fault with others, reflexively transferring to someone else their own wrongdoings.

For example, suppose your spouse always arrives late to scheduled events. On a day when the two of you are supposed to be somewhere, he or she is twenty minutes late getting ready. Finally, you rush to the car. Because you're in a hurry, you're not sure you locked the back door, so you hop out for ten seconds to check it. Suddenly, it becomes your fault that the two of you are late. In the spouse's opinion, if *you* hadn't had to get out of the car to check the door, *you* wouldn't have been late. Such transfer of blame often takes place without any conscious awareness.

Desire to punish anyone who offends them. Those with a victim mentality often find it hard to see any offense as a small one because of all the inner feelings they carry, recognized or hidden. Every injustice—no matter how small, no matter how unintentional—is perceived as a personal attack. The offenders should be punished, in the victim's opinion. And frequently, the only punishment that presents itself is to sever the relationship. Victims forsake a lot of potential friendships over rather insignificant issues.

Continued victimization. Victims continue to be victimized. They don't know how to stop. They flip-flop between being just as aggressive as possible to being so passive as to let everyone walk over them. And then they get mad at themselves. They experience tremendous anger when they realize how they allowed this victimization to happen to them *again*. They can tell you all the ways they've been victimized over the past six months—and who was responsible in each case.

Excuses. Victims can be geniuses when it comes to explaining why they are unable (or unwilling) to do something. Passivity generally marks their response style. Other people previously caused them to become victims, and now they tend to remain passive while expecting others to meet their needs. Then they make excuses as to why they couldn't deal with the issue themselves.

The media are big providers of excuses. I recently read an article about the grim job prospects for those who are now graduating from high school. If I had been a student reading the article, I would have thought, *Well, it's useless. What can I do?* By portraying high school graduates as victims of the national economy, the author provided ample excuses for times when they don't perform well.

Homelessness has become a severe problem in our society over the last several years. We recognize homeless people as victims and try to provide for them by creating and supporting shelters. Yet I would suggest that a certain percentage of people who make use of those shelters are actually irresponsible. It becomes easier for them to continue to act irresponsibly because they know they have a place to go rather than to assume proper responsibility for themselves. They see themselves as victims, while society enables them to act out this identity.

My daughter, Betsy, has taken up horseback riding. Recently she came up to me and said, "Dad, at the next horse show I'm going to win three blue ribbons." I told her, "Just enjoy yourself and have a good time, but you know I'm behind you all the way." Sure enough, at the horse show Betsy beat out twenty or thirty other people and received three blue ribbons.

That night after she went to bed she yelled out to me and said, "Daddy, thank you for believing in me." I wasn't sure my daughter *would* win three blue ribbons, but I believed she *could* do it. It made a difference that I had approached Betsy as a young woman capable of achieving her goal rather than a victim at the mercy of all her competition.

Continued struggles with the past. Victims remain victims when they never deal with the root problems that cause their pain. Those of you who have ever tried to remove a splinter from a little girl's foot may know the symptoms. The child begins to wince as soon as she sees the needle; at the first twang of pain she begs you, "Please, just leave the splinter in!" You know that removing the splinter will hurt, but leaving it in will cause even bigger problems in the future.

Victims still carry invisible emotional splinters within them. They have never found the courage to trust someone to open the wound and get to the problem and extract it. As the pain continues to become more and more intense, so do the attempts at treatment. Victims want the hurt to stop, but whenever someone becomes serious about dealing with it, they quickly retreat and deny that it's bothering them.

That's really the point of this whole book. Whether or not you feel you have been victimized by your father, I encourage you to bravely endure the process of having any embedded splinters removed from your heart and spirit. God is the Master Physician who heals and restores us to complete health. But you must do your part in holding still and bearing the pain of what will be an ongoing process rather than a momentary "ouch."

While no father is perfect, the corollary is also true: no child is perfect. While a newborn baby may appear to be wholly innocent, just wait a few months and see what emerges. Let's consider the other side of the coin in the next chapter. What developmental stages do children go through and how do they affect their relationships with their fathers?

TAKE TIME TO REFLECT

1. What images come to mind when you hear the word *victim*?

2. Put a checkmark by the following symptoms that are currently present in your life:
    fragility
    extremes in perception
    feeling misunderstood
    tremendous rage
    lack of trust or commitment
    lack of thankfulness
    demand for entitlement
    excuses or assignment of blame to others
    desire to punish offenders
    continued victimization
    continued struggles with the past

3. To what extent would you say you have been victimized?

4. What childhood situations or memories help you recall being victimized?

NINE

Growing up with Daddy

A S WE THINK BACK to our childhood years, most of us would like to have had better relationships with our fathers. People raised in severely dysfunctional and abusive home situations obviously missed out on many of the tender memories that should have been shared between father and child. But even those from "normal" homes frequently express a longing to have enjoyed more of Dad's time and attention. The more people you talk to, the more obvious it becomes that no one had Ward Cleaver for a father.

How severe is your own father hunger? A clue may be found in the emotions that escape when you remember your own relationship with your father. Some of you may recall your childhood with a strange mixture of fondness for all the good times and a touch of regret for the times that could have been better. Others will be feeling angry as they begin to remember some of what they wanted and thought they deserved as children, yet were denied. And still others are likely to resist looking back with every fiber of their being, fearful of what they might discover.

Yet when does this problem begin? No one wakes up one morning at the age of thirty, thumps a palm against his or her forehead, and exclaims, "Oh my goodness, I have father hunger!" Rather, we carry feelings within us that seem to have always been there. These feelings affect every stage of our lives, from early childhood long into our adult years. They don't evaporate with time; if anything, they grow stronger.

Much has been written about the stages of human development and the characteristics of each stage. So as not to make this discussion overly technical or complex, I like to think of four broad stages:

1. Bonding: birth to two years of age
2. Separateness: two to eleven years
3. Adolescence: twelve to eighteen years
4. Maturity: from nineteen years on up

Of course, individuals mature at various rates of growth, so any groupings by age must be somewhat arbitrary. But as a rule of thumb, certain changes are expected to take place at each of these levels of development. Let's consider each of these stages in more detail as it relates to father hunger.

BONDING

From birth through approximately two years of age, children form a strong attachment to their parents. Infants incapable of functioning on their own *must* trust that someone will provide for them. Most parents try their best. Through the process of bonding, children first experience qualities like love, trust, and value. Mature parents foster these feelings by going beyond the basic duties of feeding and diaper-changing. They try to make eye contact, play with their offspring, sing to them, hold them with tenderness, and do other things that make small children feel special.

Bonding can certainly be a time-consuming proposition. Unfortunately, many fathers tend to leave the bonding to the mothers at this earliest stage of development. Several factors contribute to this trend. For one thing, nursing mothers can naturally care for the baby more at first. In most cases, mothers spend more time reading and preparing for baby's arrival. Even with all the recent advancement in equality and women's rights, most people still perceive that it is the mother's responsibility to do the lion's share of the nurturing of a tiny baby.

Practical complications enter into the picture as well. What do you suspect happens to many fathers while gazing into the face of that first small child? They suddenly begin to take seriously their role as provider. They may feel the need to put in overtime at work to make sure the child doesn't lack for anything. Yet if they aren't careful, the child will lack for time spent with Dad. While bonding requires a certain time commitment from the father, it is certainly worth the effort.

SEPARATENESS

What typically happens after children have learned that they can count on their parents for love, affirmation, a sense of value, and so forth? The next phase focuses on establishing some boundaries that will allow children to take those first halting steps toward emotionally healthy independence. The crucial new word becomes added to a child's vocabulary: *No!*

Children aren't being completely rebellious at this stage. Imagine the immense job of sorting through everything you're learning for the very first time. Over a period of ten years or so, growing children will determine what they believe, what their responsibilities are, and what they want to become. They will learn to act in certain instances where they should, and to let others act when *they* should. As they mature, children will discover that most issues have two sides, and that they need to respect opinions that don't necessarily coincide with their own. They will struggle with identifying and coping with their often very intense feelings.

Children will also discover that they have the right to make their own choices in life. Does he prefer basketball or band? Will she be a cheerleader or a gymnast? Does he enjoy poring over his baseball card collection or roaming the neighborhood with his dog at his side—one day a pioneer and the next day a pirate? Would she rather play in the mud or bake cookies? The choices never end.

At this crucial stage a child discovers that he or she has a distinct and separate "self." While the bonding stage required an almost blind dependence on Mom and Dad, this stage of separateness can be either frightening or exhilarating. The deciding factor in most cases will be whether or not the parents provide the affirmation and confidence children need in order to feel secure about themselves.

When parents do their job, children can feel okay about making their own decisions, relating to others as unique individuals, doing some of their own problem-solving, and otherwise becoming their own persons. If parents don't become involved enough with children during this stage, however, it is very difficult for young people to acquire the confidence they need. No other source exerts as much sway as the parents.

Children ideally need the influence of both parents at this stage. While many mothers do an adequate job in a single-parent home—and may do as well as any one person possibly can—it's simply never as effective as having both a mother and father working together with the child.

A young girl learns from her father how to relate to men in a healthy way. When she feels loved and accepted by her father, nothing else seems to matter. But if love and acceptance are withheld, the void in a daughter's life may compel her to look in any number of other places to capture a similar feeling. Consequently, many young women entering adolescence end up making some bad decisions—frequently with unwanted or tragic results.

The father's influence is also vital to males during this stage. While forming his own thoughts, opinions, feelings, and values, a young boy desperately needs a role model to show him what a man ought to be. If the father is absent or apathetic, the child naturally looks elsewhere for models. He's not likely to find other good examples on the street or in the shallow characterizations on TV or in the movies. No one else will ever be as effective at combining the tough and tender qualities he will need in life as a father who spends time with him on a regular basis.

ADOLESCENCE

During the stages of bonding and separateness, parents might live under the mistaken assumption that they are succeeding in raising relatively healthy children with a minimum of involvement or hassle. However, any "sins of the past" quickly come to light during the stage of adolescence. As children go through puberty and begin to mature *physically*, they realize that soon they will need to *function* as an adult at all levels—in behavior, identity, relationships, goal setting, and so forth.

Parents who have bonded well with their children have provided a strong sense of trust, value, and confidence. If they have also helped establish a healthy sense of separateness, the child may navigate these rocky years with a minimum of difficulty or confusion. But when an adolescent stands at the threshold of adulthood without having developed such a sense of assurance, it can be a severely awkward and painful time—as many of us can probably attest.

This stage comes equipped with unprecedented peer pressure. If a father hasn't convinced the child through word and deed that people don't need a drink to get through the day, the temptation to drink will be even stronger. And if the child's need for love has not been adequately fulfilled by a parent, the sexual awakenings of the adolescent years initiate almost overwhelming cravings—as well as opportunities to find fulfillment around every corner.

How can a teenage boy act like a man if he has never seen how a real man acts on a day-to-day basis? How can a teenage girl build healthy relationships with the opposite sex if she has never been affirmed by a loving father? A mother can do everything in her power to be "both mother and father" to her children, and may succeed to a great degree. Yet during the adolescent years, most children who grew up with absent, apathetic, or uninvolved fathers will suffer the consequences. In trying to compensate for the love that has been missing in their lives, they too frequently make mistakes which haunt them for the rest of their lives.

MATURITY

The growth process never stops. Physically, we reach a certain point where we cease to grow taller, but emotionally we either continue to mature or else we regress. Emotional maturity is somewhat like climbing a steep hill in that it's hard to remain in one place. We either make progress onward and upward or else we tend to slide back downhill. We also continue to mature in a spiritual sense. The author of Hebrews calls us to "leave the elementary teachings about Christ and go on to maturity" (Heb 6:1). Jesus himself instructed us to "be perfect... as your heavenly Father is perfect" (Mt 5:48).

It might be easy to misunderstand our goal. Perfectionists usually struggle with many problems. They may come to feel that nothing they do is ever good enough. And certainly, those who live with them or work for them never seem to live up to the expectations placed on them.

Jesus does not call us to be perfectionists. We must never lose sight of the fact that we are sinners saved by grace. We are human and we *will* make mistakes. We will never achieve perfection—at least, not here on earth. Since we know we will never quite achieve perfection, we can aim toward the goal that remains ever on the horizon. No matter how far along we are in our life journey, we can always inch a little closer toward that goal.

In the freedom of sons and daughters of God, we can drop a lot of our pretenses. We don't need to act like we have all the answers; no one does. We can drop our guard and become more vulnerable. We can trust God more and ourselves less. We can quit hurrying quite so much and set a pace that is more comfortable and realistic. When we make these kinds of adjustments, the lifelong process of maturity takes on a new excitement and fascination. We may never be perfect, but each day we can be a little more mature than we were yesterday.

ARRESTED DEVELOPMENT

The physical maturation process continues to adulthood as long as we continue to eat, sleep, and exercise adequately. When these necessary ingredients are lacking, the process is hindered. In the same way our emotional and relational maturation process continues through childhood and into maturity as long as we experience affirmation, strength, and appropriate limits. To the degree—and at the stage of development—that these essential components are lacking, our emotional development is arrested.

Our adult process of maturation can be stunted or even halted if we continue to long for a father's love that we never received. As neglected children grow up, start their own families, and begin to interact with their own children, the memories of the past can come back to haunt them in ways they never would have anticipated.

Our natural response is to perpetuate the problem by treating our own children the same way we ourselves were treated. Our parents provided the model for adult behavior that we witnessed for many years. It's hard to act differently when we find ourselves in the same kinds of situations.

Yet the responsibilities of parenthood sometimes jolt people in the opposite direction. They begin to realize that there *must* be a better way for parents and children to relate than what they experienced while growing up. And when they try to pinpoint the problem, childhood memories come flooding into their minds— renewing the sense of loneliness, abandonment, insecurity, lack of worth, and other painful emotions that may have been tucked away for many years. Parents need an advanced level of maturity to deal with their own past in order to avoid perpetuating the problem with their children. Unless they do, the problem will never disappear on its own.

The absence of a father's love can influence a person at every stage of life: the need for trust and a sense of worth in a child's early months; shaping the identity and separateness that soon follows; and the need for adult role models as an adolescent. Even adult children suffer in a multitude of ways as they think back to times when a father rejected or ignored them.

Children adapt a variety of roles as they struggle to cope with less-than-ideal father relationships. The next chapter will identify several of the more common ways young children try to fill the emotional void in their lives. But first, take time to reflect back on the different stages of your own life for clues of father hunger.

TAKE TIME TO REFLECT

1. Ask your parents, siblings, other family members, or friends to recall one incident from your childhood when you bonded with your father. What did you find out from your interviews?

2. Describe several instances where you received affirmation from your father.

3. What words would you use to describe your relationship with your father during adolescence?

4. In any of the four developmental stages, list examples when you felt abandoned, abused, or neglected by your father.

TEN

What Roles Are Children Forced to Play?

WHILE CHILDREN MAY APPEAR to be weak and fragile, they are much stronger and more resilient than we often think. A child can deal with almost any single traumatic event that is followed up with love, support, and genuine concern from loving friends and relatives. The extent of damage will depend on the age of the child, the nature of the event, and any number of other factors. Yet in most cases, children will be able to "bounce back" before very long.

Lasting harm tends to occur in much more subtle ways. While any single offense may not be traumatic in itself, repeated abuse can be devastating. A child's recognition of such a pattern quickly erodes any sense of self-confidence. When father/child relationships become seriously distorted, children lose perspective. They cease to feel valued and valuable. Having learned that more is required than merely *being*, children soon turn to *doing* by trying to behave in a way that pleases the parent.

No matter how else a parent attempts to compensate, nothing adequately replaces what is lost when the child comes to this conclusion. Telling comments abound:

> "I remember when I was just a little boy, climbing into my father's lap. He would never reach for me. But I could at least climb into his lap. That's about the only positive thing I can remember."

"I remember my dad as a hard worker and I remember our family vacations. That's the highlight of my family memories, and my dad in particular. He worked hard to take us, one week a year, to a vacation at a cabin. But I don't remember any emotional closeness. Nothing strikes me as positive from an emotional viewpoint."

"My father could be smiling and talking so nice, and then could turn around and knock you flat on your back. I call it two-faced... phony. You couldn't trust him. I went to him for help when I was just a young boy—maybe five years old. I was in a cave and someone had thrown a sawhorse down on top of me. I came out and I was crying. I went up to my dad and he just laughed at me. It was as if I just didn't exist."

"My father had artistic talent. I would watch what he drew, but mine was never as good as his, so I would think, *Don't even do it*. And rather than being encouraged, I was told, 'Artists throw away wastepaper baskets full of paper until they get it right.' That was just overwhelming to me. Why even try?"

"My dad was always in the background if I would go seek him out, but he never initiated contact. My mother always told me he didn't want to bother with me."

As these comments suggest, children can be made to suffer in many ways. Most of us would be quick to agree that no child should ever have to endure serious physical abuse. Yet many of those who agree are the very same parents who subject their own children to various forms of *emotional* abuse—neglect, solitude, parental withdrawal, or perfectionist expectations. These and many other faulty ways of relating can cause children to struggle with their self-concept for years and years to come.

Many parents are not at all aware of what they're doing. Or they may know, yet not have any idea to what extent the child is being affected. But the child knows. At first youngsters react instinctively. If they're being physically abused, they hide. If they aren't receiving the love they need, they adapt in other ways. Whenever children fail to receive a father's unconditional love and acceptance, they will attempt just about anything to get attention.

Other books have described some of the traditional roles that children play in dysfunctional families—enablers, rebels, heroes, and so forth. In an attempt to keep these concepts fresh and simple, I would like to provide a slightly different approach. I believe many valid comparisons can be made between childhood roles and various members of the animal kingdom.

THE SHOW PONY

When a father doesn't provide the time and interaction a child craves, some children respond by trying to attract his attention through performance. Like a show pony, youngsters may learn a number of "tricks" to impress Dad. Boys may tend to strive for athletic excellence, desperately wanting Dad to know they can run the fastest mile, bat in the deciding run, score the winning touchdown, and so forth. Daughters may work very hard at becoming "pretty enough" for Dad to notice. Or they might try to cook special meals or imitate Mom's actions which Dad seems to especially appreciate.

Other "tricks" children learn include artistic efforts (drawings, stories, etc.), academic achievements, and musical talents. Any skill that seems to get the father to notice them will be passionately cultivated by a child who assumes this particular role. In fact, many of the children who function as show ponies grow up to be perfectionists—never satisfied that what they do is good enough.

THE WORK HORSE

While show ponies try to dazzle Dad with finesse and outstanding feats, work horses attempt to get his attention through consistent service. Both groups are attempting to get noticed for some kind of performance. While show ponies focus on the *quality* of what they do, work horses especially strive for *quantity and consistency*.

What might we see in a child who assumes the role of work horse? These are the kids who bring Dad his comfortable shoes at the end of a long day. They discover how much he hates to mow the yard on Saturday, so they give up playing with friends after school on Friday so they can beat him to it. Whatever Dad is trying to do around the house, they make themselves available to hand him tools, run errands, or do anything else that might evoke some words of praise and recognition.

Unfortunately, if fathers tend to take their children for granted, they also tend to take their children's work performance for granted as well. The child soon discovers that no amount of extra effort ever seems to draw the desired recognition. A "thank you" for a job well done offers little consolation when unconditional love is missing in a relationship. If the child continues to try to fill the emotional emptiness by constantly striving, it is likely that he or she will grow up with strong workaholic tendencies. Work can never replace love.

THE SACRIFICIAL LAMB

In homes where the father exhibits a great deal of anger or even rage, one or more of the children frequently take on the role of a sacrificial lamb. False accusations fly against the child, the mother, a brother, or a sister. The child knows from experience how terrible it feels to be falsely accused of something, along with the possible severity of the consequences. To prevent another family member from being unjustly judged and punished, the child may step in and take the blame. Here's one example told by one of five male children:

One Wednesday night when I was thirteen, my father discovered his pocketknife was missing. This was just before we left home to go to a prayer meeting at the church. He was convinced that one of us had stolen it and traded it for two pieces of bubble gum or something. So he told us that we had until we got back home for whoever took it to confess. Otherwise, he was going to beat us all.

We sat through Royal Ambassadors at the Baptist church and the prayer meeting that followed. When we got home he lined up the five of us and was ready to punish us all. So I confessed that I did it. I don't know why, other than I just couldn't bear the thought that all of us were going to get a beating for something I didn't think any of us did. I took that whipping. About two years later, Dad found that pocketknife. And he never said, "I'm sorry."

This adult man—and thousands of other men and women like him—is still carrying the physical or emotional scars of acting as a sacrificial lamb. The occurrence is far too common, the grief far too real.

THE MOLE

In homes where rage and abuse become frequent, another common role children play is that of a mole. Moles hide in dark places out of fear of discovery. The same man who told the previous story talked of his strategy of hiding:

> As a child I spent a lot of time hiding in the closet or under the house. It was much easier to just disappear. I suppose it was so easy because no one really cared where I was or what I was doing—unless, of course, they had some chore they wanted done. Often I would go under the house for hours at a time because it was a safe place. The house was on a conventional foundation. There was about four feet of clearance, and that was plenty for me. I'd say that at least forty percent of my time was spent in the dark shadows playing alone in the dirt. The best place to be when my father was around was out of sight. And I made a real effort to disappear.

A woman from a similar type of home situation echoes these same feelings: "I usually found myself hiding in corners to stay out of my father's way. My sister was more vocal, but I would just crawl in a hole. To this day, I have a very hard time expressing myself—especially when conflict is taking place. I remember hiding in closets trying to keep away from him. Always hiding. Not even feeling safe in my own house."

This response entails more than the common image of an ostrich sticking its head in the sand to avoid danger. Children who assume the role of a mole present extreme cases where the person wants to be completely out of sight, entirely in the cover of darkness. This child wants absolutely no contact with the father. The few encounters that hold any hope of communication are far outweighed by the times that are filled with hostility and pain.

THE LEMMING

The same force that pulls some people into hiding seems to push others toward a lifestyle of self-destructive behavior. The opposite response of moles is that of lemmings, noted for mass migrations that sometimes carry them into the sea to be drowned in large numbers. Similarly, some people leap out of the "frying pan" of a bad home situation into the "fire" of other unhealthy relationships. Children can suffer so much due to not receiving a father's love that they are almost literally propelled away from the family into the first open door that they find. Such opportunities do not tend to be positive ones.

The woman quoted in the previous mole example described how her more vocal older sister demonstrated lemming-like behavior:

She stands up and will fight. Consequently, we think that's why she got the more physical beatings. I got them too, but not to the extent that she did because I would just take them. I didn't fight back. My sister was gone from the house when I was twelve. She got pregnant. That was her way out. Even before that, though, she was gone most summers because she couldn't stand living in the house (which left me there alone). She was pregnant at fifteen and gone by sixteen.

Sexual promiscuity is only one of the self-destructive behaviors exhibited by children when parents fail to show adequate love. As we mentioned in chapter four, others may join gangs or begin to experiment with homosexuality in a frantic search for the love that they crave.

Some turn to the military for fulfillment. While this may not be self-destructive in itself, such a decision can often be reached out of sheer desperation rather than a genuine desire to serve one's country. One man put it this way: "All of us were eager to get out on our own as soon as we were old enough. My oldest brother joined the Army as a minor, and *my dad signed for him* to be able to enter. He had just turned seventeen. He was that eager to get away from home. He was in the Army four years and only came home once."

When a choice to enter military service is made in haste, many young men and women spend a number of years in misery until their commitment is up. Then, when they get out, these people still face the same problem: "Where can I find the love and fulfillment that I seem unable to experience?"

THE PARROT

Some children learn to cope with the lack of individual attention by becoming clones of their parents. If they aren't noticed on the basis of their individual merits, surely they will receive praise if they can just learn to do everything the way Dad would do it. They begin to parrot everything they hear. Rather than having any opinion of their own, these children learn to say what they think the parents want to hear. And maybe, just maybe, this child will get a cracker—a tangible reward of some kind.

The biggest drawback to this strategy is that the child becomes what he or she least desires to be—a carbon copy of the unloving parent. One woman detailed her childhood problems at great length and then concluded with this statement: "I didn't have the tools I needed to get on with my life. I ended up in twisted, dysfunctional messes of my own—which was a shock. I wasn't going to be like my parents, and ended up *just like* them."

Parents may indeed pay more attention to children who act more like them and say what they expect to hear. Yet a parent does the child no favors by responding in such a way. Children need to be affirmed even when they express their own opinions or act in ways that the parent may not understand (as long as the words and behaviors are simply *different* and not *wrong*). Until children are able to express themselves honestly, they will never be able to form healthy relationships with others.

THE CHAMELEON

The role of chameleon is somewhat similar to that of the parrot. The child wants to become whatever might satisfy the father. In the case of the parrot, the parent acts in a reasonably consistent manner. But in the case of the chameleon, the parent's behavior remains unpredictable or inconsistent. The child is forced to quickly analyze the state of the parent and then adapt his or her own behavior to respond to it. One lady explains chameleon-like behavior very well:

> My dad was an alcoholic, and I think of him in three distinct personalities: there was the angry daddy; there was the silent daddy; and there was the happy-drunk daddy. My family's whole home life was lived in anticipation of which one would show up. "What is Daddy going to be like when he walks in the door?" My sisters, my mom, and I would all just watch and wait.
>
> If he came in as the angry daddy, we knew we had to disappear. If he was the silent daddy, we had to keep it low—but we could hang around. We always had the most fun (and he was easiest to be around) when he was the happy drunk. But he never remembered anything that went on when he was in that state. So I knew even though it might be okay today, it wasn't going to be remembered tomorrow.

Like a chameleon, this woman found that her survival depended on how well she was able to adapt to her environment. If these kinds of kids don't "blend into the background" well enough, or if they make their presence known at the wrong time, they are in danger of harm. While craving love and attention, they know better than to ask for it.

THE LAP DOG

When a father refuses to assume the role of family leadership, a paradox can be created. His words and actions may indicate that he wants his wife and children to be strong. But when they actually begin to show signs of strength, the father may feel threatened and make life miserable for them. Sensing this paradox, children may turn to the other extreme: absolute submission. In some cases, a child can be drawn into being the confidant or "best friend" of the mother. Such a relationship often becomes very unhealthy. One man describes his experience:

> I was *physically* abused by my father and I ended up being *sexually* abused by my mother. This was never to the point of inter-

course, but she often dressed or undressed in front of me. I was never allowed any privacy. Until I was about fifteen, if I went to the bathroom to bathe, I wasn't allowed to lock the door. And typically, there was some reason for her to come into the bathroom while I was in there.

I never questioned it, though I felt very *uncomfortable*. She did the same thing once after I was married and we were visiting my parents. I had been raised with that happening. But when she came in and dressed in front of me and my wife, my wife got very upset about it. That's when my wife realized there were some potential problems with my family that I still needed to deal with.

In other cases, this role of lap dog can be intensified between father and child. When the father doesn't voluntarily show love, some children simply try to stay underfoot and look for opportunities to make their presence known. More than one woman talked about trying to do sneaky things to get Dad to notice them—like attempting to hold hands, giving back rubs, or doing other similar things. In almost every case, these behaviors proved to be responses to the father's never initiating loving interaction with them.

Parents, especially fathers, need to realize the importance of communicating their love and affection through touch. Never ignore children to the point of having them become lap dogs. Such a relationship certainly does nothing for the lasting sense of worth or emotional health of the child.

THE PROBLEM WITH ROLES

How sad that parents frequently force their children to go to the dogs, or the horses, or the parrots, or the moles, or the chameleons, or any of the other roles youngsters can be forced to play. It's not fair to the children, nor does it provide any lasting benefit for the parents. Adopting such roles just ingrains the pattern of dysfunction into the family a little deeper than before—pretty much ensuring that the child will have long-term difficulty working through his or her emotional confusion.

We hate it when we are made to fit into roles we don't want to play. Yet if we aren't careful, we make the same mistakes and force our own kids to do the same thing. If you see your children beginning to act in some of these ways, I encourage you not to wait to begin to break these repeating patterns. Later chapters will suggest some specific steps you can take, but right now you can go to that child and initiate a better relationship. You can stroke her hair or pat his arm. You can give your daughter or son a hug. You can say in very clear words, "You are very special to me. I love you."

Such expressions of love can be so simple. While many children question what their parents do or say, almost all of them are hoping to see and hear that they are loved. A little affirmation goes a long way toward smoothing over past mistakes and misunderstandings. If demonstrating love is a problem in your family, please don't wait until you finish this book. Try it now and see if it doesn't work. *Then* keep reading for more ideas and help as we consider other specific ways in which painful father memories can perpetuate themselves in our own lives.

TAKE TIME TO REFLECT

1. In what ways have you adapted your behavior to please your parents, especially your father?

2. Put a checkmark by the following roles that you have used to gain your father's love.

Show Pony	Lemming
Work Horse	Parrot
Sacrificial Lamb	Lap Dog
Mole	Chameleon

3. Which of the above roles have you fallen into most often when relating to your father?

ELEVEN

Wrong Ways to Cope

HOW DO CHILDREN COPE with the devastating discovery that their own fathers may not love them or may not be trustworthy? They may hide, or strive to please, or care for themselves, or adopt some other behavior in order to survive. But as the years go by, this problem of father hunger does not simply disappear. These famished adults still wish Daddy would express his love for them, often by something as simple as a heart-felt hug or the words "I love you."

However, our abilities to cope with father hunger *do* change. Our adult attempts to overcome the problem are often no more successful than our childhood efforts; our coping mechanisms just become more sophisticated. Victims may no longer hide in the closet, but they might hide behind a seventy-hour-a-week job. A son might move across the country to get away from his oppressive father, yet continue to tell his new friends whatever they want to hear, still seeking approval from others at any cost. A grown woman can remain unable to benefit from new opportunities to open up and be honest with other people.

The situation may become even worse when the victims see their own children reach the age at which they themselves experienced so many problems with *their* fathers. Children-turned-parents often discover that they're beginning to commit the same offenses they hated so much back when they were kids. Remember, behavioral patterns are deeply ingrained and very hard to change. If the adult children have never dealt with their internal emotional void, they will continue to struggle with the behaviors that result.

REFUSING TO FEEL—AT ANY COST

In the adult years, intense craving for a father's love usually produces one of two extremes: some suppress all emotions and try not to feel *anything;* some look for an outside stimulus that will outweigh the internal pain. First, let's look at the extreme of refusing to feel at any cost.

As children, it simply hurts too much to feel. The pain is too severe. A father's rejection or neglect cuts deep into the soul of the child. When the child rightly tries to talk about it, the father may become hostile and cruel. Most parents intuitively know when they aren't giving their child enough love and affirmation. They don't want the guilt of the child's accusations to be heaped on top of what they already fear to be true. So they circumvent the child's queries with denial, withdrawal, or violence. The child usually gets the message and stops talking about it.

After trying the *right* course of action and being reprimanded, children often try other, less healthy, ways to adapt. Children eventually grow tired of all the pain, loneliness, and fear. One natural alternative which presents itself is to do everything possible to shut it all out. These children condition themselves not to feel these hurtful emotions.

Of course, human beings cannot eliminate all negative feelings and still maintain positive ones. All the possibilities for joy, love, excitement, and other good feelings are lost as the child focuses on blocking out the bad ones. This is one reason why so many people with faulty father relationships are unable to remember large portions of their childhood. They cannot remember *anything* good about growing up.

It's not necessarily that nothing good ever happened. They simply didn't allow themselves to associate any emotions with the events. To do so they would have to risk *feeling*, and to feel might involve experiencing further pain. It seems a small sacrifice at the time to eliminate all emotions if doing so can get rid of the painful feelings that are so persistent. One woman explains how she went through this process:

My father was gone by the time I was seven. And before the age of seven he was only there very sporadically. I had no one to attach my feelings to—physically there was nothing there. I wonder if that's why I feel such a void about something others say they feel great emotions for. It seems I should have a bottomless pit of pain, but I feel nothing.

I remember getting to the point where I told myself, "He's not coming back. And I can roll around and scream and throw a temper tantrum for my daddy who is never coming back, or I can get on with my life." I did it very dysfunctionally, but I went on. And I feel like it's taken care of.

But I see the dysfunction in my family now, and people tell me it is from father loss.... I mean, I want a functional family. And if I need to deal with father loss, then that's what I want to do. But there are no feelings connected with it. And I don't know if that's because there was nothing to connect them to all those years when I was forming an idea of who I was. There was no father there for me to identify with, either positively or negatively. He was just gone.

Sometimes children refuse to acknowledge their emotions because of what has been modeled for them. When they see that this approach seems to work for someone else, they try to make it work for them as well. Traditional male heroes seem to perpetuate the myth that stoicism offers the manly course of action. In many of our interviews, John Wayne's name kept coming up as an ideal of manhood. But in the following case, the person's own father was the model responsible for the child's reluctance to show any emotions whatsoever.

I remember my father as being very aloof. There was no closeness or communication between us. But we lived with *his* father, who had an opposite personality. He was always yelling, screaming, and telling us we never did anything right. My mother would argue with my grandfather, but I always felt my father should have stood up and said something.

My brother was outspoken and was always getting into trouble. I was the one who pulled in. I always feared getting into trouble. I didn't want to be spanked or hollered at. I remember thinking to myself, *I'm going to be like my father. He doesn't show any emo-*

tion. I'm not going to show that I like something, and I'm not going to show that I dislike something. I'm just going to be like him—neutral. And I was for a long time. It's always been hard for me to show feelings.

When a child suffers because of a noncommunicative father, the mother may share responsibility for fostering a lack of feeling in the child. Sometimes the mother selfishly tries to build walls between father and child to protect her own emotional interests, thereby causing the child to become more dependent on her. Such a development is quite harmful. It not only helps destroy bonds that need to be strengthened but also prevents the child from developing a healthy sense of independence.

Sometimes the mother seems to be looking out for the best interests of the child. She may have already discovered that the father is incapable of showing love as he should. Perhaps she has been personally hurt and wants to spare the child from any potential suffering. This mother may likewise encourage the child not to express emotions. Even though her intentions might be good, the result can be just as harmful. When young children are not allowed to talk about what they're feeling or to get close to a father, they are not going to become emotionally healthy adults until they have dealt with the problem.

One woman recalls a father who would never allow anyone to question what he said. She had a number of brothers and sisters, all of whom learned quickly that Dad would be quite harsh in his treatment if they opposed or challenged him in any way. His sons were pretty tough and kept trying to communicate with him, even though they were rarely successful. But the mother stepped in on behalf of this particular daughter and tried to teach her how to avoid her father's stern corrections.

My mother always told me not to feel. If you were angry, you weren't allowed to express it. I'd get mad at Dad and she'd say, "Don't talk like that. You shouldn't feel that way." She never even asked me *why* I felt like I did. She would always back him.

Mom came from a *very* dysfunctional family. Her mother and father and her six brothers and sisters are *all* alcoholics. She is the only one who doesn't drink. I asked her one time, "Mom, what made you decide not to drink?" And she said, "Well, I guess I had to take care of everybody else." So she was the caretaker.

She never had anything. Her parents took her out of school to make her work when she was in third or fourth grade. That was her highest education. Her parents never had any respect for her, and I guess my father told her to forget them. He said, "Come on, I'm going to take you away from all this."

He paid for the wedding and bought her a wedding dress. He bought her shoes, and I guess shoes were very hard to obtain at that time. She told me, "I had a pair of shoes, Eva, and I felt like a queen. Your father saw to that." And he had a house, which he took her to. It wasn't much, but at least it was a house. So she was very grateful, and I think that's why she constantly defended him, no matter how he treated anybody.

My mother kept saying, "Eva, don't feel that way. Don't feel that way." She never really told me *how* to feel. I just knew that she was grateful and thought I should be grateful too. She would tell me, "Your daddy works hard and he provides for you." That was the answer to every hurt, I think, that I encountered. And there were a lot of them.

This mother was not trying to cause her daughter to suffer. Her intentions were quite the opposite. Yet the child, as an adult, was still struggling to develop and strengthen a sense of self-worth that had never been encouraged during her childhood. The mother had been satisfied with a less-than-completely-loving relationship with her husband. But the daughter had expected more from her father, and rightfully so.

After weighing the perceived evidence and reaching what they believe to be the best decision, some children willingly adopt a non-emotional approach to life. Others, like the woman described above, are verbally encouraged by a parent to choose that course of action. Still others, like the following man, shield all their emotions out of self-defense.

My dad was an amateur boxer. He fought some of the greater boxers in the United States. He thought I was a punching bag. When I was eight years old he said something to me, and I said no, and he hit me full force with his fist. I landed in the neighbor's yard. I remember my father beating me and then hugging me, saying, "I don't want to punish you. I love you." That was the first day I ever hated him—a feeling that continued until he was on his deathbed. My whole life was like that, and I saw some of my brothers receive worse treatment than I did. So I became a very, very good child—as long as he could see me. I was very deceptive and I learned to live in denial.

DESPERATION TO FEEL—AT ANY COST

Attempting to rid oneself of all emotions does not appeal to many people. As we have seen, some children and adults try to do so for a number of different reasons, which often stem from the pain that is felt by a father's rejection. Yet the problem remains, even when ignored.

Instead of suppressing all emotions, some people go to the other extreme. They may feel a similarly overwhelming sensation of pain. But rather than try to eliminate it, these people try to find an alternative sensation which is even greater. They look for an outside stimulus that will outweigh the hurt within them. This drive to feel something can seem to come out of nowhere and be quite frightening. One woman, who now has a husband and three children, still struggles with the pain she faced as a child—largely due to her abusive father. She says:

I had tried to work out my problems on my own for several years, but it got to the point where I knew I was in trouble because I was hurting myself. I'd burn myself. I would drink. (I had never drunk in my life except for once back in high school.) It's just so opposite, so opposite to the way I normally act. I'd run away and try to hide, I guess. I'm not sure why. I was doing things that weren't good.

It scared me because I thought I might just do something some day, not meaning to, that might hurt my family forever, and I didn't want to do that. I didn't want to have an accident or something. I would just get into a confused state. It's like my dad would be so oppressive over me that I would feel like nothing, and I would just hurt myself. It was just like he had this hold on me.

Other attempts to escape the pain of an inadequate father relationship are more common. Of course, sex offers one of the first opportunities to counterbalance previous negative experiences. Put yourself in the place of a daughter who has been rejected or abandoned by her father. If your own father won't love you, who will? Then along comes a guy who seems to have the perfect answer: a loving relationship—which he will be happy to "prove" through sexual interaction.

What makes sex such a strong temptation? The fact that you may have given up on ever hoping to experience the love that you truly need. You feel so desperate that you're willing to settle for something else—anything else—that might make you feel better. Then you find someone who offers not only *love* to fill the vacuum within you, but also *sex,* which promises to provide enough pleasure to overpower the pain you feel. It seems to be the perfect answer.

Countless people have discovered the hard way that sex is far from the ideal solution to a deep longing for love. Rather, it simply compounds the problem. If they thought it was painful to be abandoned or neglected, wait until someone uses "love" to manipulate and take advantage of them. The very person they hoped would be their "white knight" or "fair maiden" who promises love and fulfillment, may reinforce the feelings initiated by the father—loneliness, worthlessness, and terrible pain.

Instead of replacing a bad relationship with a good one, as hoped, too often the desperate sexual relationship and the painful parental relationship play against each other and cause an even greater sense of emotional friction than ever before. One woman describes her life in the wake of a father who deserted the family and a mother who refused to affirm her in any way:

> After my father left, I turned more to my mother. I think I knew he was never coming back, so I looked to her for what I needed from Dad. But the only encouragement I ever got from my mother was, "Oh, I suppose you can go ahead and try, but don't be too disappointed when you fail." She always included that buffer. I think in her own way she was trying. She had never received any comfort when *she* failed, and maybe she didn't want me to be hurt unnecessarily. But I think you need to wait until someone fails before you offer consolation.

I was so angry at her because she would not affirm me, that I would rebel at anything she said. I became a pretty unruly child, though I was only looking for love and affection. My mother never held up any hope for me. She always told me I'd turn out just like her. So when I wound up pregnant by a man I really didn't care for, I felt that's exactly what had happened.

Even though I wasn't really very interested in this man, we got married and I turned to him for emotional support. I became emotionally dependent on him. I allowed my life to take certain turns in direction that I had sworn to God would never happen. I didn't hand those controls over to God. I tried to handle everything myself. Now I can see how I got so messed up, but I couldn't see it at the time. Had I had a happy relationship with my father, I truly believe my life would have been so different.

Abandoned by her father and emotionally neglected by her mother, this woman took the first step she thought would make sense and solve her problems—she turned to sex. She even admits that in her case it wasn't so much an attraction to the person as it was an attempt to escape her emotional pain.

Sex is one of the strongest drives humans ever feel. This very natural part of being human becomes even stronger as we desperately seek an end to the emptiness we have felt so long due to the absence of a father's love. But sex is not the only outlet. In fact, neglected or abused children from the same family can turn to a variety of methods of escape as they try to find some kind of relief from father hunger. This abused son describes the family his father came from:

Most of my dad's brothers and sisters ended up with some major problems—severe alcoholism, several of them were married and divorced multiple times, two of them committed suicide. And most of my first cousins on my dad's side have some form of problem. I have two female cousins who are lesbians. Most of them have had some chemical dependence problem—alcohol or drugs. I've had one cousin commit suicide and several others attempt to. When you look at the entire picture, there's a pattern. It's an awful pattern. I don't know where it started, but that's why I'm in counseling now. My own brothers have many of these same problems, but I'm attempting to break the chain for *my* family.

When asked how he personally had been affected by growing up in a hostile household and from having so many close relatives who had no idea how to cope with life, this man answered:

I came for counseling because I suffered from depression. My testing has shown that I have major depression, a dependent personality disorder, a schizoid personality, and post-traumatic stress syndrome. And to use the words of my therapist, "I have mastered the art of impression management."

Most of the people I know and work with have no idea what I feel and would never detect anything wrong. I've worked with one client for ten years, and for the past seven or eight years we've had lunch together once a week. But I never initiate a phone call to him. He always calls me. I've never had a close friend. I've never had anyone I've confided everything to. That includes my wife. She has cried and said she'd like to be my friend. She wants to know what's going on inside. But I've built an elaborate wall, and I don't let out what I'm feeling.

THE PROBLEM WON'T SIMPLY GO AWAY

Some people determine to simply stop feeling, to whatever extent they can. They develop a blindness toward their pain. Like a small child watching a scary movie, they close their eyes and hope the unpleasantness will just go away. They sacrifice any potential positive emotions in a desperate attempt to negate the dark secrets of the past. Others turn to sexual activity, alcohol, drugs, or other methods to create a "new and improved" sensation, hoping to overpower the negative experiences they have faced in the past. They party harder, drink more, and try all kinds of excesses as they search for a new high that will work. At best, they find temporary substitutes.

The difficulty with all of these ways of coping is that the root problem remains unresolved. In the first case, repressing emotions leaves the victim with potentially intense psychological problems, such as depression, on top of the underlying pain of a bad father relationship. In the second case, the person might develop any number of addictions (sexual, chemical, emotional, etc.) and still suffer the same sense of emptiness. In both cases, the person's problems are not subtracted, but multiplied.

The man quoted above who spoke of being unable to open up to other people had been to a Rapha Treatment Center for counseling. As he was working with the staff and trying to get to the root of his problem, he began to see the lasting effects of holding in the pain he had felt since childhood. This man wrote out his discoveries and gave us permission to use them. I think you will find these excerpts illuminating:

> In the dark crawl spaces of my mind, no one could see the lone-liness, the fear, and the confusion. You see, there were things happening to [me as a] little kid that no one seemed to care about. Locked away in the dark spaces of my mind have been those memories that now haunt me. It seems like they never hap-pened, yet the anger and the tears that occur when I allow them to surface tell me, yes, it happened. How could it be that some-thing so terrible could occur, and no one ever noticed?
>
> Only a glimpse of the memories has been allowed, and it was almost too much to handle. Since starting therapy, I've probed into the edge of some really dark spots—scary, painful places that I don't really care to revisit. Is there a way to recover without reliving?
>
> Continuing to function has been really difficult during these months of therapy. The ability to deal with each day varies. Some days are better than others. I don't yet understand why there are good ones and bad ones. I just try to make it through. Another thing I don't understand is, why does everything always have to be okay? Daily it's a requirement that everything is okay. For me, it was never safe to say anything else.
>
> Actually, I don't recall my mother or father ever asking. Since becoming an adult, people ask. But it's only obligatory. No one is really concerned or interested in the truth. One thing is for cer-tain. They couldn't bear to hear the pure, unadulterated truth about what's going on in my life. To expose the inner workings and thoughts, the pain and grief, the misery and despair, would short circuit even the best listener's system. Therefore, daily I portray that everything is okay. That's the only safe way to be.
>
> If you build the "okay wall" high enough, no one else can see in. Sometimes I wonder if anyone has seen over the wall. I know

my wife has gotten little glimpses. She and the counselor have accompanied me on this adventure into the past, but only so far. They keep encouraging me to take the wall down and let them in. I wish they could understand that the wall was very carefully and meticulously built—capable of withstanding the inner pressure. Able to conceal its contents to those on the outside.

The stones are made of guilt and shame, anger and hate, terror and fear. Some of them are made of helplessness. Some of confusion. Others are numb, alone, and abandoned. Each stone has been carefully cemented into place with pain. Moving a single stone pulls the nerves that run through the mortar of pain. Obviously a wall built with these materials would attract the attention of others. Therefore it has to be whitewashed with what I call "okay." Now to all passersby, everything is okay. Pretty neat system, huh?

I forgot to mention a couple of things. The materials the stones are made of keeps growing. That means patches and regular repair. Then another coat of "okay." The wall keeps getting bigger, requiring more maintenance and repair, more mortar, and more paint. Inside there are valuable contents. They have been kept in their embryonic state, never allowed to grow and mature. Never have they been allowed to see the light of day. All available resources have been deployed to maintain the wall, and there was never anything left to nurture the captives.

One day we can talk about the captives, maybe. It might be fun to let them out to play. The only trouble is, they are all thirty-nine years old, and none of them has learned to walk or talk yet. They won't be able to come out of the dark shadows without some help.

Many of us naturally try to forget about unpleasant childhood memories that caused us pain. As children, we do what we can to repress them, or minimize them, so that we can get on with our lives. However, as adults we need to put away childish things. Those painful memories remain part of our lives, still affecting us in ways we may or may not be aware of. Like oily rags in an attic, they have the potential to ignite at unexpected times and wreak destruction.

The best strategy is to clean out these combustible memories by confronting them and beginning to deal with them. In a couple of chapters we are going to begin to work our way through the healing process. But let's first examine a few more ways memories can maintain a hold on our emotional stability.

TAKE TIME TO REFLECT

1. How do you typically respond to emotional pain?

2. How have your parents responded to emotional pain? Do you see any patterns in the ways that you and your family cope?

3. On the following continuum, put an X at the point where you see yourself coping with father hunger.

I use things (sex, alcohol, etc.) or relationships to help me feel.	I try not to feel anything at all.

4. Review the journal excerpt of the man being treated at a Rapha Treatment Center. Have you built an "okay wall"? If so, make a drawing of your wall. How would you describe your stones? How high and wide is your wall? Identify the sources of your pain by naming them on the individual stones of your wall.

TWELVE

When Women Marry Their Fathers

MANY OF THE WOMEN whom we interviewed used the tongue-in-cheek phrase, "Essentially, I married my father." They mean, of course, that they married men who are *very much like* their fathers. Why does this seem to happen?

I previously discussed how we sometimes repeat behavioral patterns over and over again, seemingly unable to change those which are personally undesirable. Women who marry men very much like their fathers—fathers whom they resent—provide one of the strongest illustrations of how an undesired pattern of behavior can continue in spite of a person's best intentions. The lack of a father's love can affect adult children in a great variety of ways, one of the strongest being in the choice of a spouse, especially for women but also for men.

Little girls look to their fathers to provide affirmation from a *male* point of view. More than likely, Mom is usually the one to notice how well they behave, how pretty they look, and so forth. But they also need to hear these things from Dad, at least once in a while. Some dads have discovered that taking their daughters out on an occasional "date" can do wonders for a budding woman's self-esteem. Young girls feel so special when they can get dressed up and have Daddy all to themselves for a few hours, perhaps going to dinner and shopping afterwards. Such happy memories will last a lifetime.

When fathers identify and address these kinds of needs in their daughters, girls are more likely to grow up feeling self-confident. A male viewpoint has confirmed their attractiveness, their intrinsic importance, their being "such a woman." As they continue to grow, women grounded in such positive affirmation won't feel as much internal pressure to compromise their standards in order to receive love from a man. A father's love and attention during a daughter's early stages can yield very specific benefits later in her life.

If fathers fail to deal with these natural feminine concerns—due to either absence or neglect—young girls are likely to continue questioning their self-worth. They will look in other places to fill the emotional void that was left empty by the father. Some are quick to become sexually promiscuous. Others struggle along until they find a spouse who will meet those long-standing needs. Without knowing it, this is the point at which their problems may be just beginning. Because these women still wish their fathers had been more attentive, they may be very strongly attracted to men who are much like their fathers—the very ones who failed to provide affirmation.

Do you see how these patterns begin to repeat themselves? Even if a father were completely unloving, manipulative, untrustworthy, or even abusive, that doesn't prevent the daughter from *wishing* he would love her. When her need for love continues to go unfulfilled, the next father figure who comes along may seem like a valid substitute. Yet usually the men such women select are *also* manipulative, untrustworthy, or even abusive. In many cases, the new husband eventually leaves, which means the woman's need for love still hasn't been achieved. So she finds someone else who was like her father and the cycle continues.

SIMILARITIES CAN BE BLATANT OR CAMOUFLAGED

Sometimes the choice of a father-like spouse is quite intentional, even to the point of physical similarities. One woman admitted, "When my father left, I missed him so much! He meant so much to me that I married a man who even looked like him—black mustache, black hair, and balding. He was even a machinist—an excellent machinist like my father was. I really admired my father. He was my source of self-esteem. I traded my husband for my father."

Of course, the resemblance between husband and father isn't always so clear. More often the likeness lies not so much in physical appearance but more in behavior, attitudes, and relationships. Sometimes the woman doesn't even make a connection between husband and father until after she has been married for a while. Some women then express dismay at the somewhat incestuous feelings that bubble to the surface along with this insight. The sexual intimacy between husband and wife can become unstable if the woman suddenly begins to focus on how much her husband reminds her of her father.

Remember that the source of father hunger is the strong craving for unconditional love. Daughters don't want a *sexual* liaison with Dad. Rather, they want love in its purest form—hugs, cuddling, verbal affirmation, stroking of their hair, being sung to, and so forth. The absence of these expressions of love leaves a massive void.

New husbands often believe that sexual intimacy within a marriage relationship will surely bring him and his wife together as closely as possible. But he may not realize that *nothing* is capable of filling the emptiness felt by such a wounded wife. The woman may be seeking a father's love from her husband, yet the husband cannot go back in time and provide the love his wife needed *during her childhood*. Both partners in the marriage remain frustrated.

The consequences of father hunger are difficult enough to deal with when you understand something about it. Imagine how confusing the dilemma can be for a couple in that situation who have no idea why they feel the way they do.

Other women may consciously try to avoid forming another relationship with a male anything like their fathers. Knowing clearly what they hated about their fathers, they want to avoid those same problems in a husband at any cost. Unfortunately, they don't always recognize the *root* of the trouble. In trying to avoid one specific behavior, they may wind up with a spouse who is alarmingly like the father in many other ways. Here is the experience of one woman who found this to be true:

I grew up with no feelings of self-worth. I think I learned at a very early age to downplay any feelings I had about my own needs. Certainly my father didn't meet those needs and he couldn't teach me how to get them met.

And yet, I married my father. The same characteristics were manifested in a completely different way, and that was the kicker for a long time. I kept saying that my husband is nothing like my father, but then I started to see that the character traits are the same. The only difference is the way they are revealed.

My father forced me to do what he wanted by being domineering and very controlling. My husband is just the opposite—very submissive, very passive. And yet he is still manipulative and controlling. I found I was being a lot more compliant when my needs were being met, so my husband could control me in that way.

A daughter's assessment of her father might be completely off base. She may *think* she detests his loud and boisterous personality. But in this case, what the woman really resented was being manipulated. Her father had done it by being powerful and controlling. When her husband used the exact opposite personality to control her, the woman discovered she hated the manipulation rather than the personality of her father.

SIMILAR RELATIONSHIP STYLES

Some women "marry their fathers" because they become accustomed to relating to men in a particular way. Even though the daughter might have a poor relationship with her father, she is forced to learn to cope. After a while, she begins to become comfortable with the relationship—as painful as it is.

Consequently, as she begins to date, guys who offer emotional health and security may seem strange to her. But when some guy comes along with the same dysfunctions as Dear Old Dad, the woman knows how to relate to him. After learning to settle for anything less than unconditional love, it is very difficult to ever hope for (or be comfortable with) something better.

Women who focus on specific character traits instead of searching for unconditional love may be in for just as much trouble. A woman might *think* what she really needs is friendship, independence, discipline, or some other characteristic. She doesn't comprehend that a father who is doing a good job of demonstrating love will also provide all these qualities.

Other women have discovered the wisdom of the maxim, "Be careful what you wish for, or you just might get it." One woman describes the pain of seeing her real father leave when she was young and then having her mother remarry. As a teenager, she had a terrible relationship with her argumentative and abusive stepfather. When she became old enough to get married, she fiercely determined *not* to get into the same kind of relationship. But even then, her problems were not over.

> My mom and I had always had our battles, but having a new stepdad go up against me made it worse. I wanted somebody who wasn't going to give me any trouble at all, so I married a very, very complacent man. He's so passive you've got to touch him every once in a while to make sure he's still alive. Now I discover I don't have any connection to him, and we're trying so hard to work on the relationship. I could at least connect with my mother and stepfather by arguing with them, but I can't connect with this man. Yet I wanted to marry him because he didn't give me any trouble.

Remember that anyone who is a victim begins to see things from one extreme or the other. Certainly, anyone who had missed out on close relationships with two father figures would more than likely be a victim of her home situation. The woman above went from one extreme of violent conflict to the other extreme of utter passivity. But as victims often find out, neither extreme may prove to be a wise choice.

A father who provides enough affirmation for a young daughter also helps her make mature life decisions. The very need to get married may be a direct result of something that is missing in a father/daughter relationship. But even marriage vows and sexual union cannot replace the genuine intimacy and sense of self-worth that so many women crave. Marriage may not be the best step to take, even though it often seems logical to those women who have not been properly loved by their fathers.

We asked one group of people, "If your relationship with your father had been one that was strong, loving, and affirming, how do you think your life would be different today?" One woman spoke up right away to say that she might never have married at all. Her generation gained approval by getting married and raising a family. Career opportunities for women were severely limited during the forties and fifties. After her kids had grown, she discovered she had many talents in the field of business.

Take note! We have no choice about the identity of our fathers. But women do have an absolute say in their choice of a husband. How sad it is to see those who perpetuate the very mistakes of the past that most distress them. And in the previous case, it is equally tragic to see someone who might have enjoyed a single life marked with accomplishments and fulfillment opt instead for being a miserable wife.

MONSTROUS DECISIONS

In summary, women who do not expect or demand unconditional love from prospective husbands are often setting themselves up for some monstrous complications. Late-night television movies suggest some of the "monsters" that can rule the darkness when genuine love is not present.

Count Dracula: Based on outside appearances, these guys seem to be quite a catch. They may well be handsome, sophisticated, and debonair. Yet beneath all their positive traits lurks the quest for control. No one can relate to these men without becoming a victim. And once they assume control, little can be done to break their spell.

Frankenstein: With the best of intentions, a woman can set out to create the husband she wants. She tries to include all the right ingredients, like strong qualities and genteel mannerisms. But as Dr. Frankenstein could warn her, she's very likely to end up with someone more threatening than loving. The potential for harm runs high.

Wolfman: Many of these guys appear to be quite normal. But occasionally, under certain conditions, they can change suddenly and drastically. Relating to wolfmen-husbands becomes much more hairy. They can become violent or dangerous, even to the ones who love them most. Then, as suddenly as it began, the transformation reverses and they return to normal. But the wife never knows when the changes will take place or how long they will last.

The Mummy: A very passive husband can sometimes be more annoying than anything else. The wife can easily outmaneuver the plodding mummy figure, but needless to say, they don't exactly make the perfect couple.

The "monster" in a husband very frequently reflects the nature of the father. Unfortunately, only too late do most women realize that "I married my father!" A devoted spouse can sometimes help in dealing with emotional problems from the woman's past, but to expect any one person to provide a lifetime of needs within a couple of years of marriage is totally unrealistic.

The first few years of marriage are difficult enough even when both people are independent and self-confident. All couples are challenged to stay on good terms as they work to generate the necessary sacrificial love, compromise, and forgiveness. When one or both individuals bring serious and weighty emotional needs to the marriage, the strain is almost always too much for the union to bear. If at all possible, it is much more preferable for individuals to deal with any problems they have with father relationships *prior* to getting involved in a long-term commitment as serious as marriage.

Many people who are reading this may be thinking, *"Now* he tells me." Well, don't despair. As we have been reminding you throughout the book, we're working our way toward some specific steps to resolving father hunger. While the solution may not be easy to discover or implement, no situation is completely hopeless. I firmly believe that God doesn't want us to suffer unnecessarily. Though severe pain from our past may continue to haunt us, it should not overwhelm our present and our future. Things *can* change. It may be too late to do anything about a lousy father relationship, but current relationships can be repaired. All of us make bad decisions from time to time, yet we can persevere through the damage if we let God show us how.

TAKE TIME TO REFLECT *(for women)*

1. If you are married (or have been married), did you marry someone who resembles your father? In what ways is your spouse similar to your father? In what ways is he different from your father?

2. Did your relationship with your father allow you the flexibility and/or affirmation to live as a single person? Why or why not?

3. Do any of the husband categories from this chapter describe your own husband? If so, which ones?

TAKE TIME TO REFLECT *(for men)*

1. If you have daughters, how are you meeting their needs for love, affirmation, and acceptance?

2. How are you similar to your father? In what ways are you different from your father?

3. Consider your father-in-law. In what ways are you similar to and/or different from him?

THIRTEEN

Hidden Problems

BY NOW, you may have found yourself responding to my description of father hunger with one of three general attitudes. Some of you may be thinking, *I understand what you've been saying, but I'm very thankful that the relationship between my father and me was loving, giving, and emotionally healthy.* Unfortunately, only a small percentage of people can truthfully lay claim to that response.

Toward the other side of the continuum, some of you may be approaching a state of panic with thoughts like this: *You've hit the nail on the head! I'm going through some of the exact same experiences and emotions that you've described.* The more you discover about the complexity of this craving, the better off you will be in the long run.

Some of you may find yourself somewhere in the middle, scratching your heads in confusion and thinking: *Gee, I don't know. I can kind of relate to what you're saying, but I'm not sure my father was that bad.* Not knowing for sure whether you've had a good or bad relationship with your father, you may not know where you stand with him now that you're an adult. Consequently, you may feel depressed and anxious, without knowing why.

Many of you were never abused—at least, not physically or sexually. You may still get together with your father on a regular basis. Things may appear to be fine. Yet you may harbor deep suspicions that something is just not quite right between you. Perhaps you have more mixed memories of a good father who sometimes behaved badly. Sometimes he may have totally missed the boat.

Maybe your father never intentionally screamed at you, never intentionally overlooked you, would never have dreamed of physically or sexually abusing you, but still fell short in some critical areas.

If you fall into this middle ground, your father hunger may be more perplexing and more difficult to resolve than those who experience extremely negative reactions. Abused and neglected children *know* they suffer from father hunger. They can point to specific actions on the part of a father and say, "See what he did to me [or didn't do for me]! That's the problem!" Perhaps you can point to nothing specific, yet still feel this unsatisfied need deep inside, which may very well be an unfulfilled craving for a father's love.

TANGLED IN FEAR, HOPE, AND SHAME

We witnessed an interesting phenomenon as we interviewed people for this book. Whenever we announced that we were looking for volunteers to talk about the relationships they had had with their fathers as they were growing up, people always seemed eager to assemble and talk. We would frequently begin by asking these volunteers to recall their positive recollections about growing up. Many groups would just sit there—silent and dumbfounded.

These people had come ready to share troubled times and memories that still haunted them, rather than warm feelings about Dad. We would often sit for long periods of time without the participants being able to think of one positive thing to say about their fathers. When we would move on to discuss the negatives, my! how the stories poured out, as if from a gushing geyser.

Then strangely enough, almost as soon as the volunteers had covered everything they wanted to say about the undesirable qualities and behaviors of their fathers, they would suddenly start peddling in reverse. They would recall *positive* memories that they couldn't identify just moments previously. It wasn't that they necessarily began to perceive their fathers as surrounded by a halo, but they did begin to remember *some* things that were positive traits. They would say things like:

> "Even though I don't ever remember him telling me, 'I love you,' he sacrificed to provide everything we needed as kids."

"He *was* an alcoholic, but he was the stability of our home because my mother was mentally ill."

"My dad was almost always either working or drinking. But the one thing I can remember that I guess you would call positive is that whenever he *was* home, I felt a real sense of being secure and protected that wasn't there when he was gone."

Those who have been victims of abuse tend to see people and circumstances as either all good or all evil. They make broad jumps from one extreme to the other. They start out seeing their fathers as wonderful—perhaps perfect—men. But eventually that trust is destroyed, and they make a long-lasting shift into seeing their fathers as bad.

Yet after having an opportunity to share their true inner feelings with someone else, they seem to be able to recall more of the positive aspects of their previous relationships. It's as if most of these people would be ready to forget everything in the past (or at least try to) if their fathers would simply say, "I realize I have hurt you. I was wrong. I love you. Let's start over."

In most cases, such a blanket admission is never going to happen. Many of these fathers may be deceased, too far along in the aging process to think straight, too set in their ways, or simply unwilling or unable to admit any major shortcomings in their past relationships. Yet the desire of the adult child to hear such words of reconciliation remains strong.

The resulting emotional dissonance can create immense confusion. On the one hand, a breach in the trust of a father stirs up in the child fears of additional hurt. The fear and doubt push him or her away from the father. And remaining close to someone after becoming convinced that that person doesn't really care for us can be very painful.

But on the other hand, few of us ever lose hope that somehow our fathers will come to their senses and somehow change for the better. We may know this is never likely to happen. Having been hurt over and over again after making the first move, we don't even expect it to happen. Yet no matter how diminished the level of hope becomes, it almost never completely disappears. We often feel like we're on an emotional roller coaster—gradually allowing our hope to inch upward, bit by bit, only to plunge into despair after another painful incident of Dad's thoughtless words or actions.

Then, on top of everything else, we frequently find that we must deal with shame as well. Some of us are ashamed of what our fathers have done and perhaps are still doing. Others experience shame based on their own actions as they rebel against a painful father relationship. Still others are shamed by their innermost thoughts about their fathers. They don't want to harbor such negative feelings about Dad, but they can't help it. And no matter how warranted these emotions may be, they still feel ashamed for such ugly feelings.

FOUR FALSE BELIEFS
CAN OFTEN BE TRACED TO FATHERS

In one of my previous books, *The Search for Significance*, I discuss four false beliefs that affect most people to at least some degree.[1] While they influence all of our relationships, I think it's appropriate to mention them here as they deal specifically with fathers. (If they seem to describe the way you feel, I would strongly encourage you to refer to this book for a more in-depth discussion.)

False belief number one: "I must meet certain standards in order to feel good about myself." This stance tends to stir up fear of failure, perfectionism, a drive to succeed, the willingness to manipulate others to achieve success, and the avoidance of risks. Many people trace this false belief to their fathers.

When children always feel the pressure to achieve, they never enjoy the sense of unconditional love that they need. The roots of fear begin with this impasse. Young children cannot process all the events and relationships they encounter, nor can they determine to what extent they or the other people involved are actually responsible. Consequently, if the father is not demonstrating genuine love, the child knows it—yet can't understand it. The result is an underlying fear that the father doesn't love him or her. And the only apparent way to generate that love is to meet certain standards.

Some fathers specifically set high standards they expect their children to meet. In other instances, the child keeps trying to do more and more, in a desperate attempt to receive love. Either avenue may lead to this first false belief becoming ingrained in the child's mind.

Once it does, it affects not only the paternal relationship, but all other relationships as well. Such children fear failure because failure, in the young mind, will prevent others from loving them. And unless others love them, they will not feel good about themselves.

False belief number two: "I must be approved (accepted) by certain others to feel good about myself." The harmful effects of this belief include the fear of rejection, the attempt to please others at any cost, an oversensitivity to criticism, and withdrawal from others to avoid disapproval. It's one thing to be rejected because you fail to meet unreasonable standards others set for you. Most of us can learn to live with that. But when we feel that other people reject us simply for who we are, that can really hurt.

The pain of rejection can be especially intense when it stems from our relationship with our fathers. After all, if our own fathers don't seem to sincerely care about us, how can we possibly expect anyone else to? That's why so many of the people we interviewed talked of hiding. They preferred to avoid any contact with a father rather than risk another painful put-down. It was better to stay under the house, in a closet, in their room, or somewhere else out of sight. Some had brothers or sisters who had moved out and become hermits to avoid further contact with people—any and all people. That's how severely the father's rejection had influenced them.

At this stage the fear continues. First we fear that our suspicions might be correct that Dad doesn't truly love us. Then, as those fears are confirmed, we fear future confrontations where he might reject us outright.

False belief number three: "Those who fail are unworthy of love and deserve to be punished." The tendency in this case is to fear punishment, punish others, blame others for one's own personal failure, withdraw from God and others, and become driven to avoid failure. No one has ever succeeded at everything he or she has attempted, but you'd never know it based on the attitudes of many of our fathers. Some of them seem to expect perfection from the time the child is old enough to function independently—all the way through adulthood. The father with this mindset can constantly downplay his own imperfections even as he demands more and more from his children.

In such situations, it's no wonder that people tend to assign blame. No one enjoys punishment, yet we come to expect *someone* to be punished for mistakes and offenses. So whenever something goes wrong, we react by quickly finding someone else to whom we can shift the responsibility. Parents blame their kids. Children blame parents, or perhaps each other. Alcoholic fathers blame dominant wives. Divorced wives blame absent fathers.

All of these individuals crave love and acceptance, yet may be unwilling and perhaps even unable to offer these things to someone else. And again, the more we can withdraw from any potentially threatening confrontation, the better off we feel we will be.

False belief number four: "I am what I am. I cannot change. I am hopeless." The gnawing sense of shame enters the picture at this point. Other consequences of this belief include inferiority, passivity, loss of creativity, and further isolation. It isn't unusual for people to recall being told by a father, "You'll never amount to anything." Those who aren't told that outright come to the same conclusion based on the father's scornful behavior. Again, how can a child overcome such a negative attitude when the source is his or her very own father?

People who are ashamed of themselves don't want to be around other people. They don't want to try new things. None of the traditional clichés work for them. They don't want to "keep a stiff upper lip." There's no way they are going to "try, try again." It is impossible for them to "grin and bear it." The hopelessness they experience seems vast and impenetrable. Losing all hope of finding a better way of life is exceedingly painful, and harmful as well.

WHAT *SHOULD* WE BELIEVE?

Perhaps you can relate to one or more of the four false beliefs listed above. If so, the key thing to remember is that they are *false*. No matter what your experience is, or what you've been told, or what you're convinced is true, please do not believe any of these statements. They are lies that Satan has used again and again to destroy individuals and families.

People who are barraged by these lies can wander through life, alone and zombie-like. Their lives seem to have no meaning. They remain unable to feel love from any source. They sense walls between themselves and others. Many of them come from "average" homes, yet feel imprisoned by blame, fear, shame, and other shadowy struggles. But the truth is that *it doesn't have to be this way.*

- Not even if your father said you would amount to no good.
- Not even if your father abandoned you as a child.
- Not even if your father blamed you for everything that went wrong in his miserable life.
- Not even if your father abused you.
- Not even if your father continues to degrade you and put you down at every opportunity.
- Not even if you're still terribly confused at this point about whether or not your father really does love you.

One of the worst feelings associated with these four false beliefs is the sense of aloneness. Each person who experiences an inadequate relationship with a father may feel that he or she is one of a kind. Actually it is far more common to find people who have experienced relationship difficulties—even serious ones—than those who had happy and healthy families. Some people hide their prior conflicts better than others, but most of us have ugly stories to tell if we are honest enough to share them.

Let me tell you about a few experiences shared by the brave volunteers who were willing to open up about their past. One woman described how her mother would always stick up for her father, even though he was an alcoholic who was frequently abusive. When sober, he appeared to be an upright citizen and loving father. But the family members knew better. They saw the effects of his disease on a regular basis. Yet the mother kept trying to convince the daughter that her father was a good man.

This woman tells a different story: "Even as a teenager, I knew better. I would tell Mom, 'No way! He's a weak person. There's just no way we should be putting up with his behavior.' I could not reconcile my mother's reaction in my heart. And my love/hate for my father caused tremendous stress. When I look back, I know I just recoiled in revulsion from him."

Even in homes completely dominated by fear of the father, a nearly invisible strand of hope sometimes seems to be present—

hope that perhaps the father will change and learn to demonstrate genuine love. One woman described some of the horrible physical and sexual abuse she consistently received at the hands of her father or witnessed being inflicted upon others. After she had admitted that she literally hated her father, we asked whether she and her father ever had any kind of rational communication.

She responded, "None. At least, not that I'm aware of. My mother says that I followed him around like a shadow when I was little. I can't comprehend that at all. It doesn't make any sense to me. But maybe I did to a certain point."

Even in the midst of this fear-filled family, this little child seemed to be clinging to a shred of hope. Fear and common sense warned her to stay out of harm's way, yet hope continued to pull her back toward her father. If she remained nearby, perhaps he would notice her. Of course, the day came when she finally gave up. While she still struggles with a despondent sense of hopelessness, she's gradually getting better as she confronts the problem directly.

A man who came from a similar kind of home described a parallel experience. During years of physical and emotional abuse at the hands of a cruel father, he had often wished his father would die and be out of his life forever. Then one night the father suffered a heart attack. It seemed that the son's wish would be answered, but for some reason this young man decided to resuscitate his father. He reflects on this incident:

> The night in August of 1972, when my father had his heart attack, is very clear to me. I have mentally beaten myself all these years for giving him CPR on the way to the hospital. Why did I do it? Why couldn't I just let him die? I think in spite of all the abuse and neglect, I really wanted to love him. And I always hoped he would love me back. Boy, was I living in a dream world! All I got was sixteen more years of neglect and verbal abuse. I might have been free sixteen years earlier if I had just let him die. I'm sorry I didn't.

A child's hope dies hard. As painful as the relationship may be, we all know deep down inside that the death of our fathers will leave the matter forever unresolved. We cling to that last thread of hope like a drowning person clings to a lifeline. Our desire to experience a father's love prompts us to inflict all manner of harm to ourselves and those around us.

Many people whose fathers aren't cruel, abusive, or apathetic also suffer the same paradoxical hope. Some adult children have fathers who strike others as ideal, while the child carries a deep resentment so well hidden that no one else can detect it. Others complain of fathers who seemed more concerned that children not do anything wrong than that they reach their full potential. In such cases, the fathers may believe everything is okay. The children *seem* to have grown up to be fine, mature men and women. Even such relatively normal father/child relationships can suffer when one or both of the parties fail to show unconditional love. Any solution that involves dishonesty or deceit can also result in fear and shame.

One woman had a loving but strict father. His willingness to accept her seemed to hinge on her willingness to obey the standards he set for her. She describes how their relationship began to fall apart: "One big thing that's always stuck out for me was that he didn't allow dancing. In seventh grade I wanted to start going to school dances, but he wouldn't let me. So I'd lie and say I was spending the night at a girlfriend's house. And I *would*... but we'd go to the dance first. From that time on there was a lot of shame and guilt in my life."

Shame may very well exist without fear. The following man is now thirty-two. Even though his father has been dead for nine years, he still struggles with the feelings of shame which began as a small child.

I don't know if you're familiar with the film *The Deer Hunter*, but it contains a scene after one of the soldiers has been forced to play Russian roulette. He's sitting in the hospital window. The doctor comes up and begins asking him questions about his name, his parents' names, and so forth. But all he can do is sit there and look out the window. He is just overcome, emotionally. He can't speak words. He's not cognizant of what he's being asked.

To me, that's a perfect picture of what I felt in my relationship with my dad, starting at a very young age. I detested him. He should have been at my baseball game, cheering me on and encouraging me. Instead, he would show up, and at times you could tell he had urinated in his pants. And the shame I felt started at the top of my head and went down to the bottom of my foot. I'm still acutely aware of it. There are times throughout the day when I will be walking and just try to shake it off... physically. It's just like a burlap sack that clings to me, and I can't seem to get out from under it.

Thanks to our fathers, many of us face a lifetime of struggles because of deeply ingrained fear or shame. Some of our feelings may be justified, yet others may be based on false beliefs. We must be careful not to be tricked into believing something that is very painful that may not even be true.

The truth is that you *can* learn to feel good about yourself without meeting someone else's standards. You don't need to gain the approval of your father—or anyone else—to enjoy a sense of self-worth. If you fail, so what? You're still a valuable person worthy of love and respect. You don't have to continue to feel unhappy with your life. You *can* change. The situation is *not* hopeless.

In the next section of this book, I will suggest some specific steps involved in the healing process. You will have to do a lot more than simply read through the material. But I urge you not to give up hope. On the other side of that smoke screen of hopelessness lies a power stronger than the one which has you defeated right now. The battle is not yet over. Victory can still be yours.

TAKE TIME TO REFLECT

1. How much trouble do you have recalling positive qualities or behaviors of your father?

2. What actions or words would your father have to do or say for you to forget everything in the past?

3. To what degree have you believed the four "false beliefs" discussed in this chapter?
   - I must meet certain standards in order to feel good about myself.
   - I must be approved (accepted) by certain others to feel good about myself.

- Those who fail are unworthy of love and deserve to be punished.
- I am what I am. I cannot change. I am hopeless.

4. How did shame and loneliness figure into your relationship with your father?

5. On a scale of one to ten, with one being *hopelessness* and ten being *hopefulness*, how would you describe your current perspective on life?

PART THREE

Relieving the Hunger

FOURTEEN

Mental Snapshots of the Past

HAVE YOU EVER BEEN out in some public place when you suddenly noticed a stranger who irritated you? You have no specific *reason* to be irritated. Some man or woman may be just talking on the phone or reading a book. Yet you form an immediate dislike for that person. I know I've had that reaction at times.

I tend to react very strongly whenever I'm in New York City. Many New Yorkers seem to ignore other people. They can step over someone sleeping on the sidewalk without missing a beat in their conversation. Or they walk down the sidewalk three abreast, not a bit concerned about anyone trying to go the other way. Personally, I get irritated around such people.

Yet I know they themselves are not necessarily the source of my irritation. We all have memories of our past, some of which might be quite unpleasant. Maybe as children we wanted desperately to be noticed and loved by our parents, but weren't. Sometimes in a crowd we see someone doing something which triggers the painful feelings attached to those memories. It doesn't have to be much— maybe just his way of standing, her tone of voice, his raucous laughter, or the way she carries her purse. But it's enough to trigger a brief mental flashback to times when we were truly miserable. Some inner threat-sensor goes off and we immediately go on the defensive. At least, I know I do.

Most people carry around a "picture album" in their heads—a collection of memories concerning key events of their past. These memories may be either pleasurable or traumatic, but they stay with us. And like any set of snapshots, we like to look at some of them frequently and with fondness. Others we keep hidden away in some remote corner, out of sight from ourselves or anyone else. We know they exist, but we'd rather not remember what we were like at that particular point in our lives, so we intentionally ignore them. Still others we may forget about completely. Then one day, out of the blue, an old snapshot turns up that we hadn't thought about in thirty years.

Our memories are like that. It's not as if we can guard against triggering certain flashbacks. Our minds work like a bizarre and complex Rube Goldberg machine. For example:

- You see a dog as you drive down the street.
- The dog reminds you of your childhood dog, Buster.
- You recall loving Buster because you were an only child, and this pet provided love when no one else was around.
- Come to think of it, there were a lot of times when no one was around.
- You wonder why one or both parents weren't around more often.
- And then, *click,* you recall how your sixth birthday was ruined because your parents spent much of the evening shouting at each other. They tried to be civil during your cake-and-presents celebration, but even as a youngster you could tell things were tense.
- As a matter of fact, that was the point when Dad stopped being home so much, which eventually led to your parents getting a divorce.

Even though the memory of your sixth birthday may have been tucked away in the recesses of your mind for a decade or more, it can be quite vivid when released. You had tried not to focus on that unpleasant experience as a child, and had done a pretty good job— or so you thought. Yet the event was not forgotten; the memory was simply deferred. All it took was some single event in your life to call it to mind, like seeing a dog who looks familiar.

Sometimes certain smells trigger childhood memories. Mothballs might bring to mind being placed in a closet for punishment.

Particular brands of aftershave can remind us of either good or bad experiences with our fathers. Evergreen scents can serve as the ghosts of Christmas past. And so forth. How can we use these mental snapshots of the past to relieve our father hunger?

THE BEST OF TIMES AND THE WORST OF TIMES

Many people cannot truthfully say they were satisfied with the relationships they had with their fathers. Yet no matter how bad the situation was and how much they regret, most people cling to a few positive snapshots of special times spent with their fathers. They may recall only one or two such incidents, but those snapshots seem to be framed in gold—as proof that the father's love was what it was supposed to be, however briefly.

One woman we interviewed had such a painful relationship with her father that she had absolutely nothing positive that she could say about him. Her childhood, as well as much of her adult life, had been oppressive and miserable. When thinking back to certain years of her childhood, this woman could not remember a thing. Yet she had one cherished snapshot that she could clearly recall.

I have one memory that I associate any kind of good feeling to. I was in a crib and I remember a blanket being up over part of the crib. I don't think I could walk, but I could pull myself up on the side. I had a cold and the vaporizer was running. (I love Vicks to this day because someone had put Vicks in the vaporizer.) And I think why I remember that is because I saw it as somebody caring for me. That's the only reason I can think of as to why I would remember it *so* vividly. I can even tell you where the crib was in the room. I have no negative feelings connected with that at all. I've always had that picture in my head.

Another woman had an alcoholic father who was absent a lot of the time. Her relationship with him deteriorated as his disease progressed, yet she could remember a few wonderful times before his drinking got too bad.

I have very positive memories of my father during my younger childhood years—five, six, seven, eight. He wasn't home a lot,

but during the time he *was* home he spent a lot of time with us—
me, in particular, because I was the youngest. I can remember a
lot of times playing with him in the yard or doing outdoor
things, like fishing. He did a lot of things with me that a father
might do with a son.

I can remember being on his lap and he sang to me a lot,
which was a very positive experience. Our family is not musical at
all, but he sang. There are many positive memories of him when
I was a young child. As a teenager, I don't remember him being
there. He was there, physically, but I don't remember interacting
with him.

Most people, even those who suffered considerably during their
young lives, tend to cling tenaciously to the meager number of
happy memories they can recall. Sometimes these recollections
seem to haunt them, lingering in their past to remind them of what
might have been. As their lives overflowed with pain and despair,
these few emotional connections with their fathers continue to feed
their cravings for genuine love and acceptance.

These same people, however, are usually not short on snapshots
that reflect how things *really* were when they were children. These
negative mental images are usually even stronger than the positive
ones and often more numerous as well. For example, the woman
who described the security of being in her crib also went into great
detail about her unpleasant memories because of her father's mental
and physical illnesses. Here is just one example of many she shared.

When I was six years old—I can identify the exact age because I
have a picture of being there—I remember fishing off of my
uncle's dock. I remember my dad being on the dock. He was
very nervous at that point. I remember him pushing me off the
dock, and I remember being under the water. I couldn't swim. I
didn't know how. And I remember being under the water, not
being able to get up, and hating my father so much. Even while I
was underneath, I was accusing him in my mind. I accused him
of pushing me and hating me.

Today my question is, "Why would a six-year-old accuse her
father of doing that and why would she hate him so much?" You
know, *something* must have caused that feeling because I was trying to imagine a similar situation with my husband and one of our

children. They wouldn't think their father hated them, because their dad loves them and cares for them. And if my husband were to happen to knock one of them into the water, they wouldn't *hate* him for that. It would be understood that it was an accident.

I have no idea if my father actually meant to push me or if it was accidental. From what they tell me, my cousin finally got me out of the water and the next thing I remember was waking up in the cabin. I have no idea. I just remember how I felt.

The men we interviewed frequently had mental snapshots of the event that finally severed the ties between themselves and their fathers. Both of the following stories were told by men who had violent and abusive fathers. They could recall, in great detail, many of the beatings they had received. Yet when asked to recount one of the strongest images of the past, they both told about a time of great *emotional* devastation rather than physical suffering. One man says:

Everyone was intimidated by my father. He was five foot two. He had an inferiority complex, even though he had no excuse for having one. I was taller than he was. I remember one day when I was about sixteen. I walked up and kissed him on the forehead. I didn't mean it as any kind of put-down, but, oh boy, talk about taking a bull by the horns. His eyes were normally a deep blue, but they got whiter, very cold. I thought he was going to drop me in my tracks. He let me get by with it that time, but I never tried it again.

Another man remembers trying to make amends with his father, in spite of all the turbulence of the past. His sincere attempt at reconciliation failed.

Probably my very worst and most ultimate rejection came when I was twenty-two. I went to see my father on his birthday. I had tried so hard to please him and somehow to earn his approval and acceptance. I planned that day for a long time. I had worked hard and saved my money to buy a pocket watch that I was sure would please him. I also got the courage to say to him something that I had never heard from him. His response continues to ring clearly in my ears. I said, "I love you," and he responded with,

"Don't say that." It was then that I knew I was a bastard. He was never my father and I was never his son.

The specific content and impact of some of these mental snapshots can be quite surprising. You would probably expect the two previous stories to have made quite an impression on the victims. Such blatant rejection would certainly be hard to forget. Yet some of our snapshots of wrenching times might not seem nearly as severe to others. The events we remember may not be so horrible in themselves, but gather into such a storm cloud because we associate them with a deeper level of negative emotions which we were feeling.

The following events were shared by a woman whose biological father had gotten her mother pregnant and deserted her. The mother soon met another man who married her and began to raise the child as his own. The daughter knew this man as her father, but he left before she was ten. When the mother married again, the daughter never got along with her second stepfather. So while her mental snapshots may not sound so terrible at first hearing, she associates a lot more feeling with them than you or I would expect. Here's what she remembers about the man who first filled the role of father in her life:

> My father worked at this factory where they made rubber bands and he used to get the biggest kick out of whipping those rubber bands at us. I was one of three daughters, and we were just little girls at the time. We didn't like being hit. It hurt. But he really thought it was funny.
>
> One time I visited him when I was fifteen. I had gone to the bathroom, and when I came out he was hiding behind the door and wearing a mask. He scared the life out of me. It triggered memories for me. He enjoyed sneaking up on me and scaring me, but it made me feel insecure. He was probably just trying to play the only way he knew how. But it had the opposite effect.

THOUGHTS, FEELINGS, AND BEHAVIORS

The snapshots we carry in our minds are not so much true visual images, but more like internal feelings. As we go through traumas while growing up, it's as if a part of us breaks off and never grows. Each piece that gets broken off evokes a certain emotion each time we think of it. Sometimes we might experience that emotion without any apparent reason at all. Other times we feel it magnified many times over.

A tremendous amount of energy becomes wrapped up in these "emotional nodules" that have detached themselves and remain inside us. They contain emotions that have capsulized within us—irrational feelings that don't go away. Let's say you're feeling lonely at the moment. If that triggers a recollection of feeling lonely in the past, it magnifies the loneliness of the present.

Even deeper than the feelings are the thoughts that originated them. The problem is that we frequently continue to respond to our emotions without ever getting all the way back to the thoughts. Though the feelings of the present magnify the past, they are motivated by certain thoughts buried in our memories and never resolved. The *thought* motivates the *feeling*, and the feeling motivates the behavior. It is senseless to spend a lot of time trying to change our behavior if we don't take a close look at what may be causing it.

If you find yourself confused about why you responded quite as dramatically as you did to some minor incident, perhaps you too have deeply embedded thoughts and feelings. Some people say the answer is simple: just pour out your heart to God. Though I wouldn't argue with that advice, I also believe that someone can't pour out his or her heart without knowing what's there to confess.

Others are quick to recommend counseling. This may also be a helpful step to take, though I would alert you that much outpatient counseling is never successful for people with deeply buried memories, feelings, and thoughts. Encapsulated emotions are very, very strong. Events in the present only scrape the surface of those passions, allowing only tiny bits to escape. Some people have kept those feelings buried and intact for many years. And keeping such powerful forces inside for so long leads to fear.

Many express fear that they will go crazy if they ever begin to release everything they have inside—like a volcano ready to erupt. Not knowing exactly what those feelings are, they don't know how to deal with them. They know their universe is getting way out of balance, but they don't have a clue why or what they should do to prevent further confusion. Outpatient counseling may not provide a significant support system for dealing with these very real and powerful issues.

If the person *is* successful in getting all the way to the core of the emotion—to the point of "lancing" the nodule and releasing the long pent-up feelings—he or she will need significant help. Our ultimate goal is to get in touch with how we felt as children (when this emotional capsule got broken off and stopped growing). Until we do, we will not respond in an adult way. We will respond as we *would* have responded as children—in a very emotional and volatile way.

Someone being counseled on an outpatient basis usually has a fifty-minute session about once a week. But what happens if this person gets down deep enough and opens up one of those encapsulated emotional nodules? The sensation may be best described as an "emotional heart attack." Such people need immediate attention. They don't want to wait a week to deal with it, but someone else is waiting for the next appointment. They don't want to go home, because they're in no condition to be around other people. Besides, others don't like to deal with people who are going through that kind of pain.

It's difficult enough for professional counselors to work someone through the stress of dealing with those kinds of intense emotional releases. When a client begins to spew rude or obscene comments, seemingly out of nowhere, a professional isn't going to take it personally. A trained counselor realizes it's only a symptom of the problem, like an annoying cough is symptomatic of a cold. In fact, increased annoying behavior may offer a subtle signal that the person is beginning to get better. Some of the emotional poisons that have been trapped for so long are finally being released.

Some people recommend hypnosis to get to the root of the problem—going beneath the behaviors to the feelings, and beneath the feelings to the thoughts. I disagree. I firmly believe, from counseling with many people, that God helps us recall our painful memories when we're ready to deal with them.

One case in point is a woman who was physically and sexually abused throughout her childhood by her father. She had blocked out a lot of the memories of her childhood—or so she thought. Now, as a wife and mother, she had come to Rapha for some inpatient counseling because of recurring nightmares and sudden changes in her behavior. She told us:

I was in counseling three years ago, dealing with another issue, and they told me I'd have to deal with my dad at some point. I said, "That may be, but I'm not going to bring it up just to bring it up. God's going to have to bring it up for me." And that's what happened six months ago. I had quite a nightmare of my dad being in bed with me. It took me four hours to express it to my husband. I was kind of paralyzed in my own bed because I was reliving it. I thought I was crazy because I was in the nightmare looking down at myself, at what was happening. I had never heard of anything like that before. I didn't know other people had similar dreams. But it scared me to death, and that's what started it.

When I had this nightmare, I fought it. I fought having to deal with this. I had said three years ago that I would deal with it if God said so. I said, "I'll do it then." And I feel like he brought it up, yet I resisted dealing with it for about four months. In the meantime, I felt like I was becoming like my dad. I was a mess. I was very withdrawn. I was sleeping—and I relate that to my dad, always wanting to be in bed. If I *was* up, it was like I had energy to burn, which was abnormal for me.

All the characteristics of becoming like my father seemed to be there. I began to compare myself to him, and I couldn't stand it. After four months I finally said, "Okay, I need some help." I think I was in bed for a whole day, going on into the night. I don't know exactly what woke me up and made me do something, but I knew I was in trouble. It was so unlike me because I'm a very social person.

This woman has a long way to go in the healing process, but the hardest part is over: she took the first step. She knows she will have to deal with unpleasant memories, to relive a lot of painful experiences. But she's going beneath her erratic behavior and getting down to the thoughts and feelings that still hold her captive. She's doing it for her husband and children, as well as herself. Another woman wrote about starting to recall painful memories after a long period of time:

My dad was the son of a pastor who preached in small farming communities. Yet when I was a small girl he would come into my bedroom at night and rape me. He died of cancer in 1983. As an adult, I had just recommitted my life to Christ when memories began to surface. I started to remember him physically beating me.

I am currently in therapy with a Christian therapist who specializes in incest therapy, ritual abuse, and dissociative disorders. I had tried to get help before, while Dad was still living with the aid of a hospice program. I would have appreciated the help, and I wanted the help, but my father didn't want anyone invading "our privacy." I respected his wishes.

When the timing is right, the memories will come. You won't need to force them, nor should you resist them. Help is available for those who recognize they need it. Hypnotism isn't the answer; quick and easy therapy sessions are a pipe dream. It's going to require emotional excavating—a lot of seeking out and digging up of those long buried, encapsulated emotions.

Perhaps you've settled for less than the best for a long time. You may not even know what you want any more. The next chapter will help you determine what you might be seeking. In the meantime, don't keep pushing these mental snapshots back into the recesses of your memory. Open up some of those dreaded albums that have been closed for so long and take another look. You might be surprised. You may be a lot closer to dealing with your past than you thought.

TAKE TIME TO REFLECT

1. Describe one time when you felt a strong emotional connection with your father.

2. Describe your most unpleasant memory of your father.

3. What painful memories did God call to your mind as you read this chapter?

4. List a few words that describe how you felt as these memories surfaced.

FIFTEEN

What Do You Expect from a Father?

I N RETROSPECT, most of us can see how our relationships with our fathers haven't been everything they should be. We probably experience some very specific regrets, along with a lot more vague sadness. Yet early in the relationship, we usually swing from one extreme to another before we ever reach any definite conclusions. Young children tend to believe that their fathers are just about perfect. These seeming giants usually have the wisdom to solve any problem and the strength to overcome any obstacle: Superman in the flesh.

Based on what a child can observe, it appears that Dad works hard, provides for the family, and spends time with them whenever he can. But as we continue to grow, those opinions usually change. We realize that our fathers *aren't* perfect, that they have faults and warts, just like everyone else. At first, we may be quite disappointed. We want them to spend more time with us, rather than be at work so much. We realize that the little bit of time they do spend with us fails to provide the sense of love and affirmation we need. We discover that sometimes hard work is actually workaholism, or that some fathers cope with their problems by abusing alcohol or other drugs.

The pendulum soon swings back the other way. We typically begin to make excuses for these all-important men in our lives. After all, since no father is perfect, shouldn't we learn to forgive them for their shortcomings? If Dad is only human, isn't it logical that he will lose his temper once in a while? If his rage gets out of control and he hits us, isn't it because he just can't help it? If he drinks to get through a rough day, isn't that understandable?

With a sobered sense of realism, many of us begin to settle for whatever we can get out of the relationship. Sure, in a perfect world, fathers come home from work, laugh at the dinner table, ask how our day went, and listen with interest as we recount any special events. But this isn't a perfect world. If Dad gets around to talking to us a few times a week, we try to be satisfied with that.

As we move into adulthood, the perspective shifts once again. We realize that even in an imperfect world, Dad is still responsible for his behavior. The fact that he had a bad day doesn't give him the right to come home and abuse us. No matter how busy they are, fathers still have the responsibility to provide adequately for their children.

But by the time we reach these conclusions, childhood may be long past. We are left with a vague sense of confusion and regret. We made excuses too long, and now our relationships with our fathers will never be what they should have been. And we need not have been abused or seriously mistreated to feel this way. Gradual but consistent neglect over a long period of time can sometimes be just as devastating to an adult child as actual abuse.

Many adults find it very difficult to express exactly what they *would* like to have received from a father. They may see what went *wrong*, yet have trouble determining what *should* have happened. Having made excuses for so long, many hardly dare to believe how short of the mark Dad really was. Others may have gotten just enough attention to know what fatherhood *should* be, but not nearly enough to satisfy their emotional needs.

To top it all off, an ugly suspicion may linger in the back of our minds: *What if Dad knew what he was supposed to do, but just didn't think I was important enough for him to make the effort?* That makes it very difficult for the adult child to look back and admit, "I wish Dad had spent more time with me on Saturdays, rather than sleeping off his hangovers," or, "Dad was nice enough most of the time, but I wish he could have *said* he loved me." Even speaking the words forces the person to confess that his or her strained father/child relationship may never be resolved.

Stating that fathers should provide unconditional love for their children is a bit too simplistic. It happens to be true, yet the statement means different things to different people. In the interviews with our volunteers, not many were quick to verbalize *specific* things they wish had been different. Yet in their stories, we were able to identify certain desired qualities. This list essentially breaks down unconditional love into some of its individual components. We could certainly name other qualities that a father needs to have. Yet these ten kept coming up again and again in our interviews. We will come back to these ten traits in later chapters as we seek ways to resolve your own father hunger.

Obviously, very few men are going to be strong in all these areas, just as few will be completely devoid of every single positive trait. But overall, effective fathers display the following characteristics to the best of their ability, while ineffective fathers fail to reflect most of these qualities in any consistent way.

Most people think they have the right to expect these behaviors from a father. In some cases they came to this conclusion because their own fathers were outstanding models of the particular quality being considered. More frequently, however, the person zeroed in on a particular characteristic because his or her own father did such a *poor* job, leaving an even more intense emotional void in the child. As you read over this fatherhood top ten, consider how your own father measures up.

TIME

A father ideally spends enough time with his children, which was one of the most commonly expressed desires we heard. Nothing else seems to translate so directly into proof of a father's love. If Dad fell short in this area, no other material gift is convincing enough to prove his love. No verbal expression, no matter how eloquent or frequent, provides an adequate substitute.

Adult children of workaholic fathers who were seldom home grieve over the loss of a loving relationship almost as much as those with absent or alcoholic fathers. Men can offer any number of reasons to justify the time they spend away from their children. They may even sit their kids down and explain why Daddy is gone so much. And the child may seem to accept his absence—for now. But later—after it is too late for the father to attend the child's baseball games, go camping together, or spend an occasional Saturday in the park—the child is likely to recall a lack of genuine love rather than an intense devotion on the part of the father to provide.

FOCUSED ATTENTION

While fathers must spend time with their children, time in itself is not enough. Many adult children recall Dad being at home a lot, but he could have been on Venus for all the good it did. Alcoholic fathers were especially not much fun to be around. Those not lost in an alcoholic haze may have hidden behind a newspaper or focused the majority of their attention on the television screen rather than on their children. Dad may have been home and *able* to devote attention to their children, yet he chose to remain unavailable.

Young children who so need to feel their father's love can be devastated to discover that they are less important to him than day-old news or Monday night football. Many of the happy stories we hear center around one shining moment when Dad put everything else aside and spent some one-on-one time with the child. But these times seemed woefully rare. Several people clung to just one or two such memories. Others had none at all.

PROTECTION, COMFORT, AND SECURITY

Perhaps no one can address our need for comfort and security as well as a father. When children are young, their lives are filled with fears. As they grow, the fears don't go away; they just change forms. We start out by being afraid of getting lost, frightened of big dogs, or reluctant to sleep alone without a night light. As we get older, we're afraid people won't like us. We may be scared of what will happen in the future: Will I get into college? Find a job that pays the bills? Meet someone who will be a good marriage partner?

Attuned fathers know what their children fear and help them face those fears. They know how much the child is capable of standing alone, and when he or she needs Dad to step in with a large dose of consolation and affirmation. When children know that Dad is there backing them up, they can overcome their fears. But when fathers make no effort to foster such a feeling of security, young children remain much more vulnerable.

One woman described how her father *had* helped her develop a strong sense of confidence: "I knew that if anything broke around our house, Dad could fix it. And I've never been afraid of storms. He worked for the electric company since before I was born and every time there was a storm he had to leave. But before he left he always assured us that there was nothing to worry about, that everything would be okay. So I was never afraid of thunder and lightning."

This universal need for protection and security shifts as the child grows. Very young children need to know that Daddy, who is "big and strong," is there to keep them safe. Nothing is too much for him to handle. Dad can fix any of the toys they break, answer any question they have, open the lid of any jar. They feel safe and secure. Later those childhood needs shift from wanting *physical* protection to wanting *emotional* security. An attentive father will note the change and provide appropriately.

COMMUNICATION

Wise fathers communicate with their children in a way that isn't vague or harsh. When Dad comes home from a hard day at work, it's hard to explain how much it means for a child to hear, "Tell me about your day." The child may be aware that Mom and Dad are very busy people and needn't be reminded all the time. But when a father doesn't complain about his own day and instead shifts the focus of conversation to the child, the youngster feels special. Children love communicating with a father who really wants to listen, without having to try to wrangle Dad's attention.

Talking to their children would seem to be one of the easiest things for fathers to do. It doesn't take any money; it doesn't require a lot of time or energy. A few minutes each day around the dinner table or at bedtime, along with an occasional one-on-one outing would more than satisfy most children. Yet far too few fathers even put forth that much effort. Here's one of the worst case scenarios:

There was no communication in my family whatsoever. I came home one day and asked my mother, "How come the piano is outside?" She didn't answer me. My dad came home, and I didn't know whether to ask him or not. I think I waited until the next day. Then I asked, "Dad, why is the piano in the backyard?" He didn't say anything. A couple of days later I came home from school and the piano was demolished. My dad had taken it apart with a sledgehammer. I never knew why. That's the way communication worked at our house. There just wasn't any. It wasn't allowed. I had no affirmation or anything else. And that affected my whole life, because I didn't know how to communicate after I got married. I still have doubts about my ability.

Communication techniques don't have to be that bizarre in order to create self-doubt in children. If fathers fail to communicate, youngsters are quick to blame themselves. They may assume they're doing something wrong, don't know how to express themselves, are asking the wrong questions, or expecting too much. Certainly, children may sometimes be able to take the initiative and become more involved in their parents' lives. Yet many adults shoulder a lot of guilt because their fathers failed to show more interest in them or open up a clear channel of communication.

TRUST

A father needs to be the child's ally. Children need to know that their father has enough trust to support them as maturity presents new opportunities and challenges. But if their father is distant, absent, or apathetic, children know he will never fill that role. In one sense, he becomes just another adult in their lives. If he doesn't trust them, who will? They will likely find allies among their peers instead, which many times brings more trouble than support.

Boys often look to their fathers to help them grow up faster. When they want to start riding their bikes on the street, play football, go camping overnight with a friend, or do any number of adventuresome things, many know what their protective mothers will say. They need Dad there, both to convince Mom and to assure them, "You're a growing boy and I started doing these things when I was about your age. I trust you. I believe in you. Be careful."

Sometimes young girls need a male point of view as well. They need a trustworthy father to pull aside and open up to. Another woman—even a mother—just can't provide the sense of self-worth they need as little girls who are fast becoming young women.

FORGIVENESS

While no child is perfect, some fathers act as if they expected perfection. If children never feel forgiven, they cannot feel loved. All youngsters are going to make mistakes, get caught in lies, accidentally break things, push the limits of authority, and behave in other ways that don't necessarily please the parents. Yet if Dad doesn't show that he forgives the child, he or she will be forced to carry the guilt—perhaps for a lifetime.

When children know they aren't likely to be forgiven, they aren't going to be so quick to confess some wrongdoing. An unforgiving father can unintentionally create a lifestyle for his children of deceit, double standards, and the need to redefine certain terms according to their own perceptions rather than what may actually be true. We will address this process of redefinition in the latter part of this chapter.

Tied into the quality of forgiveness is the father's responsibility to create a sense of "home" for the child. Someone has said, "Home is a place that, when you go there, they have to take you in." Young children need to know that whatever they do, or whatever happens to them, they can go home and find forgiveness. This quality is precisely what makes the story of the prodigal son such a powerful parable.

DISCIPLINE

The quality of forgiveness does not negate the need for occasional discipline. Children expect to be disciplined when they intentionally disobey pre-established rules. In fact, this discipline is interpreted as proof of the parents' love. Children know at some gut level that a certain number of rules and regulations are for their own good. When they refuse to comply with one of the rules, a lack of subsequent discipline confuses children. If the rules are truly for the child's own good, then how much does Dad really care if he fails to enforce them?

Of course, discipline should be applied with love and should fit the offense. It should be consistent and not administered in anger. A father who quickly flies off the handle, screams incessantly at a child, strikes the child in a fit of rage, or otherwise loses control will not reap the desired effect. Forgiveness and discipline should go hand in hand. While it may be appropriate to forgive without disciplining on occasion, a father should never discipline without expressing complete and total forgiveness.

ACCEPTANCE

Fathers may entertain big plans for their young children. *My boy is going to be the best quarterback the Chicago Bears ever had. My girl is going to be president of the United States. This kid is going to find a cure for cancer.* And so forth. As time passes, the youngster may exhibit much more of a passion for music than for quarterbacking, or prefer ceramics to politics. Those great dreams are popped like a bubble.

At such times, a loving father still accepts the child for who he or she *really* is. When children are allowed to develop their own God-given strengths, the parents might be pleasantly surprised. Fathers should do all they can to provide acceptance and affirmation for *whatever* the child's interests and achievements happen to be—as long as they aren't illegal or immoral, of course!

Not sensing approval from Dad can be especially shattering to a child's emotional development. A child needs to know that "it's okay to be me." If not, lack of self-worth and self-esteem wait upon the doorstep of that child's life. They easily feel as if they exist only for someone else's pleasure, only to serve someone else's desires. They feel like nobodies with no intrinsic value.

Related to this lack of acceptance is a craving for *touch*. As people think back to their childhoods, one frequent regret is that Dad never hugged them, held them in his lap, patted them on the back, or physically connected with them very often. Usually, if children never received tangible signs of affection, they never truly feel accepted. Wise fathers express their acceptance through both verbal and tactile means.

GUIDANCE AND ADVICE

Fathers serve as a natural source of authority for their kids. But a lot of other qualities have to be established before the child will look to a father for advice: the communication channels have to be open; the trust factor has to be in place; and the assurance of forgiveness must be evident before a child will confide in Dad about *real* problems.

Yet fathers who make the effort to provide such guidance for their children can instill values that will last throughout life. One woman remembers: "I would consider my dad a workaholic, but when he was home he was fun to be with. He was a fair man and he taught me that we pay our bills before we eat. That has helped me not to get in real bad debt since I've grown up. Because of his advice, I never charge more on my credit cards than I can pay at the end of the month."

Making bills a priority may seem like a minor lesson, but that's the point. If children are learning, remembering, and applying what fathers teach them about economics, just think what they are learning about much deeper concepts such as love, relationships, and life values. A father has great power to enhance his child's experience of life—or to leave the child confused and directionless.

PROVISION OF A ROLE MODEL

Verbal advice and guidance are important, but so is the nonverbal example that the father sets for his children. It's not enough for him to simply tell his kids what they should do. He must show them. Providing a positive role model is a heavy responsibility—a fact I know from experience! Children are watching all the time. They may choose to imitate anything: words, attitudes, personality, behavior, and so forth. If a father is racially prejudiced, his children will probably struggle with that issue as well. If the father swears, smokes, or drinks, the children may do the same—perhaps without even thinking twice about whether they should.

But on the other hand, a father who provides a positive example for his children doesn't have to lecture them so often. They pick up on and imitate the positive aspects of his character from simple observation. One man was molded by these positive memories of his father:

His manner of correcting was to put me over his knee and spank me. And he would always preface the spanking with, "Now, son, this hurts me worse than it does you." And I think he really meant that. It was very hard for him to correct me. I don't remember playing games with him or anything, but I do remember we lived on a farm with paths that went out toward the back woods. And he would hunt at different times, and I remember following him out. And because he was a Christian, he would be praying out loud and telling the Lord about his problems. I remember hearing his conversations.

This man had had his share of relationship problems with his father, yet his self-confidence and sense of humor were very evident as he spoke. In spite of the father's mistakes, for the most part he had provided an example for his son to follow.

None of us experiences all of these ideal qualities as much as we would have liked. Some of you may not remember enjoying *any* of them to any significant degree. An important element in your healing process will be the realization that their absence was not *your* fault. You deserved to have a father be there for you. If he was there, he should have made an honest effort to relate to you in these basic ways.

If your father seriously fails to measure up on this list, that's his shortcoming, not yours. Granted, you still have to live with the resulting disappointment and grief. My goal in this book is to help you deal with those feelings. Before you move on, spend some time trying to identify what you missed most in your relationship with your father. The emptiness and regret you feel has a source. Try to discover what it is. The more specific you can be, the more pain relief you may experience.

TAKE TIME TO REFLECT

1. How does your father rate on the "Fatherhood Top Ten List"? Put an X on each continuum to show the extent that your dad either generously exhibited or stingily withheld these qualities.

	Generous	Stingy
time	_____	_____
focused attention	_____	_____
security and comfort	_____	_____
communication	_____	_____
trust	_____	_____
forgiveness	_____	_____
discipline	_____	_____
acceptance	_____	_____
guidance and advice	_____	_____
provision of a role model	_____	_____

2. Describe any other specific aspects of your relationship with your father that you wish had been different.

3. In what ways have you blamed yourself for the absence of these qualities in your relationship with your father?

4. Do you find it difficult to believe that you deserved to have a father who provided these things for you? Why or why not?

SIXTEEN

New Perceptions, New Definitions

YOU WILL NEVER be able to overcome the hurts of the past until you're able and willing to reach some accurate definitions of such important concepts as love, trust, and intimacy. In doing so, you may discover that your parents lied to you. Perhaps they didn't mean to; maybe they did. Either way, until you discover what is actually true, you will continue making the same mistakes due to inaccurate data.

If you really want to confuse your friends sometime, try this experiment. Lay out pieces of paper or cloth that are different colors and then redefine the colors. For example, tell them blue equals green, red equals blue, yellow equals red, and green equals yellow. Then ask them to respond to a few simple commands: "Exchange the yellow and blue papers." "Put the swatches in alphabetical order according to color." "Pick up the two colors that would combine to form green." Performing the simplest of functions when the definitions are suddenly changed can be awkward, uncomfortable, and frustrating. Even intelligent people appear dense by having been slowed down considerably.

Consider what happens to a child who is brought up with distorted definitions of some key emotions. That child is experiencing life and making decisions based on erroneous information. How can relationships be expected to flourish, especially if the other people involved have a few wacky definitions of their own?

As an adult, you are now more capable of stepping back from your problems and analyzing them than you were as a child. You may not be very good at it, especially if you've been making wrong assumptions all this time. If you were like most children, you believed what you were told without a lot of questioning. But in retrospect, you may begin to see that perhaps you took too much of what you were told at face value. One person expresses it this way:

> As I look at my parents, I realize that I have never seen them as young married "kids." I've always looked at them strictly as adults. But my parents were very young when they got married, and the confusing things I'm working through now are probably much like what they must have gone through as well. I never looked at my dad in that kind of context—young, confused, and trying to do his best.
>
> Maybe he put his own feelings before his kids, which wasn't right. But maybe that's all he could see at the time. I just wonder if what he did isn't common to a lot of other parents. For example, I can see a lot of options for myself that would be easier right now, but I wouldn't be able to pay as much attention to my son. In a way, I feel that my child holds me back, yet I have a responsibility to him. Neither my mom nor my dad put their kids first, not really. And that hurts sometimes. I don't want my son to be able to say the same thing.

This man was able to analyze the problem, change his perspective, and make adjustments that would diminish the chances of continuing the same situation with his own son. His new perspective resulted from applying logic and reason. Other changes can require a more graphic alteration in the way a person perceives reality, such as actually seeing the conditions under which a father grew up.

For example, one woman was a first-generation American whose parents had grown up in Europe. Her father never gave her much attention, mainly because she was a daughter instead of a son. She still regrets not being able to connect with her dad. But she describes how she reached a change in perspective that finally allowed her to understand what made him the way he was.

As a child, I would pick up bits and pieces, little by little, trying to fit the puzzle together of why my father wouldn't accept me. But my healing didn't really begin until I happened to meet up with a person who had known my father as a child. I was able to go to his home back in Germany. I remember coming out of the very small cottage where he grew up and asking my mother, "How did they raise thirteen children in this little, tiny cottage?" The man who took us there turned to me and said, "They didn't stay home. They were farmed out as soon as they were able to pitch hay and do other chores."

I found out that my father hadn't had a relationship with *his* parents, because you *feed* your hired hands, but you don't love them. And that was the relationship my father had had as a child. He was somebody to help with the chores. After he married my mom and we came along, he fed us. He cared about us. He saw that we got a good education. He made sure we went to church on Sunday. We always had decent clothing. We had all the necessities of life. But he didn't believe in luxuries at all. And to him, it was something of a luxury to pay too much attention to one's children. At least we always knew where we stood.

Your father didn't wait until the day you were born to start behaving inappropriately. He had his own parent-relationship problems, stresses in life, and other factors that influenced his actions. Yes, it was wrong when he took it out on you, but as an adult you can now try to discover and understand what some of those factors may have been. As you do, you will begin to trace your faulty definitions back to their original source.

As children, we learned about life by observing what took place around us. We made certain assumptions which we believed to be true. We knew that parents were supposed to love their children, so we interpreted their actions toward us as "love." We knew husbands and wives were supposed to be close, so we may have interpreted their behavior toward each other as "intimacy." But now we realize that perhaps our perceptions were not correct after all. Consequently, we may need to formulate new definitions for some very crucial concepts. Let's take time to examine how a few of these concepts specifically relate to father hunger.

WHAT IS TRUST?

As people talked about the consequences of their fathers' short-comings, one of the major observations that kept coming up was the near total annihilation of their ability to trust other people. Once fathers abandon or abuse children, they are usually unable to put their trust in any other person. Some children, however, learn to redefine trust. Webster's defines trust as "assured reliance on the character, ability, strength, or truth of someone or something." The verb means "to place confidence" or "to be confident." These definitions would certainly suggest that trust is a choice.

But the distorted definitions of childhood may paint a different picture. We may trust people not because we *want* to or *choose* to, but because *we have* to. And in reality, that is not trust at all. Blind faith in someone is not "assured reliance on the person's character." And we may find out the hard way that such trust is in error.

For example, one woman was placed in custody of her mother after her parents had divorced. In severe need of love and affirmation, she placed a great deal of trust in her mother. At that time in the child's life, the mother was the only person who could meet those needs for her. However, this woman later discovered her trust in her mother was misplaced.

My mother had always pointed the finger at my father for me to be angry at, as opposed to herself. As I grew up, I was even told that I was supposed to have a lot of anger toward my father. But then I found out that my *mother* was the one who had the affair and caused the crisis in the marriage. I was in the hospital for depression, and they said, "You're just like your mother. You've grown up exactly like her." They also said I was feeling anger toward her. I said, "I don't have any angry feelings toward my mom." But I eventually discovered they were "frozen" feelings.

All my life my mother had been telling me that I should be mad at my dad. I had been brainwashed into thinking that my mother was such a wonderful person. Now I finally realize that I *do* feel anger toward my mother. And my father... I don't have angry feelings toward him. I know that he wasn't perfect and that he did some things that hurt me. But I have a real strong longing... a real hunger for my father who was absent.

I would argue whether or not this child genuinely trusted her mother. Perhaps she did to begin with, but what was soon established as trust was actually manipulation on the mother's part. Having trusted an untrustworthy person, the child formed a wrong definition of trust. Rather than believe that her mother would do something to hurt her, the woman simply adapted the meaning of the word to fit her circumstances.

Genuine trust is risky. Trust must be given, not forced or demanded. Yet some people try to generate trust when little or none exists. They use the facade of faulty trust to hide other feelings, such as loneliness, despair, fear, and so forth. People may appear to be trusting when they are really trying to prevent being hurt.

Perhaps you've met people who, almost right away, pour out their whole life story for you to hear. Then they move right into telling you secrets about themselves or maybe trusting you to hold their wallets or drive their cars. Is this really trust? No. Such behavior is not normal. Their goal in opening themselves up to you is to try to coerce you into opening up to them. They desperately want a trusting friend, so they offer their trust first as a ploy.

As we discussed in chapter eight, real trust is developed over time. One person gives a little trust and the other gives back a little. Then they open up a little more and *gradually* the trusting relationship is formed. When the relationship becomes one-sided, it is not based on trust—no matter what the people involved actually call it. Once trust is destroyed, it can be extremely difficult to reestablish. And when a person's own father proves untrustworthy, it is difficult for the child to trust *anyone* else—even a spouse. In fact, women betrayed by their fathers typically find it especially hard to trust another man, even a husband. Here is one example:

My father abused me, both physically and sexually. I was so scared of him that even after he died I felt his control over my life. I find it very hard to trust other people. But God sent Paula my way a few months ago who was to be the person that I would learn how to trust. I learned a lot from her. One of the most important things was that I *could* trust someone else.

I very recently started getting awful flashbacks from my childhood. It took me hours and hours to tell Paula what I saw because I thought I was... crazy or something. But I told her a little bit at a time and she never rejected me. She listened and never made me feel like I was stupid or crazy or anything. So I've begun a foundation of trust.

And, see, that's what I would like to establish with my husband. I'd like to be able to confide in him. It's not really that I don't trust him, yet it's just so hard for me to open up to him. But I've never trusted anybody before in my whole life like I do Paula. I really think I needed that relationship to begin to work through everything.

WHAT IS INTIMACY?

If we see our parents regularly hug and kiss, cuddle on the couch, ask each other's opinions before making decisions, and collectively pass love down to us, we know what true intimacy looks like. But if we see a colder, more sterile relationship between them, we may *assume* that to be intimacy. After all, it may be the only model we have on which to base our definition.

Consequently, we may later exhibit that same shortsighted behavior when we begin dating or enter into a marriage relationship. This is one reason why sexual promiscuity is so rampant. Young adults frequently perceive their relationships to be functioning at a deeper level than they really are.

Due to misperceptions and faulty definitions, the promise of trust and intimacy combined sounds too attractive for many young adults to refuse. Rejected as children, they grew up feeling a desperation for closeness. Then boy meets girl, both offer "trust" to the other in order to force a friendship, and they begin a dating relationship. Still in search of intimacy, the dating relationship soon becomes a sexual relationship. They both think they're being intimate, when in fact they're only being sexually active. They need to revise their definitions of intimacy.

Husbands and wives can live together for years without realizing they lack true intimacy. Those who aren't afraid to deal with the truth and to work hard at improving their marriage relationship just might have a chance to discover what intimacy really means. Here is a testimonial from one man who is at least making the effort.

I hear a lot of women saying they married looking for the dad they never had. But I think a lot of men have the same void and look for women who will fill it. That's what happened in my own marriage. It finally dawned on me that my children had *two* parents who were still trying to find fulfillment in a relationship that they had never gotten before.

It's regretful to go into a relationship handicapped, putting so much *unspoken* expectation on the other person without her knowing. I know when I got married I didn't think of it in those terms and neither did my wife. But after looking back over ten or fifteen years of relating to each other, it's like we have suddenly discovered, "So *that's* why we were acting that way. We were both looking for something that wasn't to be had."

People who are still emotionally empty cannot be truly intimate with each other. They have so many personal needs that they have little, if anything, to give someone else. But if they are able to alter their definition of intimacy, they can begin to move in a new direction.

WHAT DOES IT MEAN TO BE A MAN?

When the qualities listed in the previous chapter are missing in our own fathers, we may create our own definitions. We may believe that real men can hold their liquor or think of the "strong, silent type" as the ideal. We may rationalize any number of our fathers' faults in forming our definitions. As we grow older, we may begin to see a father's shortcomings and create a definition of "a real man" that is just the opposite.

In the face of a domineering wife, the father may escape by spending time at the tavern with his buddies. The son is left alone to search for a new definition of what it means to be a man. He may consider TV cowboys to be his heroes, those who cut a manly form, don't take any guff, and always win the gunfight and the beautiful lady's hand. At home this boy sees men beaten down by women, never winning, or fighting with each other all the time. He begins to think, *Where are the real men around here?* Such a scenario spells trouble for a long time to come, both with authority figures who are overpowering and with wimps who are mousy.

Sometimes we need another person to show us how shallow our own definitions of manhood or fatherhood have become. We think we have a good idea of what a man should be. Then when we see someone who provides an excellent model of a father and a man, we wonder how we could have been so blind. One person found such a model when he went away to college.

When I was a junior in college I was going to be in summer school. I met a family in church and there was a real bonding between myself and them. They had three little kids, and the kids just adored me because I gave them some attention. That family invited me to move in with them. They said, "No need in staying in the dorm at college and getting assigned a roommate you don't know. Come stay with us for the summer." That summer turned into two and a half years.

At twenty years of age I finally got to see what it was like for a man to love his children. They were glad to see their father come home from work. They didn't run and hide like I had done as a child. He came in with hugs and kisses. He'd put his briefcase down and ask them how their day was. They would have dinner together as a family around the table. And he would bring out his Bible and share a little bit from the Bible and they would hold hands and pray.

After dinner he would play a game of Sorry or Monopoly, or whatever the kids wanted to do for a while. Every night he went into each of the children's bedrooms, sat down on the side of the bed, spent time with them, and prayed for them before they went to sleep. He was an excellent model!

So now a lot of what I'm trying to do with *my* children goes against my normal nature, but it's something that I've learned as I've seen it modeled and I've tried to duplicate that. This guy's kids are grown now. And I'm just like a brother to them. We write and call each other. We get together at Christmas time. It's a very close relationship.

There are any number of ways that our observations of imperfect fathers can lead to misperceptions about what men should be. Yet from an adult perspective, we can begin to face the truth about our own fathers and look for standards that aren't quite so subjective.

WHAT DOES IT MEAN TO BE A WOMAN?

Children can also be seriously misguided in their definitions of womanliness. It is next to impossible for a woman to live with an extremely dysfunctional husband for many years and remain unfazed by the experience. Usually, the wife in such relationships also sends out some inaccurate signals to her kids. Some mothers try to cover up the shortcomings of their husbands—for the sake of the children, of course. Some get into frequent and violent arguments. Some just take over and dominate the relationship. If a father isn't being "what a man should be," neither is the mother likely to be everything a woman should be.

Domineering women can beat down even the hardest worker and best provider in the world. When the mother becomes more and more the head of the house, long-term father hunger is a sure bet for the kids. Some children see the opposite drama acted out when a domineering man marries a very passive wife. Both sons and daughters can grow up with skewed notions of what true womanliness entails—which also spells future problems when they enter into marriage themselves.

With so many misperceptions and faulty definitions abounding, we can easily misunderstand one of the most important concepts of all: *love*. If we don't comprehend trust, how can we understand love? If intimacy is confusing, how can we truly love someone? How can we receive love if we don't recognize it? How can we offer love to someone else if we have lost sight of what it is? As difficult as it might be at this stage in your life to try living according to new definitions, you need to try. Until you do, genuine love will always be "out there," somewhere just out of your grasp.

In the next chapter we will consider more of the lessons we learned about manhood and womanhood from interacting with our fathers. In the meantime, you might want to think through some other terms that you may need to redefine in your current relationships: concepts such as friendship, truth, and commitment. We could spend a chapter on each one, but suffice it to say that many of us are settling for far less than what we should.

TAKE TIME TO REFLECT

1. Can you think of any situations from your childhood that you may have misinterpreted? If so, describe them.

2. Are there any factors in your parents' relationships with *their* parents that may have influenced your relationship with your father? If so, what are they?

3. Complete the following sentences:
   When it came to trusting my dad, I could always count on:
   The most intimacy I saw in my parents' relationship was:
   My father thinks a *real* man is:
   I think a *real* man is:
   My father thinks a woman should be:
   I think a woman should be:

4. List any other terms (i.e., friendship, truth, commitment) that may need redefining in your life.

SEVENTEEN

Fathers and Sons, Fathers and Daughters

A S PEOPLE BEGIN to consider the consequences of a problematic father relationship in their own lives, many ask out of curiosity who is more affected by father hunger: daughters or sons? I can offer no easy answer to that query, but a few patterns have become clear in my own investigations.

First, in almost every case where a father was negligent, abusive, or absent, the child will have some kind of severe emotional problem later in life. It may be during a dating relationship or in the context of marriage. Or the effects may not become obvious until the person has children of his or her own. But we have yet to find someone raised by an ineffective father who didn't suffer significant, related difficulties later in life.

Second, the subsequent problems rooted in a deficient father relationship don't go away on their own. The people who learn to cope are usually those who get help—often from a counselor who can patiently help them to work through the memories of the past, the present emotional turmoil, and the fear of passing the problem along to future generations. Sometimes a friend or relative can provide the much needed support.

Yet when searching for patterns as to whether sons or daughters are more susceptible to father hunger, none seems to be evident. Both males and females whose fathers have been weighed in the balance and found wanting to a significant degree will have problems at some point in their lives. Both males and females whose fathers demonstrate regular love, affection, trust, communication, and so forth are much more likely to avoid most of the emotional snares that have been detailed previously in this book.

If anything can be determined according to gender, it may be that more women are willing to open up and be honest about past relationship difficulties and to seek help. In the groups we approached, women outnumbered men in each case by at least two to one. However, other groups that deal with chemical addictions such as Alcoholics Anonymous are frequently predominantly male. The root of many of their problems may well be a poor father relationship.

In many cases we found that the daughters were jealous of the sons and the sons were jealous of the daughters, so typical of sibling rivalry. Let's consider a sampling of comments by both men and women so that you can search for any patterns of your own. My conclusion is that father hunger affects sons and daughters equally but often in different ways. A father's love is crucial for the formation of both sexes.

FATHERS AND SONS

Sometimes a father expects a son to grow up too fast—trying to make a man out of him almost from the time the baby is born. The father does severe damage in trying to force his little boy to become an adult before he ever has the chance to be a child. The following example was told with great difficulty, amid tears and long pauses:

> My mom became sick when I was four, so I lived with four or five different families for about a year. Then I came back home and basically my dad was the one who raised us. I was already very mature. By the time I was seven, I would say I had the emotional maturity of maybe a twelve-year-old. My father persecuted me very much—emotionally. He wanted me to "grow up." And he would tell me, "I'll be there to make sure that you understand what life's about."
>
> But I didn't seem to be growing up fast enough for him. There was no escaping him. He chose to persecute me because I

was not mature. When I was about seven, I stood up to him one night when we were supposed to go to bed, and I... we all got beat. I asked, "Why do we always have to get a beating?" And he beat me... and he beat me... and he beat me.

My dad was raised in Nebraska, my mom in Montana. When they grew up, they learned to stand their ground. In my family, the way we were raised, you learned to not back down. But that's very difficult for someone who is seven years old and it left some permanent scars on me.

During my teenage years his relationship with me was pretty much one of authority. My response was to run and hide for shelter, so to speak. He was not really someone you could talk to. Everything I did was to try to get his approval. Even so, I respected him a great deal. He did have a lot of values and morals. But there was what I would call some schizophrenic behavior: "Do as I say, but not as I do."

In this case, the father's expectations were way too high for his son. In other cases, fathers went to the opposite extreme, such as the man who told us the following story:

When I was nine years old, I would work with my dad before school. Then after dinner we'd sometimes go out and work till ten o'clock at night. In all that time he never allowed me to do anything except hand him tools, which did not build my self-confidence. All I ever did was hand him tools. He would work on tarring roofs, and I would carry half-buckets of tar up a ladder two and a half or three stories high. But he wouldn't allow me to spread it. He wouldn't allow me to pick up a hammer. I was strictly a dummy, as far as he was concerned. He never allowed any of his sons to help him except the first one.

The oldest son was extremely intelligent, very mechanical, and could do anything—just like my dad. But one day he took our truck, ran away to New York, and got married. The depression hit at about the same time. After that my father would never trust the rest of us with anything. If you picked up a hammer, he'd take it away from you. Pick up an axe, he'd take it away from you. He could do any kind of work himself, but he would not allow us to do anything but hand him tools.

My two brothers ended up becoming alcoholics. One brother

was more fortunate because he went to work in a carnival and met someone who became more or less a brother to him. But when they left, I had no one to talk with. I had to fight for everything I ever got. No one was willing to spend any time with me.

Who's to say which is worse: a father who makes impossible and unreasonable demands on his son, or one who refuses to let his son develop any sense of self-worth? Both ends of the spectrum can have devastating effects on young boys who are simply trying to please Dad and get a little affirmation along the way.

Now put yourself in the place of a young boy who never receives the love and attention he needs. He's not a bad person. He tries hard and wants to please others. He grows up, gets married, and starts a family of his own. Now what? He truly wants to avoid the problems he faced in the past, yet has absolutely no idea how. Unless he has found another role model along the way, he still has no clue as to what fathering is all about. This man is likely to continue the same patterns with his own children.

One man felt very inadequate due to the shortcomings of his father. Even though he recognized in his dad many good qualities as a provider and caretaker, this man never heard his father say what a good job he had done or that he loved him. From a divorced family, the father himself had been raised without a man around the house. No blame was assigned, but the effects were apparent, especially when this man had children of his own. He says:

> When our first was born, it was a boy. I remember exactly when he was born, thinking, *Oh no, God, I don't know how to be a father to a boy.* I figured if it was a girl, I could just love her. My second child was also a boy. (We finally got a girl the third time.) I love my two boys, but I remember those frightening feelings very distinctly. I think I'm doing some things right. But how do you become the father you didn't have?

This man was something of an exception. His desire for a daughter was based on selfless logic—or perhaps plain fear. And he is doing all he can now to obtain the proper kind of guidance for himself and his family. In other cases we discovered that fathers were more selfish in their desire for sons. In some cases the daughters in the families were expected to fill those roles. Other times the daughters voluntarily tried to play the part of a son in order to get Dad's attention.

FATHERS AND DAUGHTERS

A father who refuses to accept children for who they are commits a form of abuse. Simply because a father wishes to have a son is no excuse to ignore a daughter. Yet many of the young women in our country are growing up with the impression that they are second-best, based almost entirely on their father's way of treating them. The memories of such women are striking and painful. Here's one of many:

The first time I remember getting rejected by my dad was when he came into our house, took *my* kite out of the closet, and then went to another apartment to play with a little boy. (He eventually left us to live with the mother of this boy.) They had a street behind their house and we had a cornfield, so it was safer in our backyard. I knew then that since his own children were all three girls, he wanted a boy to roughhouse with. My sisters and I stood at our patio door watching him play with this little boy. We hated that kid.

Everything was always more important to my father than his three little girls. One time we had a birthday party for him and he was too busy to come in and get his presents from us. If you had asked me about my dad during those days, I would have had some very choice words—lots of anger. I was upset and misunderstood a lot.

To make things worse, the mother in this case felt a lot of anger toward the father after he deserted the family. She did nothing to soothe the feelings of her daughters. Instead, she used their anger and confusion against him. Not only did these young girls struggle with their rejection but they also had to learn to cope with the hostility and manipulation of the mother. Much later these girls discovered that it was the mother's fault that he made no attempt to contact his daughters more regularly. After they all became adults, it turned out that the father wasn't nearly the ogre his ex-wife had made him out to be.

When fathers don't respect daughters sufficiently, the mother can do a lot to make the situation either better or worse. Here's a case where the mother tried to help:

> Mother made up for Daddy's lost love. She was a very giving person, very understanding. She shielded us from him, in one sense. I can remember being scolded by him for having two tubes of lipstick. One was pink and one was red. He asked me, "How come you have two tubes?" I said, "Well, one is pink and one is red." He said, "You only have one mouth. Why do you need both?" After the confrontation with my father, I can remember my mother saying, "Please don't flaunt any kind of extravagance in front of your father, because he doesn't understand. He's had to go without so much."

But the problems faced by this woman as she grew up were far more severe than having twice the lipstick tubes her father thought she needed. Her father's intolerance destroyed one family member, as well as produced extremely harmful consequences in her own life. If a father chooses to have a favored child, it is hard on all the other siblings—gender notwithstanding.

> In our family, the sun rose and set on the firstborn son. My father has passed away and I have mourned a lost relationship that I never had with him. He didn't know I existed, other than to discipline me. That's the only time I ever heard from him. I never heard "Well done" or "I love you" or anything like that.
>
> I grieve that my father didn't notice me or take an interest in me. I also grieve for my brothers. They lost a father also. He showed favoritism to the oldest one and ignored the second one almost as much as he ignored me. He became the alcoholic in the family and I could identify with his pain. His intelligence was far superior to our older brother's, yet he wasn't even allowed to change a light bulb at our house. Anything he wanted to do— and I do mean *anything*—my father always said no. I saw myself in the mirror of his rejection.
>
> I tried on several occasions to seek my father's favor or at least be acknowledged. But I was reminded that I was a girl, second-

rate. I kept watching my brother's progress and there wasn't any, so I knew there was no hope for me. But it didn't stop *him*. He went back time after time after time after time.

Before he died (of alcoholism), he called me from out of state. I remember talking with him at two o'clock in the morning, bonded by the shared rejection that drew us together. He just wept and wept and didn't stop crying. And he said, "You know, at least *you* had Mom."

I thought, Wait a minute here. I'm the lost child. (Even my ex-husband had pointed out one time that my oldest brother was my father's favorite and the second son was my mother's favorite.) Even if she didn't favor him, she was always protecting him from my father's hurts. She spent most of her life shielding him.

So I'm still having repercussions because of what Daddy did. I've lost my father who didn't drink, and I've lost one brother who became an alcoholic to try to cope with never being accepted as a son. My other brother turned out just like my dad, even trying to control and discipline *my* kids, so that I would be willing to sever my relationship with him. It gets lonely (and I'm not at the top).

When you take off the labels, I think the hurts of people are much the same. I think I'm progressing somewhat. Two or three years ago I was very still angry with my father. A lot of times when I'm alone, I have flashbacks of my childhood and I cry. I really cry because I miss my Daddy. I just wish things could have been so much different.

Such grieving is much more common than you might think. And in fact, grief must be expressed before healing can take place. Not everyone experiences quite as much pain as this woman or her brother, yet stories abound among daughters who tried whatever they could to draw Dad's attention to themselves. Some girls try to excel in sports to win praise from their fathers or turn into real tomboys to ease their dads' disappointment that they were not sons. Many still relive the few memories they have when the barriers came down for the briefest amount of time.

Just when you might begin to suspect that every father prefers boys, you find a strong example of just the opposite. Here's one such story told by the only daughter in the family:

I have four brothers and I'm next to the youngest. My brothers all felt they didn't receive sufficient love or attention from my dad. I was the type that, if I wanted a hug, I'd just go up and get it myself. And for me it was okay because I was the daughter. My parents had waited for years to have a girl and when I finally came along it was a special thing. My brothers all wished for the relationship I had with my dad. But my relationship wasn't a whole lot better than theirs. It was so performance-oriented.

I can't really say I didn't feel loved by my dad, though. He was judgmental and perfectionist, yet I felt really loved by him. But then, sometimes I had to wonder if he loved me just because I was his daughter. We had a very special relationship, but was that just because it was cross-gender? Sometimes that's a major concern I have. Did he love me just because I was a girl?

Other daughters learn that they shouldn't even attempt to be very close to their fathers. Emotional closeness seemed to be taboo, especially as they reached puberty. As one woman said, "I got a very strong message from my mother that fathers and sons should spend time together and girls should bond with their mothers. I was discouraged from being close to my dad."

We also talked with many women who naturally felt closer to their fathers than their mothers, with whom they might have had more conflict. One remembered only good things about her dad: "He was fun to be with. He was gone a lot, and I think he was a workaholic. But when he was home he wasn't crabby with us like my husband is with my kids. I always felt comfortable to go talk to him about anything. They say girls tend to talk to their mothers. But I never talked to my mother. I always went to my dad. I still do."

If you can find any patterns in these stories, fine. But it seems to me that the realities of these people's lives come down to one basic truth: children want and need love and affirmation from two parents. They desire to be loved and accepted by both a mother and a father.

When one parent doesn't genuinely love a child, the child automatically compensates. Some children will try even harder to get the attention of the distant parent. Others will give up on that parent and try to form stronger bonds with the other one. When you toss in other factors such as manipulation by one or both parents, misperceptions on the part of the child, workaholism, alcoholism, and simple birth order, a young child can have way too much to try to handle.

Daughters don't cope with these things any better than sons. The boys aren't any stronger than the girls. Both sexes hurt. They both suffer. And before either of them can get over the pains of the past, they both must learn to grieve the losses of their childhood.

TAKE TIME TO REFLECT *(for sons)*

1. What kinds of expectations did your father have for you?

2. In what ways did your father help or prevent you from developing a sense of self-worth?

TIME TO REFLECT *(for daughters)*

1. To what extent did your father make you feel second-best?

2. What methods or actions did you use to draw your father's attention?

EIGHTEEN

Getting on
with Your Life

THE WITTY PLAYWRIGHT, George Bernard Shaw, once made the following observation: "Home life as we understand it is no more natural to us than a cage is natural to a cockatoo." Perhaps he too struggled with some of the issues discussed in this book. If so, he evidently coped with them by developing a strong penchant for sarcasm and cynicism.

Children who experience abuse, neglect, or other mistreatment by their fathers may respond in any number of ways depending on such factors as age, intensity of the offense, repetition of the offenses, and so forth. Some people withdraw, hide, and try to become as invisible as possible. Others rebel and continue to challenge the misappropriation of parental authority. Some look anywhere and everywhere else for the love that is missing in their lives. Some continue to humbly try to please their unpleasable fathers.

Yet all these people have one thing in common. Before they can find some relief from their pain, move on with their lives, and stop passing along those harmful patterns of behavior, they must go through a grieving process. This is usually accomplished sometime during their adulthood, when they are able to look back over their lives with greater clarity.

GOOD GRIEF

Most victims of father hunger have much to grieve. To begin with, many of them have been bearing heavy emotional burdens for a long time. Emotional pain may be expressed in the form of rage, numbness, wide mood swings, depression, or any number of other symptoms. All of these can be traced to a common source: an inadequate or completely absent relationship with Dad. The victims of father hunger grieve because they've suffered so long. They grieve over the mistakes they've already begun to perpetuate with their own children. They feel a heavy sadness for the current state of their lives.

As the grieving process continues, these sufferers reach a deeper level of remorse. Just as they might mourn the death of a close friend, they begin to grieve for the "death" of their own childhoods. It becomes increasingly clear to them that they will never be able to enjoy the innocence of youth. It was taken from them and they could do nothing about it. They cannot go back in time. All they can do at this point is to provide a proper burial for the childhoods that died long ago.

Sometimes the grief over the past is accelerated by a circumstance in the present. One woman observed how well her husband related to a young female family member and found that it stirred up painful memories of what she had never experienced:

> The emotional connections that fathers have to their children are so incredibly important. I never had that, even though I had three different fathers. God gave me three chances to have a dad and I never connected with any of them. It's been a major hurdle in our marriage, because so far I haven't been able to have any emotional connections to my husband, either. I watch him with his niece and he seems like a totally different human being. The love and caring come pouring out. It's wonderful, and I miss it, and I mourn not having it. I feel this sense of jealousy.

Sometimes the person has misinterpreted the problem. Years can go by when we think the source of our problems are in one area, when something completely different may be at the root. When we finally discover the truth, we tend to grieve the loss of all that time of stumbling around in the dark. This scenario is very typical of alcoholics:

I'm a recovering alcoholic. I used to think all I needed to do was get a handle on the drinking and the rest of my life would straighten out. Of course, I found that not drinking is the easiest part of the whole program. I've had this yearning, though. I'm almost sixty years old, and about twenty years ago I first started trying to break out of what I had come to feel was a personal prison. I went off in a lot of half-cocked directions and used a lot of misguided methods, but it wasn't until twenty years ago that I found there could be a better way, and it took me until about two years ago to work through all my feelings.

It's the only thing that's ever made any significant difference in my life. I'm just now starting to understand where my father was coming from. I'm beginning to realize that he went through practically all his life feeling the same way I was feeling. He felt rejected, abandoned, controlled, manipulated, and all those other things. So we ended up being very much alike on the inside.

I don't know whether or not he would ever have admitted that he had any needs. He was always right. There was never any possibility that he was not absolutely right in everything he said and did. Whether he could ever have come to the point of trying to unsnarl his life, I don't know. But *I* finally did. I sure know he left me in a mess and I've had considerable anger over that. It was one of the first things I needed to do—work through all the anger I was still harboring toward him.

Some people would like to think that they can simply forget about the past—just leave it behind them and walk away. Remember the mental snapshots and memories we carry with us? The feelings of our childhood haven't disappeared and they haven't changed. They will continue to affect us in various ways until we uncover them and grieve the losses which they signify.

MOVING BEYOND GRIEF

Grieving, however, is of little use if it doesn't further the healing process. After years of repressed memories and denial, followed by a period of anger, grief is a logical next step when someone begins to confront the pains of the past. But the goal should be to work *through* the grief—not to get stuck there. Sometimes we find people who can help us discover constructive ways to move ahead; sometimes we come up with our own creative methods.

One woman with an unmercifully abusive father could not stop thinking about how much she had been under his control. The father died, leaving the relationship unresolved and leaving the woman still with a need to express herself to him. She tells this dramatic story about how she finally gathered the nerve to confront her father.

I remember going to his grave. It was the end of February. I still felt like he had this hold on me, like I was in bondage to him or something. I took off from my house at about eight o'clock at night and drove to where his grave was, which was about an hour and forty-five minutes away. I was determined that I was going to have it out with him. He's dead, but I'm going to have it out with him, right? Brave soul!

I left with the intent of killing him, you know, even though... he was already dead. When I was almost there, I stopped at a store and bought some liquor, even though I don't drink. But I didn't want to lose any courage. I wanted to face him. It had snowed quite a bit that day and there was about four feet of snow on the ground. When I got to the cemetery, I couldn't get back to his grave because they hadn't plowed all the way in the back. I was so angry because I was thinking that he had *won*. He still had control over me.

Since I felt like he had won, I drank what I had bought. Then I stayed there for quite a while because I still had enough sense to know I shouldn't be driving while I felt the way I did. I finally got home at about three thirty in the morning. My poor husband had no idea where I was. I was going through a stage where I would have all this stuff inside of me, and I didn't know what to do with it. I thought I was going crazy, with all these intense feelings.

That took place on a Saturday night, so I said to myself, *Well, Dad won. I'm going to get up for church tomorrow, even though I'll only get a few hours sleep.* And the next morning I was real cocky. I put on a black dress, red belt, red shoes—I just got real duded up. My father had called me a prostitute and a whore many times, so I felt like I was just being what he always thought I was. I still had the sense that I was never going to be free of him.

I went to church with my "strong face" on. I talked to a few people and then my best friend came up and asked me how I was doing. I said, "I'm doing fine." She looked me straight in the eye and said, "You lie." Then I kind of broke out of the facade I was putting on.

We went into the office and talked for a few minutes. She asked, "What do you need to do?" I said, "I need to go back. I have an obsession to go back and have it out with Dad." So we did. It took us about five hours to find him because I didn't know exactly where his grave was. It turned out to be a flat stone and with all the snow we disturbed a lot of graves that day. When we finally found his, we had to chip through about two inches of ice.

I asked my friend to leave and I spent about two hours there by myself. I still couldn't yell at him. I don't know why not. I just had a lot of emotion inside. I did walk around a while. I found the bottle I had thrown away the night before and smashed it over his grave. I also had a knife with me and I messed up his gravestone pretty badly. I found some relief from that, but he's still with me and I'd like to be rid of him. I remember walking away from his grave toward the woods, feeling like he was walking behind me. It was like he was out of his grave, following me. I didn't sense any peace at first, but I did eventually. I felt fairly good when we finally left.

One grief-resolving technique used in our Rapha Treatment Centers is to have people write a letter to the father who had mistreated them. One person who had come to us for inpatient treatment of several problems discovered that the relationship with his father was at the root of many of those issues. His father, too, had already died. We encouraged him to write a letter to his father anyway, to provide an outlet for his feelings. Here is a portion of his letter (reprinted with his permission):

Dear Dad,

It's not easy for me to write you. After all, why should I? You can't read it. Even if you could, you wouldn't, would you? You were never interested in me or anything I did. Why did you and mother even have me? How could you bear a child and never be even remotely interested in him? It seems after five others you would have realized that, to you, kids were a nuisance. I thank God that Mary Louise only lived two weeks. She was spared a life of hell on earth.

It amazes me that we could live in the same house for the twenty years that I was there, and we never spoke to each other. There was never a conversation or a communication with you. Everything was a direct command that demanded absolute and direct obedience. Did you ever look at a report card? Did you ever consider attending a school play or coming to watch a ball practice? Where were you when it was time to share the joy of winning? The times we were defeated, there was no one there to help me bear the pain.

This man's letter went on at length, grieving the poor relationship that had been established. And while the finished result may appear to be just words on paper, the effect on the writer can be quite therapeutic. After a father has died, one of the few courses of action for the adult child is to be brutally honest about his or her feelings. By expressing them, even in retrospect, that person can take one more step toward healing.

Besides taking action to heal a damaged past relationship, we must also be willing to admit to the things that *we* have done wrong. The father may have been responsible for ninety-nine percent of the problem, yet we need to take responsibility for the one percent that might have been our fault. And usually the ratio is not nearly so skewed. Here's how one man put it:

As part of my recovery, I have recognized my own responsibility—where I was at fault for enabling the system to go on. On the twenty-eighth of October, 1983, I leaned over the side of my dad's bed and kissed his forehead. And I was the last one to see him alive. He'd been in the hospital for about a year with cancer. I feel very touched by this now. I was sad, because it hurt.

But I can remember going into high school—and growing eight inches and putting on eighty pounds in one year. I remember thinking, *Now I've got the power. Now it's my turn.* And I remember times when I would pick him up and throw him in the house. That was my sin. I recognize it now. For me to go on and be a father some day, I needed to take responsibility and turn from those things. And yet, it can be an insidious thing for me because of who I am and the gifts I have.

I thank God for recovery, because of the rigorous honesty required. Sometimes you get sick and tired of being sick and tired. I miss my dad. And I wish... I'd give my right arm for three hours with him, knowing what I know now.

Grieving is necessary to find peace of mind. So is taking action toward healing and taking responsibility for our own wrong behaviors. The ultimate goal of these steps is to experience the freedom of forgiveness.

FINDING FORGIVENESS

If your father is already dead or otherwise beyond help, you might wonder, *What's the use of trying to dredge up all these old memories? It's not going to do anybody any good.* True, it won't restore the relationship with your father that you missed out on. If your children are already grown, you have probably already made mistakes with them that you regret.

But without sounding selfish, you need to forget about those people for a moment. Until *you* regain an emotionally healthy outlook on life, you are likely to continue doing things you don't really want to do. If for no other reason, *you* are important enough to work through all these unresolved issues. You need to see beyond the father who let you down, realize you aren't to blame, and know that healing is precious for your own sake.

As one woman put it, "Yes, it would be wonderful if I could change things with my kids, but no, I can't. I've come to accept that as a parent I did the best I could to raise my children under the circumstances I was in. I'm not extending any blame backward into the previous generation or forward into the next one. I'm only looking at myself where I am right now, and at what I need to do to become a whole person."

Another woman was quite honest about how she had kept trying to put off dealing with her past. She had tried a lot of things to patch the problem rather than confront it, which had not worked. But she was beginning to sense that she was approaching the fresh sensation of freedom.

I didn't have a father. I came from a broken home. My parents divorced when I was thirteen months old. I vaguely remember seeing my father approximately four or five days a year and at Christmas time. He was a stranger to me then, because I didn't really know him. But he would show up with many lavish gifts for one of us three children. My mom thought he hoped one of us would return to him, but I don't know if that was true.

When I think of memories of a dad, I think of total vacancy— a complete void. I've spent fifty years trying to fill that void. It has tainted every relationship I've ever been involved with, though I didn't know it was a totally subconscious action on my part. Yet through the grieving of that tremendous abandonment I felt, even though I didn't know I felt it, I've discovered a huge freedom which feels tremendous.

I'm not through grieving, I don't think. Things surface from time to time that take me back into my past. But now I'm willing to face it and that's the exciting part. I never had any idea of the amount of hurts and feelings I had stuffed and stuffed and stuffed. If you had asked me even a year ago how I felt about my dad, I would have told you it didn't make any difference. I didn't have a father, so it didn't make any difference. But now that I'm in recovery, some of those feelings are coming out. I'm not done grieving, but I see a freedom coming and that's exciting.

The exciting part for me was finally seeing myself as a little girl who was demanding a father. I wanted that love and acceptance and I was trying to get it from everybody. I didn't realize until I went into counseling that God intended for me to have that kind of nurturing when I was a little girl, but I didn't get it… and I'll *never* get it, no matter how much I want it. Once I passed puberty, it was too late. So I must grieve. And when I talk about grieving, I mean crying and telling myself that I'll never have what I wanted so badly.

That's what's so exciting—the freedom that I don't have to be searching anymore. I deserved better, but now I can grieve that loss and get on with my life.

You need to forgive your father for any ways in which he might have failed you—to whatever extent you're able to do so. You need to forgive your mother if she looked the other way when you were hurting so. You also need to forgive yourself for wrong behaviors or for nursing grudges—even if much of it seemed justified by what you faced. You also need to recognize that you had reasons for thinking and acting as you did.

Refusing to deal with the issue doesn't help. Holding grudges may make Dad suffer, but then, so do you. The ability to receive and offer forgiveness for past offenses is your best option for finding freedom. You may not be able to forgive (or feel forgiven) right now, but keep in mind that it will come to pass if you seek it.

Refusing to confront the pains of the past or refusing to go through a grieving process is like refusing to go to the dentist to have a cavity filled. The pain won't simply vanish of its own accord. In fact, that toothache is going to bother you until you let a dentist deal with the source of the pain. I don't know of anyone who enjoys getting teeth drilled, yet when the pain gets bad enough, most are willing to do anything to get rid of it.

The key to healing is to take action *before* the level of pain becomes so severe. At the first sign of pain, it is wise to try to find the source of the problem. And just like wise dental care, it doesn't hurt to give yourself an "emotional check-up" every few months or so to make sure that no new symptoms have cropped up.

Grieving, taking responsibility, and finding forgiveness are steps in an ongoing process. You can't decide to do it and get it over with today or this week. It will take time and effort on your part. It may require the help of trained people or caring friends. But the result will be well worth anything you have to go through. No pain will be greater than that which you keep so well hidden inside.

One invaluable resource in this process of reconciliation is our own family members—the people who are most likely to understand our own pain and hunger. I will suggest some new ways of relating to our families in the next chapter. Are you ready to move forward? Even though the way ahead may prove rough at times, you have everything to gain and nothing to lose, except your pain and hunger.

TAKE TIME TO REFLECT

1. How does the suggestion of grieving over an inadequate relationship with your father make you feel?

2. What recent circumstances have stirred up some memories from your past? How did you deal with those memories?

3. Which of the suggestions for working through your grief seems most effective for you?

4. To what extent have you experienced forgiveness and freedom?

NINETEEN

Feelings about God the Father

So far we have been dealing primarily with the physical, emotional, and relational problems that result from not receiving enough of a father's love. But what about the spiritual dimension to this problem? Our ability to receive the love of our heavenly Father can become severely distorted when our earthly fathers fail to meet our needs to a significant degree.

For some, the entire concept of "father" becomes repulsive. Father may have been the person who neglected you... who forced you to measure up to certain standards before he would acknowledge you... who may even have abused you physically or sexually. Most of us had to live with a father, no matter how we felt about him. And some of us could hardly wait for the day we could move away or even be rid of our fathers forever.

Meanwhile, many of us whose earthly fathers failed every day in ways small and great may have attended church on Sundays. Preachers told us that we have a *heavenly* Father. An *all-seeing* Father. An *all-knowing* Father. An *all-powerful* Father. An *eternal* Father. Perhaps nothing could have been more disturbing than to think of God in terms of Father—yet there it was in black and white in the Bible.

Jesus himself told us that God is our Father. What if you were living a daily hell at home, then going off to church once a week only to hear that a judgmental and eternal Father awaited you in the afterlife? Needless to say, you would not have been comforted by such news.

Powerful *feelings* about God the Father, whether right or wrong, tend to brew and stew in those who suffer from father hunger. Just as we sometimes form incorrect definitions due to our misperceptions about such things as love, intimacy, and trust, we can also develop a very distorted image of God. Many of us continue to struggle against assigning to God the characteristics of a human father who may have been cruel, inconsistent, or simply uncaring.

After we first focus on some of these intense feelings, I will talk about what I believe to be some of the facts. In the meantime, be assured that God is big enough to handle any feelings we have toward him, however negative they may be. We may form some very unflattering opinions about God, and that's okay. God doesn't hold grudges. Besides, our misperceptions are not usually our fault.

I simply ask you to apply the same process I recommended in redefining other essential emotions of life: step back and try to weigh all the existing evidence objectively. It may be next to impossible at this point to be impartial, but I encourage you to try. Working through these feelings may very well make a huge difference in bringing the healing you seek.

GOD AS THE JUDGE

The establishment of certain performance standards is one of the most common problems with fathers that then becomes projected onto God as well. After living for years with a man who granted acceptance or affirmation on a clearly conditional basis, it becomes almost unthinkable that God would not have similar—if not higher—standards. If we aren't "good enough" to receive the love of our own fathers, how can we ever expect to be "good enough" for God?

One daughter's struggle to perform in order to gain acceptance eventually led to her becoming involved in a very legalistic, ritualistic, rule-bound church. She felt the need to work out her own salvation, yet feared she could never do things well enough to please God. As she says, "It's very hard for me to believe that God accepts me, because I was never accepted unless I performed perfectly. I had the concept of God that I'm not acceptable unless I am perfect. I believe he accepts everyone else, but I can't believe it for *me*."

Another woman formed a different opinion. She didn't feel the need to work for God's approval in the same manner that she had to work for her father's approval. Rather, she felt she had *no right* to come before God until she had somehow earned her father's approval. But she could never quite please him. She still struggles with the concept of God as an all-loving, all-forgiving Father.

Another common problem is that of trying to develop a sense of self-worth after a father has left the family for some reason. One woman's father had left his wife and children behind, moved away, and remarried. She kept up infrequent contact with him—enough to realize how well he was doing with his new wife and family. Her feelings proved to be common among those from similar situations:

> To this day I still have a problem believing that I'm important enough to God, even in the small details, that he would care enough to forgive me time and time again—that he really wants to give me all the things he talks about in the Bible. I'm not that important. I'm just not important enough! I also sense that he is impatient. He's *tired* of having to go through the same things over and over again. He doesn't want to be bothered, but when he *has* to be bothered, he's impatient. So for a lot of years I said, "I'll take care of this problem myself. I'll handle this one, Lord." Meanwhile he's up there going, "Oh, please, trust me. I'll take care of you." But I never heard him. I wouldn't. It would hurt too much.

Sometimes our misperceptions of God are compounded by other father-figures. Not only do we read a lot into God's nature based on the way our fathers behave, but we also watch our ministers closely. We know that they're supposed to represent God, and—being only human—they sometimes contribute to our wrong impressions. One woman shares about how the similarities between her father and her minister skewed her concept of God:

> It's not that I didn't believe in God, but I had an inability to really *trust* him due to the fact that my father wasn't consistently there for me. I mean, the protection would be there *when he was*

there, but when he wasn't there we would always wonder, *What if something happens while he's gone?* Now when bad things happen, I wonder, *Why wasn't God there?*

In the church I grew up in, the minister boomed out from the pulpit. I can remember the few times I sat in church with my parents. He would pound on the pulpit to make a point and he had a loud voice that projected. To me it sounded like he was shouting and reprimanding and judging—which was what my father did. He shouted. He reprimanded. He judged. He punished. And I have a real hard time thinking God is sitting up there loving me and forgiving me. It just wasn't true of my earthly father. It isn't true now.

My father established very high expectations that I've never met, that I'll never be able to meet. That's just the way it is and it's hard for me to relate to a God who keeps saying, "You're okay. For today, you're okay. You may have made a big mistake, but I still love you and accept you."

I know it's in the Bible. I read it. I hear it on tapes. I hear it from ministers. I see it in books I read. But for it to really sink in and get from my head to my heart, that's really tough. And I believe that's because of the earthly father image I had.

Another man expressed similar concerns of how imperfect clergymen tainted his view of God. His father had been rather passive, so that he didn't have a high opinion of men in general. When he tried to become involved in a church, he had problems:

I grew up Catholic. To me, priests were not male role models. They were "no gender," to my mind. Later in life I began to attend Protestant churches. The first church I was in, the pastor was found to be counseling—and doing more than counseling—most of the women in the church. The church fell apart because of it, so that was a blow.

The next church we were in, the membership fell apart because of mismanagement. So it's been difficult for me to really get involved in a church, especially when one man says, "Well, this is the way we're going to go." My response is usually, "Great. But you're going to go without me."

I have a reluctance to really give, because you feel like you're going to lose it. You don't want to risk any more. You say, "The

Lord knows what he's doing," but after the third or fourth time you wonder, "What's he going to do about it?"

The tendency of ministers to confirm what our fathers model for us is never as strong as when one's father *is* a minister. It is rather common for the children of ministers to experience difficulties. The person who stands in the pulpit each week and challenges the congregation to live a more godly life is just as human as anyone else. However, no one sees that as clearly as the minister's spouse and children. When the kids see things at home that contradict what he says and stands for as a pastor, it affects them in a variety of ways. Here's the story of one "preacher's kid":

So much of my Christianity was caught up in my dad's performance-trap orientation. He had high expectations for his kids. I became Sunday school teacher, Sunday school superintendent, the whole gambit. I felt that my walk with Christ was reflected with how involved I was with church—how many days I was at church. If the doors were open, I was there. I always struggled with the concept that I had to perform to be accepted. I knew it wasn't right, but it still was how I felt.

Another problem was that I didn't see my dad's Christianity at home often. I saw him reading the Bible to study for his sermons, but we didn't have family devotions. We prayed a grace around the table, but that was all the prayers we heard—not even at bedtime. Maybe when I was younger Mom would tell us Bible stories, but that was all the training I got at home.

That has become a real struggle for me with my husband. I want to see him as a spiritual head of the house. When *he* doesn't take that role, then I'm going to take it. I'll go in there at bedtime and I'll say prayers for my children and talk to them about spiritual things, but I feel a big disappointment with my husband because he doesn't fill that role.

I'm still very much caught up in the performance trap, though I'm working on it. It's been very healthy for me to step back from the church and to be uninvolved lately, because I needed to do that. I was addicted to religiosity. My husband and I both were. Of course, Satan's always there to whisper in my ear, "Hey, you know, they really *need* someone in this position to do something. *You* can do that."

And do you know? I *can*. But I don't want to *need* to do it. I know God loves me no matter what. Yet that's been a major problem for me—almost hypocritical to be the "preacher" on Sunday mornings. I think it's true of almost every minister's kid—they don't see their dad acting out at home what he's preaching. I realize that nobody is perfect and I didn't expect my dad to be. But to have had personal devotions at home would have balanced that out for me.

HOW DO WE COPE WITH SPIRITUAL CONFUSION?

Some of us become rather creative in coming up with ways to stay close to God without having to sort through all the problems of our past. Several people spoke of separating the nature of God the Father from that of Jesus. Because they had an essentially negative image of God and didn't want to think of him as any kind of father, they could relate more closely to Jesus. One woman expresses feelings which several other people seem to share:

> I see Jesus as a big brother. I can relate to the fact that he came to earth and talked about us being brothers and sisters. It may be because I had an older brother and there was something special between us. I have a better feeling about my brother, certainly, than my father. I think of Jesus as an earthly figure who was more willing to offer forgiveness and acceptance.
>
> I think that's one of my saving factors—that I can accept Jesus as my Savior. I can accept that he sent the Holy Spirit to be a Comforter. And I'm able to get in touch with those things easier. But when I envision him in heaven sitting at the right hand of the Father and start to think about the Father, then I have some problems.

Yet some people cannot let God off the hook that easily. If God were any kind of loving force at all, why did they have to undergo such pain, humiliation, and emotional destruction at the hands of an abusive or absent father? One woman talks about trying to establish a relationship with God in the wake of a father who gave her up for adoption to a sexually abusive stepfather. You can get some idea of her intense feelings of abandonment.

It is hard for me to have a relationship with Christ because it means trusting, loving, and feeling loved by a male figure. I don't remember my dad ever saying he loved me except when he was having sex with me. That wasn't the right way. When I was a teenager I was looking for other ways of love, too, just to be accepted for who I am. And it was hard, very lonely. Even in my marriage, it seems I had to learn how to be dependent. I had to learn not to do things for myself. I was so independent and stubborn in my ways. I wanted to do one thing and my husband wanted me to do another until I don't know who I am. It creates such a demand for dependency.

I feel like I'm in this trap that I can't seem to get out of, because I'm independent but now I have a husband. I was independent before and did pretty much as I pleased. I had a car, my own checking account, a job, and I paid for my schooling myself. Now I feel like everything's caved in. My husband doesn't want me to work. We have so many financial problems. I was crying last week because I just couldn't deal with some of the situations with our finances. He has been laid off a lot, and it makes it hard to depend on God. I also just went through a miscarriage.

All the time I was thinking how I wanted to serve the Lord. I felt like I gave everything on the altar like Isaac was given on the altar... and then I had the miscarriage. I got very angry. It was even hard to look at baby commercials, Gerber commercials, diaper commercials, or to hold someone else's baby. And then I see how my kids are acting. They're acting like *me*. And I don't want them to act like me. My husband's yelling at me and I want to stay as far away from him as much as I can, because that's what my dad did. It brings back a lot of memories and haunts me.

With my relationship first with my father, and then with my husband, I have a hard time surrendering myself to God. I feel like he has left me alone... that he's not even watching what's happening... that he's not taking care of me and getting me out of the situation.

Many women hunger so for a father's love that they easily fall for men who seem to be everything they had hoped for as little girls needing a daddy. Perhaps a male supervisor with whom a woman spends long hours at work may seem to be an irresistible magnet. Others become infatuated with the pastor at church who seems so loving and kind. Often these women are married with children of their own, but the attraction can be very insidious and powerful.

They can even start behaving in extreme and uncharacteristic ways, unable to exert control over a particular obsession. These episodes usually dissipate gradually without reaching the tragic conclusions of a "fatal attraction," but they often exact a terrible toll in terms of shame and guilt. One woman who developed this sort of obsession toward her boss ended up blaming God for not providing the love she needed as a small child. She shares her confusion:

> I'm married. He's married. I'm a Christian with very strong convictions about women who go after some other woman's husband. I always thought that was terrible, yet I feel no conviction in this setup I have. I never went through that stage with my father and I feel like I have a right to my father. I feel like this drive is my right, because I never had it as a child. I never faced the reality that it's not possible, you know, and it's like I'm having to learn that lesson now.
>
> The pain and hopelessness I'm feeling is really incredible. Someone tried to tell me that grieving was exciting, but I don't think so. I've seen a little hope, but I still feel very much anger just talking about not having a father when I was a child. I'm very, very angry at God. All my life I've been searching for something—a love I couldn't attain. It's very painful, but I'm also learning that most of my life I've denied my feelings and haven't been honest with myself or other people. I'm learning to be honest.
>
> Yet for me to be honest with God at this point is to say, "I'm angry with you, and I don't feel like faking my Bible studies and praying." That's where I am right now, which is very unusual for me. I was raised as a religious person, and I thought I had to be on track with the Lord. I'm going through a hard time. I don't know how God's going to get me back on track, but I'm not going to worry about that today.

As bad as this woman is feeling now, and as much as it hurts, I believe that it's okay for her to feel angry at God. She's right. It wasn't fair for her to be without a father when she was growing up. She shouldn't be suffering the intense pain she feels now. It's not her fault. I don't believe it's God's fault either, yet I truly believe God understands these intensely negative feelings we have toward him. He will patiently wait as we go to him crying, kicking, and screaming. And he will be there with his arms held out to us when we finish venting our feelings.

The fact that this woman can express her anger toward God is a giant step toward finding emotional healing. She probably doesn't believe that at this point, but many people who have been through similar situations are willing to testify to this reality. The sooner you are willing to become brutally honest, the sooner you can work through the pain that has been holding you captive for so long.

One reason we need to be honest about our feelings is that we may be wrong. Feelings can easily fool us. But if we're not honest about them, we never get around to discovering the truth. I encourage you to be completely honest about any feelings you have toward God, especially those you may not even want to admit to yourself. God honors truth. He will not be judgmental if you express how you honestly feel. Spend some time trying to identify any negative feelings you may have of God as a father. In the next chapter, you can compare the impression you have with some facts you can be sure about.

TAKE TIME TO REFLECT

1. How do you think your relationship with your father has affected your perception and/or relationship with God?

2. List some words that describe how you feel when you think of God as your Father.

3. How has your pastor or priest helped shape your concept of God?

4. Do any of your feelings toward God make you feel guilty, embarrassed, or afraid? Why or why not?

TWENTY

Facts about God the Father

Suppose you are selected to serve on the jury for a murder trial. From the first moment you see the defendant, you just know he's guilty. You can feel it in your bones. He has slicked-back hair, shifty eyes, an expensive pinky ring, and an arrogant voice. But as a dutiful member of the jury, you watch and listen as the evidence is presented. To your amazement, your mother is the surprise key witness for the defense. She testifies that she saw the defendant during the time when the murder was committed. According to your mother, there can be no doubt that this guy is innocent. Other credible witnesses and evidence prove your initial feelings were wrong.

What do you do when the facts don't support your feelings? Do you stand by the way you feel? Or do you reluctantly change your way of thinking?

Feelings can be quite deceptive. You may feel a deep resentment toward a father who wasn't there when you needed him or who mistreated you in some subtle or obvious way. That is certainly a valid feeling. However, that same feeling may be directed toward a spouse, people in other relationships, or even God. Those feelings may be just as strong, but in these cases are not necessarily accurate.

Feelings change; facts don't. And the key to lasting emotional health is to meticulously separate distorted feelings from facts. Let the facts stand on their own. Take a close look at them while they're not intertwined with all those feelings you've carried around for so long. Your spouse may not be nearly as similar to your father as you thought. Your father may not even be as terrible as you remember. And, most importantly, you may start to see God from quite a different perspective.

THE CASE OF FACT VERSUS FEELING

Maybe you've carried grudges against certain people for years and years. Perhaps a bully pushed you off the swingset in the third grade. You might have felt intense anger or even hatred toward him as Mom sprayed on the Bactine and bandaged the scrape on your elbow. The wound healed in a couple of days, but the angry feelings lingered. Sometimes they linger for years.

Suppose you happen to meet that person on the street twenty years later. You are both very different people than you were in third grade, but it's very likely that your feelings are going to be the same. Your first reaction might be to run up to him, point to your elbow, and scream, "Look what you did to me." The stinging wound is still fresh in your memory. You still harbor those feelings of anger or hatred. But then the facts begin to sink in. You realize that enough time has passed to heal the wound and that the other person is no longer a playground bully. Who knows? You and a childhood enemy may end up being best of friends.

In a similar manner, you may have kept alive feelings and accusations toward your father ever since childhood. You might still wear a big bandage to prove how badly you were treated. But now it's time to remove the bandage and take a closer look. In many cases the wound is still deep and in need of treatment. Yet in other instances, the wound might not be nearly as bad as you remember. Memories sometimes fool us. If a huge bandage covers a slight scratch, perhaps you've been judging your father too harshly for many years.

That's why it's so essential at this point to deal with *facts*. No one wants to receive love from a spouse or from a god who is cast from the same mold as an oppressive father. But once confusing feelings have been removed and clear distinctions made, you may find new sources of love, acceptance, and affirmation that you never noticed before. You may discover new levels of closeness and intimacy that you never thought possible. As you learn to deal with feelings *and* facts, your perspective takes a thrilling shift for the better.

I'm not at all saying that feelings are not real. They most certainly are. And therein lies their ability to absolutely incapacitate you. Your feelings are very real; they just may not be justified.

Feelings can interfere with emotional healing. Put yourself in the position of a little girl whose father is frequently violent and verbally abusive. Nothing the child does is good enough. The father is never pleased. When she fails to carry out a command to the father's expectations, the father beats her. This kind of relationship has taken place for as long as this girl can remember. There seems to be no hope for escaping her father's harsh treatment—at least not for many more years.

But what if a neighbor reports the father's cruelty? Agents of the child protection agency come to the home and remove the little girl from his care. The father is arrested and imprisoned. His daughter is put up for adoption and is soon taken in by a loving and caring family.

How would this little girl act? Would she truly expect better treatment? Probably not. All she knows is violence and anger. That's what she expects from her new parents as well. And for a while, no amount of love is going to sink in. This child has been conditioned for further failure. The new parents can buy gifts, take their adopted daughter on exciting vacations, and spend a lot of time with her. But with her lengthy history of abusive treatment, it's going to take a long time for this little girl to even begin to trust her new parents.

The *facts* are that the new parents truly love this child. But it's going to take a lot of time, patience, and a new level of trust for this young girl to comprehend those facts. Her *feelings* are still too strong and overpowering.

ADOPTED INTO GOD'S FAMILY

The facts are clear. God loves you. He didn't want your father to neglect you or to abuse you in any way. He's sorry that you're hurting. He wants to help. Right now your feelings may be far too intense to allow your heavenly Father to comfort you, but he's willing to wait until you're ready. God adopts each one who comes to him through Christ. He wants to provide his children with the love, nurture, affirmation, acceptance, and self-worth that they may have never received from anyone else.

This concept of adoption is not something I'm making up. It's biblical. I refer you to the eighth chapter of Romans. It's a bit long to print here in its entirety, but it's one of the most uplifting passages of Scripture. If you are currently struggling with any of the results of father hunger or feelings that you can't seem to overcome, I would suggest that you read this chapter every day for a week. Then, each day focus on one of the promises from the passage. Here are a few to get you started:

- No matter what else might be wrong in our lives, God will not condemn us when we put our trust in Jesus. (Rom 8:1-4)
- Peace is possible for us when we learn to be controlled by the Holy Spirit. (vv. 5-9)
- Even though we will suffer in life, we can be assured that we are God's children and heirs. We should not be afraid. We have every right to address God as "Abba" (Daddy). God has adopted us! (vv. 15-17)
- The suffering we face now, as bad as it may be, is nothing compared to the good things in store when we finally receive the full benefits of God's adoption. (vv. 18, 22-23)
- We can be confident as we place our hope in God, even though we can't see him working all the time. We must learn to be patient. (vv. 24-25)
- We aren't strong enough to handle our problems on our own, but the Holy Spirit is there to help us. (vv. 26-27)
- God works for good in all things in our lives. (v. 28)
- Since God is for us, nothing can possibly harm us. (v. 31)
- It is impossible for *anything* to separate us from the love of God. (vv. 35-39)

These statements are facts, whether or not you can believe them at this point. As you learn to trust your new adoptive Father, you can begin to loosen the grip of your past and any negative emotions which still control you. These facts may not correlate with your present feelings, but as you learn to more effectively identify your distorted feelings over time, the facts will become more apparent.

Let's review the ten qualities listed in chapter fifteen and consider to what extent God meets each criterion.

Time. We will never be able to complain that God doesn't spend enough time with us. Since we often do not sense his presence in our lives, we may assume that he's far away. Psalm 46:1 tells us otherwise: "God is our refuge and strength, an ever present help in trouble." Note the key words: ever *present.* Anytime you need access to God the heavenly Father, he is there. All day. All night. Every day, even weekends. God doesn't disappear when times get tough. He doesn't desert his children. He always has time for you. Jesus himself made this promise, one of the last things he said while he was still on earth: "And surely I will be with you always, to the very end of the age" (Mt 28:20). God will be there for you when you need him. That's a fact.

Focused attention. Our heavenly Father isn't just hanging around until we call on him. He takes an active interest in our lives and activities. Each individual is important to God. After all, he created each one of us and gave us unique personalities and strengths. According to Scripture, "even the very hairs of your head are all numbered" (Mt 10:30). No one knows you like God does. If you still have your doubts, spend some time reading and rereading Psalm 139. Here is a portion of it:

> O LORD, you have searched me
>   and you know me.
> You know when I sit and when I rise;
>   you perceive my thoughts from afar.
> You discern my going out and my lying down;
>   you are familiar with all my ways.
> Before a word is on my tongue
>   you know it completely, O LORD.
> You hem me in—behind and before;
>   you have laid your hand upon me.
> Such knowledge is too wonderful for me,
>   too lofty for me to attain....
> For you created my inmost being;
>   you knit me together in my mother's womb.

> I praise you because I am fearfully and wonderfully made;
>> your works are wonderful,
>> I know that full well. Ps 139:1-6, 13-14

Protection, comfort, and security. God is all-powerful and capable of protecting us from whatever might harm us. However, our heavenly Father usually doesn't fight our battles for us. Rather, he equips us with spiritual "armor" (Eph 6:10-18) and promises to take care of us. God expects us to show up on the front lines and "fight the good fight of the faith" (1 Tm 6:12).

We can count on God's protection, comfort, and security in the context of our spiritual struggles. But he doesn't choose to eliminate all conflict from our lives. When the fight threatens to be more than we can handle, he provides a number of promises for us to count on. Again, Romans 8 is a good place to find comfort in trying times. Scripture also assures us that "the one who is in you is greater than the one who is in the world" (1 Jn 4:4). We are commanded to "cast all your anxiety on him because he cares for you" (1 Pt 5:7). And these verses from Isaiah describe God as the one who will not grow weary in protecting us from all harm.

> Do you not know?
>> Have you not heard?
> The LORD is the everlasting God,
>> the Creator of the ends of the earth.
> He will not grow tired or weary,
>> and his understanding no one can fathom.
> He gives strength to the weary
>> and increases the power of the weak.
> Even youths grow tired and weary,
>> and young men stumble and fall;
> but those who hope in the LORD
>> will renew their strength.
> They will soar on wings like eagles;
>> they will run and not grow weary,
>> they will walk and not be faint. Is 40:28-31

Communication. God is not nearly as remote and detached as some people suppose. He communicates with us through a number of channels including Scripture and the Holy Spirit, as well as close

Christian friends who are there to offer support and advice. And even more exciting is the fact that God likes to hear from us as well. Sure, he knows what's going on in our lives. Yet as we learn to talk to our heavenly Father about it, we sense that he truly cares. We begin to detect his will for our lives and the communication channel grows stronger. If God hasn't seemed too close lately, I urge you to respond to this challenge issued by Jesus in the Sermon on the Mount:

> "Ask and it will be given to you; seek and you will find; knock and the door will be opened to you. For everyone who asks receives; he who seeks finds; and to him who knocks, the door will be opened.
>
> Which of you, if his son asks for bread, will give him a stone? Or if he asks for a fish, will give him a snake? If you, then, though you are evil, know how to give good gifts to your children, how much more will your Father in heaven give good gifts to those who ask him! In everything, do to others what you would have them do to you, for this sums up the Law and the Prophets."
>
> **Mt 7:7-12**

Trust. You will never find anyone as trustworthy as God. David expressed it well: "Some trust in chariots and some in horses, but we trust in the name of the LORD our God" (Ps 20:7). Jesus confirms his own trustworthiness as well: "I am the way and the truth and the life. No one comes to the Father except through me" (Jn 14:6). Jesus doesn't just represent truth. He *is* truth. What Jesus Christ says is fact. No matter how our feelings may seem to contradict these facts, we can trust that Scripture is correct.

We said previously that trust is a two-way commitment. You may not be very trustworthy sometimes, yet God allows you to make your own decisions. He invites you to receive all that he has to offer. God the Father even sent Jesus to earth to die for your sins. But he still allows you to make your own decisions, for right or wrong, and he will not violate that trust. Nonetheless, the sooner you begin to respond to God's gentle nudging, the better off you will be.

Forgiveness. Forgiveness is certainly one of God's strong points. It doesn't matter what you've done. It doesn't matter how long you've done it. If you're sorry about something you've said or done and truly repent, God will forgive you. Completely. Instantly. Forever.

The price was high. Jesus died to make possible the forgiveness of our sins (Eph 1:7-8). But as we go to him when we've done something wrong, we quickly discover that the forgiveness we receive proves that Christ's death was not in vain. The key to receiving complete forgiveness is honest and open confession of sins: "If we confess our sins, he is faithful and just and will forgive us our sins and purify us from all unrighteousness" (1 Jn 1:9).

God doesn't take our sin lightly. We cannot go around sinning without regard to the consequences and expect God to come along and clean up behind us. We must search ourselves to see if sin is present (Ps 139:23-24). When we discover something that isn't right, we should immediately confess it to God. *Then* we can find total forgiveness.

Discipline. Because of our parents, we may have come to think of discipline only in negative terms. Yet we shouldn't automatically equate discipline with punishment. Our heavenly Father can help us discipline ourselves to develop good habits and become more spiritually mature. As we obey his commands, we grow in faith. Of course, sometimes discipline does take on a corrective nature. But even then, as children of a heavenly Father we shouldn't expect harsh judgment. God's discipline is a sign of his love:

> And you have forgotten that word of encouragement that addresses you as sons: "My son, do not make light of the Lord's discipline, and do not lose heart when he rebukes you, because the Lord disciplines those he loves, and he punishes everyone he accepts as a son." Endure hardship as discipline; God is treating you as sons. For what son is not disciplined by his father?... Moreover, we have all had human fathers who disciplined us and we respected them for it. How much more should we submit to the Father of our spirits and live!... No discipline seems pleasant at the time, but painful. Later on, however, it produces a harvest of righteousness and peace for those who have been trained by it.
>
> **Heb 12:5-7, 9, 11**

Acceptance. Forget about all those performance standards you've come to expect from God. He won't make you say dozens of prayers before he accepts you. You won't have to have perfect attendance at church for a year. He invites you to come to him just as you are. You may need to change certain things, sure, but God accepts you first. Later on you can work on those problem areas.

In fact, God the Father promises to help you. If you're envisioning something akin to the twelve labors of Hercules before God will consider you for membership into his kingdom, guess again. "You see, at just the right time, when we were still powerless, Christ died for the ungodly.... God demonstrates his own love for us in this: While we were still sinners, Christ died for us" (Rom 5:6-8).

We also mentioned previously that acceptance has a lot to do with the sense of touch. If you read the Gospels carefully, you will see that Jesus was always showing his acceptance of others by touching them—even lepers, who were both physically diseased and spiritually unclean. And when Jesus' own disciples scolded the little children who came to listen, we are told that Christ "took the children in his arms, put his hands on them and blessed them" (Mk 10:16). Jesus did for complete strangers the very thing many of us craved as children from our own fathers.

Guidance and advice. Many of these passages have talked about God the Father and Jesus his Son. But when it comes to receiving the help, direction, and advice that we need on a day-to-day (and sometimes minute-to-minute) basis, the third member of the Trinity is at our disposal. When Jesus came to earth and prepared to return to his Father, he promised to send a "Counselor" who would always be there for us.

The Holy Spirit serves as that Counselor for those who have put their faith in Christ. One of the last things Jesus told his disciples was this: "If you love me, you will obey what I command. And I will ask the Father, and he will give you another Counselor to be with you forever—the Spirit of truth. The world cannot accept him, because it neither sees him nor knows him. But you know him, for he lives with you and will be in you.... The Counselor, the Holy Spirit, whom the Father will send in my name, will teach you all things and will remind you of everything I have said to you" (Jn 14:15-17, 26).

Provision of a role model. People describe God in all sorts of ways. Some see a man with a long beard, tossing thunderbolts at will. Some perceive a judge. Some think of a kind, grandfatherly type. But if you want to know what God the Father is *really* like, the secret is to look at Jesus.

The Gospels provide an amazing amount of information about the teachings and actions of Jesus. We see his love, forgiveness, and sacrifice. We see him healing the sick and exposing the phoniness of the religious leaders of his day. We see a person with whom we would really like to be friends. One day one of his disciples stated that although he knew Jesus, he didn't really know what God the Father was like. Jesus replied, "'If you really knew me, you would know my Father as well. From now on, you do know him and have seen him.... Anyone who has seen me has seen the Father'" (Jn 14:7-9).

The parable of the prodigal son tells us more about what the Father is really like. (A better name might be the Parable of the Forgiving Father.) Put yourself in the place of the child in this parable and then see how God the Father feels about you—no matter how you may have treated him in the past. The reunion of a lost child and a loving heavenly Father is always cause for celebration.

"There was a man who had two sons. The younger one said to his father, 'Father, give me my share of the estate.' So he divided his property between them.

"Not long after that, the younger son got together all he had, set off for a distant country and there squandered his wealth in wild living. After he had spent everything, there was a severe famine in that whole country, and he began to be in need. So he went and hired himself out to a citizen of that country, who sent him to his fields to feed pigs. He longed to fill his stomach with the pods that the pigs were eating, but no one gave him anything.

"When he came to his senses, he said, 'How many of my father's hired men have food to spare, and here I am starving to death! I will set out and go back to my father and say to him: Father, I have sinned against heaven and against you. I am no longer worthy to be called your son; make me like one of your hired men.' So he got up and went to his father.

"But while he was still a long way off, his father saw him and was filled with compassion for him; he ran to his son, threw his arms around him and kissed him.

"The son said to him, 'Father, I have sinned against heaven and against you. I am no longer worthy to be called your son.'

"But the father said to his servants, 'Quick! Bring the best robe and put it on him. Put a ring on his finger and sandals on his feet. Bring the fattened calf and kill it. Let's have a feast and celebrate. For this son of mine was dead and is alive again; he was lost and is found.' So they began to celebrate." Lk 15:11-24

According to Scripture, God the Father perfectly meets all the criteria for fathers listed above. Perhaps you are still skeptical or even afraid to hope that it could be true. But I think the facts are clear. I didn't always think so, but I do now. I'll explain further when I finish my own story in the last chapter.

TAKE TIME TO REFLECT

1. Do you believe that God loves you and cares for you, that he wants to adopt you as his own child? Why or why not?

2. Which one of the promises from Romans 8 means the most to you? Why?

3. In your own life, to what extent do you believe God has either generously exhibited or stingily withheld the ten qualities of an ideal father?

TWENTY-ONE

Change Begins
with You

SUPPOSE YOU OWE one thousand dollars to a finance company to keep your car from being repossessed. If you come to me for help, how would you respond if I go through my pockets and come up with only seven dollars? You may scoff and say, "A fat lot of good that's going to do!" Or you might express thanks and genuine appreciation for what little help I can offer.

Then suppose the next day I unexpectedly receive an inheritance of five thousand dollars. I might immediately think of your need. If you had insulted me the day before, I would probably be very reluctant to let go of twenty percent of my windfall right off the top. But if you had shown sincere gratitude for the little I could contributed the day before, I might be inclined to sit down and write you a check for the rest.

Emotional healing works in somewhat the same way. When I suggest that you simply "trust God as your heavenly Father" in view of what may be intense pain, it probably sounds like a seven-dollar answer to a thousand-dollar problem. I know you would prefer to have a list of seventeen things you can do to permanently eliminate the problem of father hunger from your life.

You need to realize that *you* didn't get yourself into this situation. You were the victim, at the mercy of a father who hurt you in ways that may seem impossible to repair. And since someone else forced you into that emotional pit, you need someone else to help you climb out. No one is better suited in this case than God. Your heavenly Father has both the power and the desire to personally demonstrate the love you deserved from a father all these years.

I know it's impossible for you to suddenly begin trusting, loving, opening up, changing, and doing all the things necessary to overcome father hunger. But if you are grateful for whatever little bit you *can* do at this point, more significant healing will soon follow. Or you can choose to reject any help that God offers at this point and trudge on as you always have—on your own, with an ever-expanding emotional black hole within you that robs you of any bit of joy, peace, laughter, or hope you try to manufacture.

Actually, one of the first steps in letting God work in your life is quite simple, though not necessarily easy. You need to learn to be a child again. When you were living with your parents, you may have wanted to grow up and get out of the house as soon as possible. You may have been robbed of many of the joys of childhood. If so, I believe that God wants you to experience what it means to be *his* child. He wants to provide all those qualities I discussed in the last chapter. Later on, you'll be expected to do some harder, more adult, things. But first, let's consider how claiming your identity as a child of God can satisfy your deepest longing for a father's love.

BEING A CHILD AGAIN

Some of the saddest stories we heard in our interviews were the fun things people regretted *not* being able to do as children. As you begin to risk being a child again, you are likely to anticipate a similar response from your heavenly Father. But try to remember that God is more than a Father. He is also the Creator of the universe— which includes you. Those inner desires you may have to write, or sing, or draw, or play, or whatever, were put there by God. Nothing makes God happier than to see his children doing what he has gifted them to do! He gave you those talents not just for your own good but for the good of all his other children as well (1 Cor 12:12-26).

One woman spoke of how difficult it was to express herself as a child because of the way her parents refused to acknowledge her talents and interests.

I used to love to draw and try all sorts of new and different things, but the creativity I tried to express as a child was always put down. I was told, "That's stupid. That's silly. That's out of the norm." Anything I tried to do that was individualistic or creative was put down, so I learned to just hold that inside.

Now, with help, I'm just beginning to realize that I have the talent... and I have the ability... to create. But it has affected me a lot, such as learning to relate to people, to have healthy relationships, to learn to express myself, and to *risk* expressing myself. It's a big risk for me to just put something on paper because I was so criticized as a child.

Even my being creative with dressing and my appearance has been a problem for me. I remember one time very distinctly. I was sitting in a chair and my father was across from me on the couch. I asked him if I was pretty, and he said, "No, you're *not*. Anybody who asks that kind of thing and wants to think of herself as pretty is very selfish and self-centered and inconsiderate."

I got a lecture for just asking, so I learned never to ask and never to make a fuss over myself. And I'm just beginning to learn that it's okay to get involved with personal hygiene and things like that. It's *healthy* to take care of yourself. It's *healthy* to put on a little make-up or try to look pleasant. But I still struggle with it.

This woman's creativity was a reflection of God's own creative nature. Yet her parents squelched it. They destroyed her interest in creating new things. Now, years later, she is rediscovering the childhood joy of creativity. And it shows in her facial expressions as she talks of her newfound passion.

Being a child can be a lot more fun than being an adult. Laughing and having a good time is not only okay but should be encouraged. If you never had the opportunity, what's stopping you right now—other than the shadows of your past? Ask God the Father to provide new glimpses of what life as his child can be like. If you missed out on the joy of childhood, he can provide it for you now. If you desperately need a sense of peace, it can be yours for the asking. If you just need someone to love and accept you as you are, you have found the source of all love.

All these wondrous gifts are available as we recognize and claim our place as children of God. When you sit in God's lap and let him love you in this way, he will clear out all those poisonous emotions and incapacitating memories that may hold you captive and replace them with his living and powerful Spirit. When he does, the results will be just what you need, what Scripture calls the fruit of the Spirit: love, joy, peace, patience, kindness, goodness, faithfulness, gentleness, and self-control (Gal 5:22-23). How long has it been since these characteristics have been evident in your life? How much longer are you willing to wait until you begin to taste them?

Children also tend to be more vulnerable than adults. They often take more risks in opening up to new people. They aren't quite so concerned with what others think. Able to be more themselves, carefree children try to make friends with almost everyone else. If others don't respond, they soon look elsewhere for friends. We need to regain that sense of vulnerability.

When we lose a sense of who we really are, along with the self-worth that flows from that personal identity, we set ourselves up for more and more problems. We learn not to trust people, especially those who may remind us of our fathers. We may develop friendships with individuals who seem needier than we are so that we can project an image of "having it all together." Meanwhile, we may shy away from those whom we perceive as equals, terrified that they will see our weaknesses and make fun of us—just like our parents sometimes did.

As a child of God, the heavenly Father can rebuild in you a genuine sense of self-confidence and value. He created you. He is your parent in the truest sense of the word. He wants you to realize how truly important you are to him. As this kind of recognition takes hold, you will more willingly take the risk of opening up to other people. If someone doesn't like who you are, no big deal. God does, and that's more important. He can direct you to people who *will* accept you for who you are.

It may seem silly to think about becoming a child again. It may seem frightening. But the *fact* of the matter is that you can put your trust in God and become, literally, his adopted child. When you do, he will work with you to restore all the things you may have given up for lost. He will provide the emotional healing necessary to see your circumstances from a new perspective and get on with your life. He will renew the childhood excitement and enthusiasm you may have missed. Enjoy it!

BEING AN ADULT

Eventually, God will show you how to be an adult as well. Some of the behaviors you previously considered to be "adult" may in fact be very childish. But after you learn what it means to be God's child, you can discover how to be a more mature and healthy adult as well.

You may argue that it's difficult to start depending on God so heavily when you can't even see him. That's true in a sense. After you've spent a lifetime learning to distrust other people and doubting that anyone really cares about you, it's not easy to put your faith in an invisible Being. So in addition to trying to get closer to God, one of the first adult things you need to do is to find a *human* role model as well. This may take some work, but the results are well worth the effort.

Some people have gone through their entire lives without ever meeting anyone who provided a good example of what a father should be. Most of us have at least had glimpses of what we're hoping to find. One woman shared about being with her girlfriend's family. She enjoyed the jokes and laughter, the display of affection, the lively conversations, the smiles on the father's face. Of course, she had to battle envy, wishing her father could be more like her friend's. But at least she had the opportunity to see healthy fathering in action.

Your father may have tainted your opinion of adults as a whole. Nevertheless, you can find other people who truly *will* care about your spiritual and emotional growth, who will help you in any way they can. One of the best things someone else can do for you is to provide some accountability on your part. When you regularly talk with someone else about your efforts to change, it's not nearly as easy to get stuck. Those in whom you confide can challenge you to keep moving forward when the going gets tough.

Another adult action is to find constructive outlets for your feelings. First, you need to foster that sense of total honesty that young children exhibit—until they learn the "adult" technique of hiding their true feelings. Honesty isn't always pleasant, yet it is essential to any kind of growth. Here's one example of unpleasant, even frightening, honesty. This young woman was the oldest daughter of eight brothers and sisters. She didn't specifically detail what had taken place in her home when she was young, but she spoke very clearly about the effects.

I finally got to the point where nothing was worth living for. I started walking around thinking, *Where's a gun? Where's a gun? I need to blow my head off.* I became suicidal. I got through that with the help of a support group. And because of that, now *I'm* the crazy one as far as my parents are concerned. But I'm getting better. They can live like that, but I'm getting better.

They still have kids at home, and it hurts me because my nineteen-year-old sister is now wrapping cords around her neck... and sitting on cliffs... because she saw what my father did to me. She learned how not to feel, because if you felt, you got smashed. I hate my parents. I hate them right now because they're killing my brothers and sisters. And I don't know how to deal with it. I would rather kill them than watch them methodically annihilate my brothers and sisters emotionally. What's it going to take, a death?

My suicidal tendencies meant nothing compared to knowing my sister is now going through the same thing. I have two sisters. We all had sex before we were married, looking for some kind of love. I just... I can't deal with these feelings. I think of my father and my hands are around his neck. I just can't see why one suicidal daughter wasn't enough, why there had to be another one, or why my brother is in another state so isolated he won't let anyone know where he's living. But according to my parents, "There's nothing wrong with our family. We're okay. It's not that bad." But damn it, it is. It's horrible. Kids are wanting to kill themselves. It's terrible. And I hate my parents for not facing the truth.

This young woman is still in the initial stages of letting others help her, but *at least she has begun.* Getting started is often the hardest step. She's being honest about her feelings toward herself and her parents. As terrifying and painful as that truth is, it's what will allow her to find lasting help and emotional healing.

Being a mature adult also involves learning from our mistakes and correcting whatever inappropriate responses we may have made in the past. Sometimes we can't go back and change the things we would most like to do over again. In such cases, we can only draw on our heavenly Father's unlimited source of forgiveness. One man tells of behaving in the same pattern in which he was raised. Now that he is finding healing, he regrets these violent actions and is trying to live a new way.

Being brought up by such a violent father had an effect on me. One time when my mother was visiting with us, my first wife hit me over the head with a dictionary and I almost hit the floor. I never said a word, but I felt just like my father instead of me.

I said, "Mother, I think it's time for us to take you home now." We took her home—a thirty-mile drive each way. I didn't speak a word in all that time. But when we got back, my wife walked into the house and I went in after her. She went in through the kitchen, then the dining room, and then the living room. I was right in back of her. When she finally turned around, I hit her and she hit the floor.

Violence was all I knew. I had never hit her before. I loved her more than I loved *me*. But she had crossed my boundaries—she hit me in front of my mother. If she had hit me without being in front of my mother, that might have been a different story. But she hit me in front of my mother, so I got her. I put her down.

If I had it to do all over again, it would have never happened— knowing what I know now. Now I know that *her* father was an alcoholic and it was wrong for me to hit her. It was stupid of me. It would be just like running my head into a wall. Completely stupid. And I've regretted that all my life and I wish I could apologize to her now. But I haven't seen her in twenty-five years.

This man has since dealt with the pattern of violence in his life. He and his abusive father reconciled on the father's deathbed. Even though it's too late to change some things, he understands. And he continues to try to deal with the pains of his past, as he becomes emotionally stronger day by day. He attended several of our group interviews and expressed appreciation for the opportunity to talk about many of the things that he had kept bottled up for so long. Getting it out and talking about it in the group sessions had a fantastically curative effect.

When you get your past off your chest, you can get on with the healing process. You will see positive changes take place in yourself. Yes, you will still have lots of unpleasant memories and emotional baggage from your past. Yes, you may have done any number of things you regret. But with God's help, you can see positive changes begin to take place in your own life.

Your relationships won't get better until you are ready to pay the price. And you won't be ready unless you learn to bask in the freedom of living as a child of the heavenly Father, as well as work toward becoming a responsible adult. Quit complaining about him, her, or them. The only pronouns you need to concern yourself with—for now—are *me, myself, and I*. Doing nothing while you wait and hope for others to change is not a very adult way of handling a crisis. Do something. For your own emotional health, I encourage you to do it soon.

TAKE TIME TO REFLECT

1. What are some things you regret not having been able to do when you were a child?

2. What particular areas or abilities (artistic, musical, poetic, athletic, etc.) would you like to explore?

3. List some characteristics of the kind of person you would like to have as a *human* role model. Then begin looking for a person who closely fits that description.

TWENTY-TWO

Starting over with Your Father

YOU CAN NEVER ERASE what has already happened or begin all over again from scratch with your father. Unfortunately our lives are not like tape recorders with simple erase buttons which we can push whenever something goes wrong. But I do believe you can start *over* in any relationship—once you have corrected your misperceptions from the past and created new definitions for the future. I'm not saying any of this is easy, but it is well worth the effort.

Perhaps you have an ongoing relationship with your father, albeit a strained one. You are in an ideal position to start over by applying the tools in this chapter. Maybe you have no idea where your father is now. Maybe you know, but the emotional damage you've suffered is so severe that you can hardly stand to think about him—much less *be* around him. Some adult children see the swordplay from the father/son reunion of Luke Skywalker and Darth Vader in *Return of the Jedi*, the *Star Wars* sequel, as nothing compared to what might happen if they attempted to reconcile with their own fathers.

Whatever your situation, God will provide the love, grace, and strength necessary to move forward in that special relationship. The following stories of those who have gone before you offer proof positive that reconciling with an emotionally distant father can be a wonderful and unexpected experience.

What if your father is already dead? Your memories of him may be more miserable than merry. Reconciliation, no matter how desirable it sounds, is now impossible. Perhaps even talking about the possibility of getting back together with your father only deepens your depression. What can *you* do? As I mentioned in a previous chapter, one of the things we have people do at our Rapha Treatment Centers is to write a letter to their fathers—whether or not they send it and whether or not the father is even alive. This exercise allows hurting people to crystallize their feelings, to recall any positive memories, and to express any negative ones. If nothing else, the person says goodbye from an adult perspective rather than as the little boy or girl who was previously under the complete control of someone who mostly caused them pain.

Another very helpful avenue if your father is already dead is trying to draw closer to other family members. Frequently, the wives of abusive, alcoholic, or apathetic husbands suffered as much or more than the children. Sometimes a new bond is developed between mother and child after the father dies. Working through painful memories together can be extremely therapeutic for everyone involved. We will focus on these relationships in the next chapter.

As I have mentioned previously, this may not be the right time for you to attempt any kind of reconciliation with your father. If you're still working through your own emotional turmoil, keep at it. Yet once you have begun to see your past more clearly—more from an adult perspective than a childish one—you may be ready for the next step. If you still have the opportunity and the ability to initiate a reconciliation, make the most of it; don't assume the opportunity will last forever.

The biggest question in the your mind at this point might be, WHY? After all this time, after all the pain, after all the opportunities that your father may have had to set things right with you, why should you even make the slightest effort to reconcile with him? According to the people we talked with, I can actually give you several good reasons.

MAYBE YOUR CRAVING FOR ACCEPTANCE HASN'T CHANGED

Don't forget what caused this problem in the beginning. When you get all the way back to its source, you hurt because you deeply want your father to assure you that he loves you and cares about you. At some point, you started blaming him for neglecting you, drinking too much, abusing you, or whatever. But such accusations are merely symptoms of the problem. The real "disease" is the scarcity of love from your father.

You may have written off any hope of establishing a meaningful relationship with your father long ago. You may have convinced yourself that you don't care one bit what happens between you from now on. But if you are absolutely honest with yourself, don't you still want to hear Dad say, "I love you and I was wrong not to say so for all these years"?

Maybe you don't. Maybe you have finally given up altogether, thrown in the towel, so to speak. But a lot of people would be willing to forgive almost anything if they could hear their dads express love just once. One woman shared about wanting to hear those precious words from her seventy-five-year-old father who had always been a perfectionist. She had even worked for him for years, receiving approval by working her way into his heart. But her deepest hope remains that someday he will tell her, "I love you."

She says, "He was a good provider, but never gave of himself emotionally. Today I'm very distant from my father. I can barely stand to be around him sometimes. But he's beginning to reach out in a way he never has before. He still does some of his condemning, critical things, but at least he's reaching out. In some ways I like that, and I think, *My gosh, where is this coming from?*"

This woman has waited somewhere in the neighborhood of fifty years to hear an expression of love from her father. In all that time, her basic desire hasn't changed. After being in recovery for over two years, she has changed the way she thinks about herself and her father. But that hasn't altered the way she feels, her deepest cravings for her father's love.

MAYBE YOUR FATHER IS MORE OPEN TO CHANGE THAN YOU THINK

We shouldn't be too quick to resign ourselves to the status quo. Everyone can change. Even your father. Even you. Sometimes an irresponsible father finally realizes he has a problem and *he* gets help. If he finds a sense of emotional stability before you do, it can cause a lot of resentment. This man was responsible for your pain and suffering, yet he is now able to be at peace and get on with his life while you may still be miserable. Here's one scenario:

> It took me a long time to get back the trust in my father. After he entered recovery, I just sat back and said, "Yeah, right! You've made promises before." I didn't believe for a minute that he was really going to stop drinking. He had tried to do so two or three years previously. So for me to begin trusting my father—no way. But I began to see something real was happening, because he started reaching out to other people.
>
> Then I became very angry. I thought, *Where was this when I needed it?* When I came home from college they had a sixteen-year-old girl who was living with them. I hated her, because *she had my place.* I saw my father giving her love and discipline that I never received. I had been allowed to do whatever I wanted to, which was to me as bad as not having any freedom. I knew no way of setting boundaries for myself and here I see my father giving this teenager… How dare they give her all that love and discipline? Where was *mine?*
>
> So at that point I joined a recovery support group because I was so angry. I wanted to be a sixteen-year-old again. I figured, *You are all better now, so start treating me the way you are supposed to treat a daughter.* I had no way of having an adult relationship with my father until I worked through these issues and until I acknowledged, "You hurt me." I was fortunate because my father was in recovery first. I could go to him and say, "Dad, you hurt me. I've been scarred because of what I saw, what I heard, and what I experienced."
>
> I had to work through all those feelings of loss as a child to realize that my father could no longer be the daddy I needed as a little girl. That was gone. I remember one night breaking into tears with him. I was so angry and he said, "What is your problem? What do you want from me?"
>
> I wanted him to be my father during those years when he wasn't. He didn't know what role he played anymore, because he missed all those years too. How was he to deal with this twenty-one-year-old daughter coming to him? He couldn't put me on

his knee like he could when I was six. So even after a parent is in recovery, there are still problems. It is still difficult. Yet by the grace of God, now I can look at him as a friend and I can go to him. I know I can.

Though this relationship is still a bit strained, at least father and daughter share hope for a more complete reconciliation. If the father had never sought help for his drinking—and never received a clearer perspective as a side benefit—the daughter might not have discovered how much of a difference a good support group could make in her own recovery.

The most effective strategy is for both father and child to get help as they try to hash out the problems of the past. More commonly the child finally becomes willing (or desperate enough) to get advice from other people who have coped with similar problems, or else from professional therapists. Most of the time the father doesn't choose to try counseling. In that case, the adult children shoulder more of the burden of reconciliation.

MAYBE YOUR FATHER ISN'T AS
MUCH AT FAULT AS YOU THINK

Sometimes we make certain assumptions about an absent or neglectful father that prove to be untrue, even though we may have carried those assumptions for a number of years. Sometimes another family member has provided us with erroneous information about the absent father.

If you have never dealt with your father about the problems you had with him in the past—one-on-one and adult-to-adult—you owe him at least one opportunity to explain himself before you write him off forever. In working through her own father hunger, one woman discovered that her mother had not only misled her about her father's leaving but had outright lied about him to gain the daughter's loyalty.

I have very few memories of my father and they're very detached. He moved away and I didn't see him for seven years. I thought I had dealt with that and it's only been within the last few months that I've been able to consider that maybe there was more to the story. Maybe it wasn't that he was just an awful man who didn't love me, didn't want me, and didn't care about me.

After receiving some counseling, I went to see him. I had decided maybe there was another side to all the negative things my mother was telling me, so I went down to talk to him about it. I found out that a lot of the things I had been told were a result of the bitterness of my mother. I had been told that he was too busy running around with other women to be bothered with me and that I cramped his style.

But he talked about good times when I was very small. He said, "You know, I always had a knack for getting you to sleep." And he told of how he would get down and wrestle on the ground with me and my sister—we were thirteen months apart—and that there were some good times. But he stopped coming around after he and my mother got divorced because he didn't feel welcome.

The thing that surprised me about him was his honesty. I didn't expect him to be so truthful. What an adult he was! For forty some years, I had never seen that. My mother threw temper tantrums. My grandmother threw temper tantrums. My grandfather acted like a child, hiding in the corner. The kids I grew up with had very dysfunctional parents. Most of them were divorced. So it was astounding to see this man behave like an adult—and treat *me* like one.

Dad was involved in his community and with his new kids. He treated them with respect, not with the emotional manipulation my mother used so well. He would love to have had a relationship with us. I think it's very sad that he allowed my mother's dominance to keep him away from us. I know when I talked to him he was very sorry. He had never gotten the impression that things were as bad for us as they really were. But my mother had fixed that by telling us, "Don't bother with him, because he won't believe you. It's only going to be worse when you're with him."

Now that I'm over my anger and bitterness, now that I've calmed down and sorted things out, I really think my father was as lost and confused as I was after he left. Maybe he was one heck of a lot bigger man than I gave him credit for. But by the same token, I needed answers as a child and I didn't get them.

If a father wasn't around much during your childhood, it's pretty easy to saddle him with most of the blame for what goes wrong in your life. Perhaps he deserves it. Perhaps not.

MAYBE YOUR FATHER HAD GOOD REASONS FOR ACTING AS HE DID

The great majority of men don't father a child and then consciously decide, "I'm going to make this kid's life a living hell." It may sometimes *turn out* that way, but the father isn't so much *choosing* his actions as he is acting the only way he knows. Building a better relationship with your father should involve finding out whatever you can about him. Ask questions; listen with an open mind. See what you can discover about *his* parents, grandparents, economic status as a child, friendships, and so forth. All these forces combined to help shape your father into the kind of person he became.

It certainly wasn't right or fair for him to take any of his own misfortunes out on you. Yet if you can see beyond your father's improper actions or shortcomings to some of the specific sources that may have initiated his behavior, you should be better able to draw closer to him. For example, one man speaks with deep regret of seeing the effects of alcoholism on his father. Yet he became more understanding after he found out more about what had caused the drinking. His father started out as a fun-loving, social drinker. During the Depression and the early war years, he wanted to enlist but couldn't because of having five kids.

The grown son began to realize what an ego problem that had created for his dad, how staying home from the war had humiliated him in a lot of ways. People would say, "Oh, yeah, you had all these kids just so you wouldn't have to go to war," as if his dad knew the war would happen and started having kids in 1925 in order to avoid military service! His father began drinking more and more heavily as a way to anesthetize his feelings. As the son learned to see his father as a human being with human limitations, it became easier to try to reconcile the differences they had. His biggest regret was that he hadn't started sooner:

> I felt bad because it was shortly before my dad died that I just started to know him and to relate to him without feeling pres-

sured. I was grown, had started my own family, and had a house of my own. I know he always expressed that he was proud of the way we all turned out. His first family had a lot of problems. But he started over with us and was glad that we were turning out well. He would say he didn't do anything to deserve having kids turn out so well. He always expressed that verbally to us, though he never hugged us or anything like that.

I think when he died I was most angry because I felt like there was still unfinished business. I don't know how my brothers and sisters felt. I'm finding that each of them saw Dad and Mom differently because of their age and because of sides taken in previous arguments. So there was good and bad.

Sometimes it is enough to be able to say "there was good and bad." If we never make any effort to get back together with our fathers, we can spend the rest of our lives with memories of all bad. Depending on the father's sins of the past, you may never reach an "all good" stage, but you might be able to try to understand and forgive enough to draw a bit closer together than you've been in years.

IF YOU KEEP PUTTING IT OFF, YOU MAY WAIT TOO LONG

The previous story wasn't the only one we heard of a father who died before the adult child could restore the relationship to any degree of satisfaction. Many of our volunteers spoke with regret of the finality of a father's death. For some, it was only then that they found out some things that really surprised them about their fathers.

One woman had memories of an angry father, a disciplinarian who never gave praise, a touch-me-not person who was very silent and religious. It wasn't until she stood at the side of his casket that she learned what a generous man he actually was. Because of her father, many families had made it through the Depression or some other time of turmoil because he had given without expecting anything in return. She learned that he tithed to the church and held a lot of other Christian values which had been kept in the shadows by his inability to show emotion.

A man who had suffered repeated physical abuse at the hands of his father had at one point left home "for good." He spoke of how his father's lack of acceptance had affected his life in many ways. Several marriages had failed. His sense of self-worth had been shattered. He had not been allowed to have the education he desperately desired. He had more reasons than he could count to blame his father for what had happened to him. Yet he was surprised at how much a last-minute reconciliation meant to him:

> My father and I hated each other my whole life, but he did forgive me on his deathbed. He was paralyzed and couldn't talk, but his eyes focused. After about five days of my standing there, waiting, his eyes finally focused and he saw me. He grabbed me, pulled me down on the bed, and hugged me with his one good arm.
>
> I thank God that happened. I watched him while I was waiting there those four or five days. It seemed as if he was arguing and fighting with the angels. It was terrible. And there he was, unconscious, his eyes not focused, going through all this. And then his eyes focused, and he saw me, and grabbed me. It seemed like... I believe we forgave each other at that time. I know we did. And I think that was a real gift from God to keep me from blowing my brains out during my crazy, mixed-up life.

Your father's treatment of you may have been abominable. You may have hated him with a passion. Yet death is final, nonretractable. If your father dies, you will still have all that unfinished business with nowhere to go. Your father won't be there, but your feelings will. For your own peace of mind, if not your father's, you should give serious thought to attempting a reconciliation.

Now that you're an adult, what's the worst that can happen? Your father may act the same way he always has. If so, you have nothing to lose from making the effort. And you have much to gain. Even if you are rejected again, you will at least have the consolation that you tried. And if Dad cooperates with your efforts to make peace, your memories will be all the better in years to come.

TAKE TIME TO REFLECT

1. How did the challenge to reconcile with your father make you feel? How do you think your dad would respond if you approached him?

2. Do you think you've made any false assumptions about your father? If so, what are they?

3. List some factors that may have influenced the way your father related to you.

TWENTY-THREE

New Ways of Relating with Other Family Members

COPING WITH FATHER HUNGER would be much easier if the only people affected were you and your father. Some victims would gladly give up all contact with the man who abused or neglected them if they could just get on with their lives and other relationships. Yet as we have seen, the effects of a damaged father/child relationship are both broad and long-lasting.

When someone doesn't receive enough love from a father, most of his or her other relationships are affected—perhaps *all* those relationships. Trust is lost; vulnerability disappears; forgiveness becomes impossible. Family members may go from being close allies who agree that Dad is a monster to fighting among each other at the least little disagreement. Outsiders aren't allowed to get close enough to choose one side or the other.

This disruption of family unity further underscores the importance of reconciliation to whatever extent possible. If reestablishing love and forgiveness do not offer motive enough, the personal hope of being released from the victim role in all of your other relationships *should*.

Think about it. If the number-one man in your childhood seemingly rejected you, isn't it far preferable to have allies in your family rather than more enemies? As you look back on those turbulent years from an adult perspective, you may see that some of your past behavior toward other family members was in fact unwarranted. Perhaps you also need to initiate reconciliation with your mother and siblings.

Even beyond the bounds of our birth families, our other relationships suffer as well. If our fathers didn't relate to us properly, we and our spouses are likely to have a number of problems. We may feel especially strong pangs of fear and regret as we see ourselves beginning to treat our own children in some of the same ways we were treated by our parents. This important issue of relating to your children will be the subject of the next chapter. But first, try to think through the ways that your other relationships are being affected by father hunger.

Perhaps you're already well aware of the shortcomings in your family relationships. Or perhaps you've never given it much thought. When raised in a home where dysfunction is the norm, we might be quite shocked to come into contact with a family whose members enjoy healthy relationships. This can be especially jolting when the contrast is between one's own parents and one's in-laws, as one man discovered.

In my childhood I was extremely overweight. I didn't receive a lot of overt abuse, but there were a lot of subtle things... subtle shame... expressed verbally through my father, which affected my family emotionally.

My wife's father and mother are involved intensely with each other and because my father is dead, I have to struggle to keep from being extremely bitter or jealous of them. I see her family at holiday gatherings *functioning—not dysfunctioning.* They are reliving good experiences and regaining anything they may have missed out on. I feel like I'm supposed to jump into this setting and be Richie Cunningham and say everything's wonderful. But my childhood wasn't "Happy Days."

The good thing that I have learned from being in recovery is that there *is* balance—and one of the realistic things that I've learned is that my father taught me a great work ethic. I can also see how I've taken that to the extreme because of growing up in a dysfunctional home. My identity and self-worth come from my work. What my recovery and spiritual growth have taught me is to take my pain to the Cross and ever so slowly take steps toward trust and toward understanding.

It was important for me to learn to make choices based on my true feelings instead of responding automatically as a victim. I've seen such positive changes in myself, and I fought against those positive things for the longest time. I had to realize that I either keep going in my dysfunction—my disease—or I recover. It has required a lot of pain and rigorous honesty, but I don't regret it one bit.

This man learned that emotional healing cannot take place in a vacuum. You don't just isolate yourself and get better. You still have to interact with all those people who have annoyed you for so long—mother, spouse, siblings, children, in-laws, whomever.

THE MOTHER AND CHILD REUNION

Many times an abused or neglected child doesn't limit his resentment to the father who actually did the beating or who left home. In the child's mind, the mother shouldn't have *allowed* it to happen, so she is equally guilty. The breach of trust initiated by the father is so devastating that not only do we refuse to ever trust him again but we also refuse to trust the mother. Later, through the eyes of an adult, we frequently see that Mom was just as much a victim as we were. Even when fathers and children never get back together, the mothers and their adult children can reunite.

One woman was repeatedly sexually abused by her adoptive father. She was only nine or ten at the time. After his death, her relationship with her mother was beginning to deteriorate as well. But in her case, honesty prevailed.

My father died in 1966. I never said anything to my mother about what Dad had done to me until October, 1991. I probably should have told her sooner, but at the time I just didn't feel that I could. After my dad died, my mother went through a hard time with severe depression. She also went through a change and I never knew who she was going to be—if she was going to be my nice mom or... I almost felt she was a demon-possessed woman. There were times when she actually threw me across the room when I came home on the weekends. I wouldn't know whether to step into the house or not.

But I finally opened up and told her how Dad had abused me as a child and I'm so excited because I've kept it bottled up for all these years. I was finally able to admit it to my mom. Our bond is a lot closer now and we've been able to work things out. I think the process you have to go through sometimes is not just for your own problems. Sometimes I think we go through things in our lives not mainly for ourselves, but to help out others.

Another woman tells of the special bonding she and her mother experienced after the death of her father. As it turned out, they both were feeling a great sense of freedom, though neither wanted to be honest about what they were feeling. She shares:

One of the things my mom told me that had the most profound impact on my life—and I was well into my forties when she said it—was, "You know, some days I feel guilty being so happy." That summed up the whole situation for me as well. My mom had suffered right along with us kids. In my adulthood, I finally did come to know the complete, unqualified, accepting love of a parent. My mom loved me unconditionally, and we became very good friends before she died. That was a blessing to me in very many ways.

Even if your father is beyond reach for reconciliation, perhaps you can find a new ally in your mother. It could be, as in this woman's case, that both of you are suffering alone. If you get together, you may see that the suffering won't be doubled, but lessened considerably.

SIBLING RESENTMENT

Many of the people we talked with spoke of having more problems with brothers and sisters than anyone else in the family. You might think that since siblings experienced so much common pain, they would form close bonds—in much the same way that war buddies form alliances that last their entire lives. This may be true for brothers and sisters when they are still young; they tend to do whatever it takes to help each other out. But during adulthood, the diversity of their lives frequently becomes a greater obstacle than the shared rejection of childhood.

The harm done by an inadequate father takes its toll in a number of ways. In the same family, one child might suffer from severe depression; another might withdraw and isolate himself from the rest of the world; one might engage in homosexual activity; and another might get some professional help and restore her emotional health. Needless to say, these four aren't likely to be warm and chatty over the potato salad at the next family reunion.

If the adult children reach approximately the same level of emotional recovery, they seem to relate pretty well. But when one is farther along or farther behind than another, resentment usually outweighs any ability to get along. Seeing a brother or sister regain a degree of emotional health that you haven't been able to reach can be quite threatening. Sometimes the hurting sibling even begins to defend Mom and Dad with a fierce sense of protection.

In one group discussion, three women spoke of having this same experience. One said sadly, "I don't know if I'm ever going to be able to work through the problems I'm facing because of what my parents have done to me. Yet my sister keeps saying, 'Why can't we all just go out to lunch and have a good time?' Impossible!"

A second woman piped in, "My five sisters keep asking me, 'Why are you trying to assign blame? Why are you trying to blame Mom and Dad?' I'm not. The problems are multigenerational. I can see how they have come down through the generations. But they have to stop somewhere. *Someone* has to understand recovery for the good of the rest of them."

The third woman, who has two younger sisters very close in age, has worked hard to understand her dysfunctional religious background and home life in terms of why she acts the way she does. But one of her sisters doesn't understand.

> She thinks it's disrespectful and wrong not to just forgive and forget. Don't pay attention to past problems any more. Put on a happy face. Go on with life. She refuses to deal with what happened to us. She's off doing her own crazy things, including alcoholism, drug use, and such, yet she tells me, "Sometimes I want to disown all of you, because you're all acting so crazy. Why can't we all just love each other?"

This issue of resolving sibling rivalry seemed to trigger a lot of stories from people. But as we went on with the interviews, other people spoke up who had progressed even farther with their emotional recovery. They had noticed that after they had made significant progress in working through the problems in their lives, the other siblings finally stopped resisting the truth.

The old adage is true: Nothing succeeds like success. When one family member is eventually able to overcome most of the pain of the past, learn to laugh again, and become strong enough not to act in the same way toward other people, brothers and sisters are going to want the same thing. They may not make it easy for a person to get to that point, yet they quickly change their minds when they see the extent of change that is possible.

HUSBANDS AND WIVES

A person searching for a father's love puts a great deal of pressure on his or her spouse. While no amount of love from another person is likely to compensate for what is missing from the father—at least not for a long time—it seems that victims expect their spouses to miraculously manufacture enough support and affirmation to ease their emotional pain.

When this healing doesn't take place right away, the person often goes to the other extreme. Instead of trying to become more intimate with the spouse, the wounded person withdraws. We lose sight of the fact that intimacy requires time. If it isn't immediate, we don't want it. So we become distant from the one person who might be able to help us. If husband and wife both feel insecure due to a father's rejection, the potential marriage problems are multiplied.

God's intention for marriage takes on a new perspective in such situations: "For this reason a man will leave his father and mother and be united to his wife, and they will become one flesh" (Gn 2:24). As we have seen, leaving father behind is no simple matter. Yet the bond of marriage is so important that husbands and wives should commit themselves to dealing with the issue of their own sense of father loss *for the sake of each other*, if for no other reason.

Some of the people we talked to had voluntarily submitted themselves to inpatient counseling for depression and other symptoms.

In most cases, these people had experienced a lot of abuse or neglect from their fathers and were having pretty serious marital problems as well. One woman who had been abused by her father desperately wanted to establish a sense of intimacy with her husband. She told us:

> My biggest problem, and what we've been seeking help for, is not being able to have any kind of a relationship—whether it be sexual, or whether it be communication, or intimacy, or whatever you want to call it. It's almost nonexistent, and I would like to see changes made.
>
> I'd like to be able to have a sexual relationship with my husband that's beautiful, rather than being tolerated with clenched fists and disgust. I definitely would like to see that as a change. I'd like to be able to be a mother and not a child. I'd like my children to have an adult mother. I'd like to be able to be consistent. I want to be stronger for them and know how to deal with some of *their* problems. I feel like I've been stuck as a child. I've always felt like a child. Always. And it's not a pleasant feeling when you're thirty-seven.

One spouse can do a lot to help the other toward emotional healing, but it's not easy. One man initiated counseling and treatment because of severe depression and other symptoms. But he credited his wife of sixteen years for the fact that he was finally able to come for help. He himself felt utterly helpless to change, even suicidal at times. But her patient understanding and support pulled him through. She even formed a network of friends to watch out for signs of trouble during the worst times.

When both spouses have significant emotional problems based on their childhood, major problems can result. But if both are committed to getting better, they can form their own two-person support group as they seek help. Intimacy may not be possible for them at this point, but commitment to each other will do for now. The intimacy will come later.

Even though she and her husband both came from dysfunctional families, another woman held onto the belief that God designed them to work together and create a balance for each other. And in fact, their individual strengths seemed to fill in the gaps for one another. She says, "I think that even when both people have such limited resources, they can make it together as long as they keep working at strengthening the relationship and don't cave in to their fears."

God works to heal emotionally damaged individuals, but many times he chooses to work through other competent people who can patiently see the hurting person through the painful healing process, all the way to emotional health. If you're in a family relationship that is being shaken because of emotional crises from the past, I encourage you to get help. I will offer some advice along these lines in the afterword.

Too much is at stake to let friends and loved ones drift out of your life because of circumstances that seem beyond your control. In many cases, those other people want to see you get better more than you do. People who really love you don't want to see you suffer. They can see how much it hurts you, and it hurts them as well. You might be surprised how supportive your friends and family can be if you go to them for help and advice.

Even if your relationship with your father ended long ago, does it still feel like an oppressive weight in your life—like an albatross around your neck, destroying every new relationship you try to establish? Seek help from family members. Sometimes it won't be possible for you to make amends with them right away. In any case, it won't be easy. But then, the only way you can be sure whether or not it will work is to try. Don't you think it is worth the risk?

Having suffered through the pain of father hunger in your own life or seen its damaging effects in someone close to you, I'm sure you don't want to infect another generation with this dread disease. Parents naturally want to spare their children this kind of deep pain. If fact, many have found this single fear to be a huge motivating factor in their being able to work through the healing process for themselves. How can you avoid father hunger in your own kids? We will consider this question in the next chapter.

TAKE TIME TO REFLECT

1. Are there other victims who have been affected by your relationship with your father? If so, list them.

2. Does reconciliation need to take place in any of your primary relationships, such as mother, siblings, or spouse? If so, why?

3. List some steps you could begin to take to reconcile with these family members.

TWENTY-FOUR

Avoiding Father Hunger in Your Kids

P EOPLE HAVE DIFFERENT levels of tolerance as they deal with the problems that result from father hunger. Some are quick to seek help as they suffer with the personal pain which ensues. Others put up with the *personal* pain, yet feel deep remorse if they see their own problems affecting a new spouse or perhaps another family member. It is at that point that many begin to address this issue.

Some have an even higher threshold of emotional pain. They aren't motivated to take action by their own problems, and perhaps not even by the problems they see in other people. After all, those other adults should be able to handle conflict, stress, and personal pain. Yet the point at which most people finally get serious about finding help is when they see the same problems begin in their own children.

The pain of father hunger hasn't gone away. The parents still feel it. And while they may prefer to put up with the emotional unrest rather than go through the demanding process of healing the emotional wounds, they definitely don't want their children to experience similar lifelong hurts. Many people who have put off dealing with their problems for their own peace of mind will finally take action on behalf of their children.

The adults of today have been labeled the "sandwich generation." As life spans are beginning to increase, many people find themselves having to care for aging parents as well as trying to bring up their own children. In such cases, you can see how the issue of father hunger becomes so significant. Many people still feel responsible for their aging fathers, even though they may still be hurting from less than ideal relationships during childhood. While being confronted with the grievances of the past—and perhaps fast becoming emotional wrecks—they are also dealing with their children. Many youngsters are sharp as tacks. Even if all the right things are said, they will often pick up on the nonverbal communication taking place between Mom or Dad and Grandpa.

More and more people are beginning to recognize that much of their own undesirable behavior was initiated due to poor parenting by either Mom or Dad or both. The reason their parents didn't do a better job can often be traced to the fact that *their* parents made the same mistakes. And as far back as they can follow their "psychological family tree," they can detect the same dysfunctional behaviors being repeated over and over and over again.

Suddenly it becomes clear to today's parents that unless *they* themselves break the cycle, their own children will fare no better. My primary intention in this book has not been to make you a better parent. Many such books are already on the market. However, one very positive by-product of dealing with father hunger in your own life is your ability to recognize harmful patterns and eliminate them before your own children are affected.

Let's again turn to the list compiled in chapter fifteen of what most people look for in a father. Those same desirable traits characterize what your children hope to get from you. As we work our way through that list again, I will add some examples from the lives of the people we interviewed—either positive or negative ways of how they have begun to relate to their children in response to dealing with their own faulty father relationships.

SPEND TIME WITH YOUR CHILDREN

Children know their parents are busy people, but they also sense that they make time for the things that are important. Parents will occasionally work day and night to meet a deadline at work. They will come home from work exhausted and yet go on to mow the lawn, wash the clothes, balance the checkbook, and do other things that just have to be done.

Yet if Mom or Dad never seem to make time for the child, the only logical conclusion is that the child is not a priority. While parents are making time for important concerns, time with their kids should be at the top of the list. As far as a child is concerned, time translates into love. So when a parent never manages to spend time with the child, what's the child to think?

One of the men we talked to had a father who neglected him most of the time. For the most part, the only interaction he had was when the father became violent and abusive. This man tells of his struggle to overcome his own tendencies to behave in the only way he had ever known.

I've never been physically abusive with my children. I've threatened. I've caught myself over and over again with my hand raised... just to the point of knocking them across the room. I've been a Christian for nineteen years and I've tried to counter that behavior I learned from my father. So every night I try to go and tuck my kids into bed, spend some time with them, and let them know I'm interested in them and their lives. I try to ask them questions about their day and to make a point of always telling them that I love them.

My oldest daughter has a difficult time right now telling me that she loves me. She's thirteen. I don't know how much of that is due to adolescence... being a teenager... and how much might be a carryover from when she was just a little tot, before I began to be aware of the effect that my parenting had on me.

GIVE EACH CHILD FOCUSED ATTENTION

If you have more than one child, keep in mind that each one needs to feel unique and special. So while time spent with the children is good, it also helps to single out each one from time to time.

Moms and Dads can easily become frustrated with their children when they don't respond in the manner anticipated—especially if the parent is consciously trying to avoid making the same mistakes he or she has faced. We need to remember that even in the best of families, children are going to do childish things. We want to help them mature into healthy and capable adults, but we should never come to expect consistently mature behavior from a child or teenager. Even after all the time spent with them, including focused attention, kids are sometimes going to act like kids.

One father explained how hard he had tried to be available to his children when they were young. But as they entered the teen years, he struggled with new feelings and challenges. "They're fighting for room and doing it in extreme ways. And I don't want this. I feel kind of offended because it's like now they're turning on me. I find myself responding in anger to what they're doing. At least I'm able to see these things and start dealing with them."

Even when the results aren't what you anticipated or hoped for, be patient. Children are going to be childish at times. But by giving time and individual attention, the long-term results are likely to be positive ones.

PROVIDE PROTECTION, COMFORT, AND SECURITY

In addition to time and individual attention, a father is perceived as the source of protection, comfort, and security. But frequently the father isn't around. He may be gone—due to death, divorce, or choice. What are children to do then? In such cases they look to the mother, which sometimes causes an overload. One woman speaks of the insecurity she felt because neither her father nor mother had *consistently* affirmed her.

My father was a traveling man and my mother tried to cover for him when he was gone. I think the greatest thing she could have done would have been to validate my feelings—to have been honest and admitted that she had the same problems with my father as us kids did. But she assumed almost a dual personality. When he was gone she was very loving, accepting, nurturing, and caring toward us. But when he came home again, she would withdraw completely from us and withhold her love and affection just as he did. We got such a mixed message. If she had been able to be honest with us and validate our feelings, we would have felt a lot better about ourselves.

Another woman tells how she tried to affirm her children, even though she received little if any sense of comfort or security from her own parents:

> It amazes me, with the background I came from, that I didn't repeat all the same mistakes with my children. I don't know why. I was not a Christian when I was raising my children, yet I was able to do totally the opposite. To me, that's supernatural. I was able to hug and hold them, and say the words that I never heard. I don't understand it, but I think it's neat. Total honesty with God is what set me free.

It helps when the father is there to act as the protector of the family. But even when he isn't, the mother can still try to provide a significant sense of comfort and security.

INITIATE COMMUNICATION

It doesn't take much effort to open up and talk to your children. They are thrilled when asked their opinions on various matters or simply treated as partners in conversation. They may not always show their excitement or respond right away, yet when a parent repeatedly initiates conversation, the child will eventually become more comfortable in communicating.

Verbally communicating love is very important as well. Many parents assume their kids *know* they are loved, but this isn't always the case. The words need to be spoken. It seems that the people who missed out on this aspect of a father relationship are sometimes most eager not to repeat the same mistake.

> I don't ever remember my dad saying he loved me. This year he retired and moved away. The kids and I went to visit him. I can give him a hug and I get the hugs back, but I never remember him *saying* he loves me—not once, not even on my wedding day. That hurts. Remembering these things has set me off these last couple of weeks since we came back from vacation. I'm not very free with verbal praise and affirmation, either, but children just need to hear those words. I am trying to get myself to say "I love you" a lot

more often and to get my kids' father to tell them as often as possible. You need verbal affirmation as well as physical contact.

As we learn to offer verbal affirmation more freely, our children will be able to receive things they might not necessarily want to hear. One father gives an example:

> I sat down with my younger daughter and explained to her that I couldn't go to all her intramural basketball games because I'm an accountant, the games were on Saturday mornings during tax season, and I was expected to be at work. She had four games and I went to two of the four. I made a point of coming home and talking to her about the two I wasn't able to attend. I've also made a point, when I find that *I'm* wrong, of saying I'm sorry and asking my children to forgive me for poor judgment or whatever. I try to explain that I'm human and that I've never been a parent before, and that I only get one chance. And I'm sorry I have to practice on them, but I want to do things right.

MAINTAIN TRUST

If a person's trust in a father is destroyed, it is extremely difficult for the person to trust anyone else again. People with such fathers find it hard both to trust their children, and to be trustworthy models *for* their children. Yet children need to be sure they can trust their parents and they need to believe that Mom and Dad trust them as well.

One woman had lost all trust in her father—and rightly so. She had been beaten physically and abused sexually. Later in life she struggled as a mother. Because of her childhood, she had come to abhor conflict. So when a disagreement began between two of her children, or her husband and one of her children, she had a lot of trouble dealing with it. She credits her husband with helping her to grow in the area of giving discipline when necessary.

> Thank goodness my husband's background was totally different than mine. I remember that up until my daughter was six years old, I would have to leave when my husband spanked her. I knew

he wasn't beating her, but it *felt* like he was because of the things I had been through. I think it had to do with the father-to-daughter relationship. I didn't feel the same way when my sons were spanked. I would like to be able to have all those emotions in a healthy way. I'd like to be able to be angry and stay in control. I just shake when I'm around anybody who's angry or where there's conflict.

When my children were younger, I could control them. Because I couldn't handle conflict, I would control all the situations instead. I don't know how I changed or why, but I realized that sibling rivalry was healthy for children. It's how they learn to interact as adults. I had to learn to trust them to work some things out on their own, without me manipulating them.

Trust is a two-way street. We must learn to act in a trustworthy manner so our children can count on us and feel free to be themselves. Then we must learn to trust them. Over time, the trusting relationship is something that both parent and child will come to value.

FORGIVE FREELY

Trust and forgiveness go hand in hand. When we trust others, even the best of people will let us down from time to time. When we put trust in our children and they don't come through as they promised, we can choose to either forgive or condemn. If the child is truly sorry, forgiveness can be a much more powerful lesson than condemnation. But either way, the child is likely to remember the lesson for years to come.

One man had felt too much condemnation from his own father to ever wish the same on his son. His father beat him for the least little thing. He says,

I swore I wouldn't turn out that way. I didn't treat my kids the way he did me. People in our church even told me I was supposed to beat on them, and I said, "No, I refuse to do it." If I raised my hand to my son, which I had never done, he would probably take one look at me and start to cry. He *knew* when he had made a mistake, and it was completely senseless to do something to this child when he already knew he made a mistake.

It seems easy to "teach a child a lesson" when he or she doesn't perform to a set of standards. Sometimes discipline is certainly necessary. But forgiveness is a lesson that needs to be taught a lot more often. Some children never learn it—at least, not from their parents.

DISCIPLINE WITH LOVE

When discipline *is* necessary, it should be done with love. Even God—the only truly righteous and perfect model we can find—exercises discipline with love (Heb 12:6). No one is more entitled to judge and condemn, yet our heavenly Father always shows mercy even in his discipline of errant children. Should we, with all of our imperfections, do any less with our own sons and daughters?

Each time you need to discipline a child, either verbally or otherwise, you should ask yourself, "To what extent will my child see my love through this discipline?" Very few of the people we interviewed had any kind of positive experiences to share about being disciplined. Yet the unreasonable punishment so many of them received enabled them to be more sensitive in disciplining their own children. They especially didn't want to be harsh in the way they had experienced from their own fathers.

SHOW ACCEPTANCE

Discipline is received a lot better if the child believes beyond a shadow of a doubt that he or she is still accepted by Mom and Dad. If punishment is ever perceived as a lack of acceptance, then irreparable harm can be done. It is next to impossible for children who never feel accepted to properly nurture a child of their own. One man tells of how he was guilty of perpetuating the father hunger problem without even knowing it:

When I was in fourth grade my aunt was visiting. I came in the house really happy, and yelled, "Mom, I got some good grades today!" My aunt screamed, "Self-praise stinks!" From that time on I never got good grades. I figured it wasn't worth it. I asked my mom years later, "Why didn't you say something to her?" She said, "Oh, I really just felt sorry for her."

When my daughter was about twenty years old and married, she accused me of never affirming her. When she confronted me, she was in tears. I didn't deny it. All I could say was, "You're probably right. I'm sorry. I didn't realize that." Because I was already in Al Anon, I realized that I had never been affirmed in my life. I was never encouraged. I was definitely discouraged in everything I did.

That is one of the horrible side-effects of growing up with a violent, abusive, or neglectful father—the sins of the fathers can be passed along to future generations without the person even knowing it. Parents need to consciously affirm and accept their children, whether or not they have a positive role model to follow.

OFFER GUIDANCE AND ADVICE

Fathers who spend time with their children, devote individual attention to each one, communicate with them, show forgiveness, and so forth are likely to be the first ones to whom the children go for guidance and advice. But if such qualities are lacking, children will be a lot more reluctant to ask. What aggravates the situation for those with inadequate fathers is that the children need even more guidance and advice in knowing how to cope with the lousy father. This puts a lot of pressure on the other parent to see that the children get help. Many times it is simply too much for the solitary parent, in which case help may need to come from other sources.

One woman told of finding out that her father had been having an affair when she was a young girl. No one gave her any guidance or advice in how to handle that harsh truth. She struggled with it on her own for most of her childhood and it had some very negative effects on her. Later, after she was married and had children of her own, she discovered that her husband was having an affair. Not wanting her daughter to go through the same painful confusion, this woman took action.

She says, "My husband and I began marriage counseling, I started attending a support group, and I put my oldest daughter into counseling as well. I know what I felt like when I was twelve and my daughter is now ten (and very mature for a ten-year-old). I don't want her, twenty years from now, to experience what I've been through."

Our children need guidance and advice at a variety of levels every day. Parents need to be available for them and help them in any way that is appropriate.

PROVIDE A POSITIVE ROLE MODEL

The one thing that essentially all of our interviewees agreed on was the answer to this question: "If a father doesn't do what he's supposed to do, can a mother ever effectively compensate for him?" Almost every person answered, "Never!"

But in lieu of having a loving father in the home, the next best thing seems to be to find the child a positive, male role model. If this step isn't taken, sons tend to feel a sense of lostness as to who and what they should be. Daughters tend to keep looking for the love they've never found, frequently in physical entanglements with a succession of male partners.

One woman told of having never been affirmed by her distant father. And she was one of the many who became sexually involved with someone before she was really ready. Her father was never really there for her. This woman speaks from experience:

> Mothers in homes where the father has left or is seldom around need to find a good male role model for their children—Boy Scout leaders, other family members, or even teachers. My mother barred any male influence from us, but we needed it so badly we tried to find it ourselves. I had an uncle who was influential on me for a while. My sister's high school teacher was a Christian who helped her deal with things. She got to the point where she could go to our dad and talk to him about why he left. Another sister was quick to bond with boyfriends and *their* fathers. She met with some abusive treatment that way. Parents can't just pawn their kids off on anybody.

This woman never received the love she wanted from her father. Yet she kept in touch with him for one main reason—her son.

Although her husband had abandoned her, they had reestablished a shaky relationship and she wanted her son to benefit from it if possible. She goes on to say:

> My father is now very ill. His disease is terminal and he is going to die soon. My son will be at the funeral. After he mourns the loss of his grandpa, he's going to have good memories of this man—memories that I don't have. He's going to be able to say, "I loved him and had special times with him." That's one good thing I can give my son out of this. The only positive thing I can see is that, very carefully watched, my father has been able to be a good grandparent to my son. It shouldn't have to be that way, but at least it's something.

Strong role models aren't always easy to find, but they're out there. Even though it may take a bit of work on the parent's part, the search needs to be made. Of course, the best option—if possible—is for the father to become more involved with his children. Even if the relationship between father and mother has been severed, the father should not give up on the children he left behind. He can still be a model for them, if he is willing.

It sounds so simple: To be a good parent, just be the father you wish you had had. But pitfalls abound. Time is tight. Stress at work is taken out on children at home. Sometimes the father isn't even in the home anymore and the mother is trying to be both Mom and Dad to her children. And few men are capable of fulfilling all the roles listed in this chapter.

Where can we turn when we experience our powerlessness? God the Father is waiting to provide all that we need. But as we discussed in chapter nineteen, turning to God can itself be a major obstacle in light of our father hunger. Let's focus on the spiritual ramifications of father hunger in the next chapter.

TAKE TIME TO REFLECT

1. To what extent are you willing to break the patterns of dysfunctional behavior in your family?

2. How would you rate yourself on each of the top ten qualities of a good father in regard to your relationship with your children?

3. What other specific areas do you need to work on in your relationship with your children?

4. List some steps you will take to improve your relationship with your children.

TWENTY-FIVE

God the Father Wants to Satisfy Your Hunger

L ET ME STATE without hesitation that I don't believe that reading any one book will have a significant effect in *eliminating* the feelings or *correcting* the behaviors related to father hunger. The problem has taken years and years to form, with the source covered over by layers and layers of various coping mechanisms. It's not going to be corrected so easily.

My goal has not been to provide a quick fix, but rather to coax you to take off the bandages and see the extent of the wound. If this goal has been accomplished, you will be prepared to look for help among your spiritually and emotionally mature friends, your pastor, or a trained therapist. If you discover that your wound is more serious than most, I would urge you to consider some inpatient treatment at a qualified clinic. Some people require more intensive help than is possible during a fifty-minute session once a week.

The problem of father hunger does not lend itself to a miracle cure. Even when you begin to see the problem clearly and make efforts to overcome it, be prepared for a long process—even with the help of others. The distorted thoughts and behaviors stemming from father hunger are deeply embedded. Your goal from this point onward should be progress rather than instantaneous healing. It may seem to get worse before it gets better, but as soon as you catch the first glimmer of emotional recovery, you won't be sorry.

THREE COMMON PITFALLS

Three specific pitfalls may trip you up if you aren't prepared for them: guilt, perfectionism, and hopelessness. Unless you maintain realistic expectations, they are likely to prevent you from finding the emotional healing you desire.

Guilt. In the jumble of feelings that will probably surface, guilt will be predominant. You'll feel guilty for things you've said and thought. You'll feel guilty for what you think you should have done in the past to avoid the problem to begin with. You'll feel guilty for not being a better child, parent, or spouse.

Guilt is a devastating emotion, one which should not be tolerated. You must force yourself to remember that the past is past. There's no going back and changing it. As much as you might like to "quantum leap" into the past and change history, that's not possible. You must deal with the present by starting from where you are and moving forward from here.

One woman describes the stranglehold of guilt in her own life:

Other people have concrete things to blame their fathers for, such as alcoholism or violence. My father had some affairs, but there was really no specific source like alcohol to blame. He was a workaholic, quick to become angry, and aloof toward the family.

So far I'm the only one of four siblings who is seeking emotional recovery. It's an awful feeling sometimes. I feel very alone. My husband and I have always been the ones the others came to when they had some kind of problem or needed a place to stay. We were making up for many of the things my siblings lost, emotionally, with my father.

My father is approaching seventy now and all of a sudden he's finding that he needs us for the first time in his life. I think people like him have a tendency to forget the abuses they have caused. (I've been trying to work through some of these issues because of the dysfunction that has become obvious in *my* daughter.) He's coming to me, praising me all of a sudden as an adult and telling me what a good job I've done raising my family.

Now that I'm grown, he finally gets around to saying, "I'm so proud of you"—because he knows he's going to need my help as he ages. I *want* to tell him, "You left all of us behind when you met that new woman who thinks you're so wonderful. Where is *she* now?" I have forgiven him and I've tried to learn to hate the sin but love the sinner. But what do you do when he's coming back because he wants help and you're not ready for it? I feel guilty for not wanting to be there for him.

After a lifetime of longing for a father's love and attention, this woman is not quite ready now that the time has come. Her feelings are completely understandable, yet her underlying sense of guilt holds her back.

A person's guilt over the past sometimes increases the farther a person travels down the road of emotional recovery. After working through this process for a couple of years, one man was able to tell a group some of his deepest regrets:

I'm in a job right now that involves going into other people's homes and seeing the way that they interact. That sometimes adds gasoline to the fire as I continue to work through the past problems with my father. My greatest regret probably is that I feel that I don't have the capacity to be accepted by others who are so willing to accept me. They're *so* willing. One consequence is that during the past seven years I have not spent enough time with my wife's family. A lot of times I project negatives I got from *my* father onto my father-in-law. I always set him up so that at the slightest thing he does wrong, my attitude is, "See you later." Rather than finding the affirmation I need, I keep others at a distance.

This man's regret can either initiate a deeper degree of healing or else become twisted into a sense of guilt that prevents him from moving on. The choice is his. You will find that you have similar choices to make as well.

Perfectionism. Those who have developed perfectionist tendencies face a paradox. Before they can get better, they have to learn to be not as good—at least by their definition. All their lives they have been striving to meet unrealistic expectations and thus have failed. Consequently, they just keep trying harder.

Emotional recovery for these people will require them to do something almost unthinkable: settle for less. They must learn that neither they—nor anyone else—can be perfect. Occasional failure must be tolerated. Doing one's best is all that can be expected. One woman talked about her own struggle with perfectionism which grew out of a strong pressure to please her dad. She was a black-and-white thinker: something was either right or wrong, with no gray area, no room for mistakes. She has had to work very hard to overcome that attitude as a supervisor.

Sometimes our fathers are guilty of expecting too much from us. Other times, even when we're trying to find emotional healing, we tend to expect more than we should from our fathers. Even when they express willingness to get help and try to change, we can't expect them to become totally different people. We can neither set them on a pedestal nor resign them to the deepest pit. One woman is gradually learning this lesson:

> What I learned was that God did not take and *change* my dad's personality, yet he began to use it in a more constructive way. That man I knew who used to rage at my mother still has that same intensity about things that are important to him. And I didn't like that because it brought back all those negative memories from childhood. I thought, *Oh no, my father is the same man!*
>
> I wanted my father to be totally different. I wanted him to be *not* the man I knew, but he is. It's just that God has begun to replace the negative expressions of his personality. But there are times even now when I hear him talk a certain way, and *bam*, I'm right back to being a teenager. I keep having to work through and deal with that.

As we make progress toward emotional healing, we may begin to see our problems more and more clearly. Emotional recovery doesn't necessarily rid us of problems, but it crystallizes them so that we can begin to unravel them.

Hopelessness. Most people who confront the problems of their past go through a period of hopelessness, or even despair, before they begin to get better. When they see the first glimpse of what emotional health can be like, some of them feel an immediate sense of loss for all the years they will never regain. One woman had been stifled by her parents—never allowed to express herself in any way other than what *they* felt was appropriate. Now that she is able to see what caused her problems, it is painful for her to overcome her own reluctance.

> A lot of times I don't try new things because I don't want to find out I can do them. I think it's a type of denial. If I do something new, do it well, and discover a little self-esteem from what I can do, I have to admit that my family was wrong. It brings back the pain of all those years. It's easier for me to say I just can't do it. It's just not for me to do. My talents lie in other areas. Because if I do it *now*, I have to see how much better my life *could* have been. I don't want to acknowledge how abusive and neglectful my parents really were.

I believe this woman will move beyond this stage. As she rediscovers suppressed talents, the joy will win out over the pain of not having expressed them for so long. But it will take time. At this point, she senses a great hopelessness, but those with whom she is sharing feel great hope for her.

GOD'S LOVE OVERCOMES HOPELESSNESS AND FEAR

In co-hosting a national talk show several years ago, I interviewed a couple who had been friends of mine for many years. They had gone through some very difficult times. After the woman ended up in a mental institution, the experts told her she would never again be able to live a normal life and that they as a couple would no longer be able to live as man and wife.

Even though my friend felt desperately confused and very hopeless, she persevered and eventually recovered. On that show I asked her, "How did you make it? How did you hang in there?" This woman thought a moment and then said, "When I could think of nothing else, I simply thought, *Jesus loves me.*"

"Jesus loves me." That statement is one of the first things we learn as children growing up in a Christian family. It is the most critical factor in our walk of faith; it is the key to successful emotional healing. Yet it is very important to distinguish between intellectually *knowing* that Jesus loves you and personally *experiencing* the love of Jesus Christ. Are you personally experiencing Jesus' love? If so, why do you spend so little time truly experiencing his love? And finally, how can you begin to experience more of the love of God?

When I ask people if they love God and believe that Jesus loves them, many of them are quick to say yes. Yet looking at their lives often fails to indicate that anything about God truly excites them. When was the last time you met someone who had fallen in love who didn't *know* it and *act* like it? People *know* when they are in love. They are consumed by it; their lives are focused on it. And if you are experiencing God's love, you are for sure going to know it. His love is so awesome that it dominates us and produces a profound sense of worship.

The most consistent emotion many of us experience is not love but fear. It drives us. It pushes us. It's there day and night. When growing up, we're afraid of our own family members. We're afraid of being beaten. We're afraid of being rejected. We're afraid of being abandoned. As adults, we're afraid of what we're doing to our own children and spouses. Even when we try to regain emotional health, fear can rule us. We're afraid of what we might discover. We're afraid of what we *do* discover. We're afraid we're going to change. We're afraid we're not going to change.

It is impossible to consistently feel fearful and at the same time drink deeply of the love of Jesus. Some of us may think we are depending on God, yet if we also experience tremendous amounts of fear, something is wrong. The Bible tells us that "God is love. Whoever lives in love lives in God, and God in him. Love is made complete among us so that we will have confidence on the day of judgment, because in this world we are like him. There is no fear in love. But perfect love drives out fear, because fear has to do with punishment. The one who fears is not made perfect in love" (1 Jn 4:16-18).

There is no fear in love. And without personally experiencing God's love, our relationships with him become rituals. We simply go through the motions. Worship without experiencing his love seems worthless. Sin seems more seductive. Blessings become burdensome. Money and achievements fail to satisfy. Without experiencing God's love, faith becomes an intellectual exercise and religiosity just another addiction.

I have learned these painful lessons from personal experience. In chapter one, I started telling you about my own experience with the issue of father hunger. Now that you understand the huge obstacle we must come against, I want to tell you what helped me to cope with my own longing.

MY STORY, PART TWO

I accepted Jesus when I was six, yet for most of my life, I experienced very little of God's love. It wasn't that he didn't love me, yet I *experienced* very little of his love. For one thing, I was confused about God's Word. I thought that God gave us the Bible so that we could find what we needed and wanted in it. In other words, if I needed comfort, I would read a Scripture that says God is the God of all comfort. Then I would say to myself, "Self, God is a God of all comfort. Be comforted, self."

God's Word is certainly important, but we are called to relate to *God*—not merely to words on a page. We must be very careful not to simply take his Word and use it as psychological advice. We should not stop with the mere reading of Scripture. We need to allow God's Word to lead us to the divine Author and very Source of life himself.

During much of my Christian life, I had stopped short of fully experiencing the love God had toward me. I would receive insight into why people acted as they did or else receive direction and guidance for my own life. Yet somehow I never really believed that God would be personal to *me*, that he would ever deal with *my* emotional needs.

Traumatic events from growing up can affect both our expectation and our ability to receive what God so freely offers. I explained my childhood situation in the opening chapter of this book, as well as some of the other challenges I faced. I created a way of relating to my parents that didn't hurt so much and then adapted that non-feeling behavior in my relationships with others. Then it carried into my relationship with God as well.

I also found it difficult to expect good things from God because of the difficult times I had experienced as a younger adult. Hard times will either bring us closer to Jesus or else cause us to shut ourselves off from him. My Vietnam experience and some problems I went through after I returned home had quite an effect on me.

Given all of these personal struggles, I have been absolutely amazed to see all the things that God has accomplished through the ministry of Rapha. Thousands of lives have been touched through the counseling and other resources, and the glory for all those things goes to God.

I had previously gone through hard times with a bit of resentment, yet with the determination to persevere. That's one of the common reactions to difficulties in life. From my childhood, I had gotten so good at "manufacturing" comfort for myself that I never allowed God to take over. I suppose I never felt the need—at least, not where I alone was concerned.

So how did God finally get through to me? I remember it as if it were yesterday. I was sitting in my library when the truth finally hit home. I said, "Lord, I'm just not able to make it on my own. Unless you touch me, I cannot make it."

My first step was to realize that I had no other avenues available, that I must allow God to work in my life. The second lesson he taught me was to come to him in praise. I finally understood that curious phrase in Scripture: "a sacrifice of praise" (Heb 13:15). Going through difficult times made offering praise feel like a sacrifice. I came to see that we're supposed to *continually* praise God and be thankful to him, especially when we face circumstances beyond our own control.

And finally, God taught me to pour out my heart—the good, the bad, and the ugly (Psalm 62:8). I may limit what I tell other people, but I have learned to keep *nothing* from God. Not long ago I remember complaining to God, telling my heavenly Father that I really didn't enjoy trusting him. I knew I was *going* to trust him. I had gratefully learned that I didn't have any choice but to trust him. But I didn't *enjoy* it. Not even a little bit. I intellectually knew that I was supposed to look at my circumstances as a great adventure in trusting God. Yet I had to tell him, "I don't like this. I wish I did. I wish I were confident. I *want* to be confident and enjoy the times I have to trust you for certain things. But to be honest, my heart is not there yet."

I truly believe that God wants us to be honest and pour out our hearts to him. He already knows what's there. We have nothing to fear from the truth. And as we find the courage to be honest with our heavenly Father, we discover the power of his love that breaks the bondage of fear.

Father hunger, and all the problems that arise from it, is like a deadly poison that spreads and kills. It kills relationships; it kills love; it kills hope. But the antidote is God's love. When you truly start to *experience* his love, life begins again. Hope is restored and forgiveness becomes possible. Emotional health springs from the ashes of years of damaged relationships. I know. I've been there. I pray that soon you too will know this glorious reality.

TAKE TIME TO REFLECT

1. Are you experiencing more fear than love in your life? If so, list some things which may be intensifying your fears.

2. Do you truly believe that God cares about and wants to deal with your emotional needs? Why or why not?

3. To what extent do you struggle with guilt, perfectionism, or hopelessness? Do you have realistic expectations for yourself? Your father? Your spouse, children, and other family members?

4. Take the time to write a letter to God. Pour out your heart to him—the good, the bad, and the ugly. Cast it all upon him who cares for you.

Afterword

WHEN A BOOK DEALS with a difficult issue, a common tendency is to focus on the problem more than on the hope of getting past it. We have quoted from many people who have endured painful struggles with father hunger. Some could hardly bear to speak of their fathers after all the hurt they had experienced. But, for the most part, those people were dealing with the issue and getting better. Emotional healing is on the horizon for them.

But lest I leave you with the wrong impression, let me close with an example at the other end of the spectrum. When a father *does* provide the emotional support his children need, very little can destroy that special bond. Even death is unsuccessful. At a recent funeral, a woman gave the following eulogy for her father:

> Some of our first impressions of our heavenly Father come from the example set by our earthly father. My loving relationship with God is a direct result of my dad's life: showing unconditional love for his family; having a firm but loving hand, coupled with a gentle spirit; never pushy, but always being there when we needed him; always being willing to forgive our mistakes, and then never reminding us of them. All these things describe our heavenly Father, but live in my heart because of the life of my father.
>
> One of his greatest wishes, winning the Big Lotto so we could split it and live comfortably, caused my one disagreement with him. He couldn't understand that he had already given us all we would ever need, and more. I feel rich just thinking of him. I believe true happiness can only be attained by knowing Jesus Christ as your personal savior, and by knowing my dad. I can think of no person who, after meeting my father, had an unkind thing to say about him.
>
> We miss my dad deeply. His passing opens an empty spot in our lives, but not in our hearts. The eighty years God gave him leaves us rich in memories in which he lives on. We are thankful for those memories. We draw comfort knowing that because of them, as we say goodbye today, we can still say as we used to, "See you tomorrow, Dad."

For some readers, it may be too late to develop this strong bond of love. For others, it may not be a feasible goal because of any number of circumstances. Whatever your own situation may be, you must start from where you are. Even if it takes years to accomplish this goal, receive encouragement from the fact that for some people it has already become a reality. If you believe a new relationship with your father is even remotely possible, isn't it worth the effort?

Your Father in heaven understands how you feel—the bitterness, the pain, the anger, the hurt, and everything else. He doesn't want you to continue to suffer. God waits to offer you the relationship with a father that you never had. Please don't give up on your search until you find a mature Christian friend or counselor who can both understand what you are going through and explain how God is able to help you find the healing that has eluded you for so long.

If we can be of help to you, please let us know. Rapha is a Hebrew word for "healing." When we chose a name for our ministry, we felt this word best reflected our goal. Rapha Treatment Center is currently a leading provider of Christ-centered psychiatric and substance abuse treatment. We also are committed to assisting church leaders and Christian professionals in meeting the spiritual, relational, and emotional needs of their communities through conferences and support group leader training.

Rapha Resources is a new division of our ministry that makes available books and other printed-word products on topics we feel people need to know more about: codependency, sexual abuse, eating disorders, understanding your children, relating to parents, and getting unstuck so you can move ahead with your life. If you would like more information about any of our ministries, please call us 1-800-383-HOPE or contact us at:

> Rapha
> 12700 N. Featherwood, Suite 250
> Houston, Texas 77034

If you or a loved one needs help with the issues discussed in this book or with any of the other related issues mentioned, we encourage you to seek help. There *can* be an end to the pain, the guilt, the shame, and the overpowering sense of hopelessness. May you find it soon.

NOTES

TWO
The Powerful Influence of a Father

1. See also Robert McGee, Pat Springle, and Jim Craddock, *Your Parents and You* (Houston and Dallas, TX: Rapha Publishing and Word, Inc., Second Edition 1990).

FOUR
A Broader Famine in Society

1. Robert Bly, *Iron John* (New York, NY: Vintage Books/Random House, 1991).
2. *Newsweek*, June 24, 1991, 47.

THIRTEEN
Hidden Problems

1. Robert McGee, *The Search for Significance* (Houston and Dallas, TX: Rapha Publishing and Word, Inc., 1990).

Other Books of Interest
by Servant Publications

Mothers and Daughters Making Peace
Judith Balswick with Lynn Brookside

Mothers and Daughters Making Peace explores the delicate dynamics of the mother-daughter relationship, the deep and sometimes troublesome bond that profoundly affects an adult daughter's self-esteem and life choices.

In this insightful and practical book, Judith Balswick helps readers to develop a healthier relationship with their mother; learn new ways to respond to conflict; learn to listen, set boundaries, and handle criticism; give and receive forgiveness. *$8.99*

Unstuck
Carolyn Koons

Carolyn Koons presents fascinating new insights into human development which reveal that adults, no matter what their age, have an immense capacity to grow. *Unstuck* debunks old theories and common;y held beliefs that have kept many people stuck in their past and dreading their future.

Unstuck calls readers to a profound psychological and spiritual awakening which will give them permission to change and grow. For all of us who are living longer and staying healthier, this is the guide to help us through those challenging life passages, which can lead to greater spiritual depth and deeper life satisfaction.

$16.99

Available at your Christian bookstore or from:
Servant Publications • Dept. 209 • P.O. Box 7455
Ann Arbor, Michigan 48107
Please include payment plus $2.75 per book
for postage and handling.
Send for our FREE catalog of Christian
books, music, and cassettes.